The Low-FODMAP Diet

Cookbook For Beginners

365+

Easy & Simple Recipes with **21-Days Meal Plan** to Soothe Your Gut and Heal Your IBS

Mellisa Trantham

CONTENTS

Chapter 3 Meat Recipes 35

Chapter 4 Soups, Salads And Sandwiches Recipes 65

Chapter 5 Vegetarian And Vegan Recipes 74

Chapter 6 Sauces, Dressings, And Condiments Recipes 84

Chapter 7 Salads And Sides Recipes 93

Chapter 8 Snacks & Desserts Recipes **104**

Introduction

Welcome! I am Mellisa Trantham. I am a cookbook author and recipes developer.Since from high school, I've had digestive issues, which have ranged on the spectrum from mild to severe. Sometimes they'd be slightly annoying; sometimes I'd have to cancel plans and lie in the fetal position on the living-room couch at the last minute. For that my friends stopped asking me out.There was a lot of anxiety and guilt going on with me. I was constantly worried about getting sick while out of the house. My parents took me to a multitude of different gastroenterologists who diagnosed me with irritable bowel syndrome (IBS), but they only asked if I was stressed out, and offered few to no solutions. A few years ago, I went to see a new gastroenterologist who introduced me to something called the low-FODMAP diet. She also recommended I work with her dietitian. It was the first time in all my years of suffering that someone was interested in what I was eating and how much, instead of just pushing medications at me.After completing the elimination diet, I realized it was those types of foods that were making me feel so sick for all these years. That was a great relief for my families even. They have been worrying my IBS for so many years. Thank you for all the love and care.

If you are reading this book, chances are that you have irritable bowel syndrome (IBS) or another digestive problem. The symptoms are intrusive and impacting your life. You are here because you need help.You have come to the right place. I am going to provide you with the solution for your digestive problems. This solution will heal your gut, balance your spirit, and result in a healthier and happier you.We are going to be embarking on an exciting journey. A journey that will change your life.

Our brain and digestive system is highly connected. That means that healing your gut can make you brain fully functional. A healthy intestine has also been linked with better immunity, greater energy, and sharper focus. Don't those sound amazing?Healing your IBS symptoms will lead to improvements in every part of your life.

In this book, you will receive all the knowledge and skills to begin the low-FODMAP diet. I'll explain the why, the how, and the when. I will provide you with a 21-days meal plan to keep you on track. I will tell you what food you need to eat, what food you need to avoid, how to implement your Low-FODMAP diet and loads of other information.

You will find more than 365 Low-FODMAP diet recipes of my favorite. All are gluten-free, and many are allergy-friendly, vegan, or vegetarian. After those 21 days I promise you will feel much healthy and energetic.

Are you ready to heal your IBS symptoms, improve your energy, and embark on the path to a healthier and happier you?Let's get started!

Chapter 1 An IBS-Overview and The Low-FODMAP Diet

An IBS-Overview

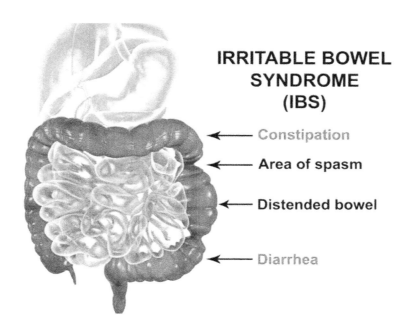

Irritable bowel syndrome (IBS) is a common gastrointestinal disorder that affects around 15% of the population. Males and ladies of various ages are affected. Excess flatulence, stomach bloating, distension, pain, or discomfort, and changed bowel habits are all symptoms (diarrhea, constipation, or a combination of both). The intensity of these symptoms varies from day to day and week to week. Because IBS is diagnosed based on the pattern of symptoms, it's critical to rule out other disorders with similar symptoms, such as celiac disease and inflammatory bowel disease (IBD), which can potentially be mistaken for IBS. Before starting a low-FODMAP or gluten-free diet, everyone with IBS symptoms should be evaluated for these illnesses, so if you haven't already, talk to your doctor about getting tested. However, keep in mind that IBS and other digestive diseases can coexist.

FODMAPS CAUSE IBS

FODMAPs all have the same characteristics:

1. They have a low absorption rate in the small intestine. This implies that many of these molecules skip past the small intestine without being absorbed instead of traveling straight to the colon. This is due to their inability to be broken down or their delayed absorption. Our capacity to digest and absorb various FODMAPs varies from person to person: Fructose absorption varies from person to person; some people do not produce enough lactase (the enzyme needed to break down

lactose), and the capacity to absorb polyols (which are the wrong shape to pass easily through the small intestinal lining) also varies. Fructans and galactooligosaccharides (GOS) are poorly absorbed in everyone since none of us can digest them.

2. They are little molecules that are eaten in high doses. The body tries to "dilute" tiny, concentrated molecules by pumping water into the gastrointestinal system when they are poorly absorbed. Extra fluid in the gastrointestinal system can produce diarrhea and interfere with the gut's muscular activity.

3. They're "quick food" for the bacteria that exist in the big intestine naturally. Billions of bacteria live in the large intestine (and the bottom section of the small intestine). If chemicals aren't absorbed in the small intestine, they make their way to the large intestine. These food molecules are seen as rapid food by the bacteria that reside there, and they are swiftly broken down, releasing hydrogen, carbon dioxide, and methane gases. The length of the chain determines how rapidly the molecules are fermented: In comparison to fiber, which comprises considerably longer chain molecules known as polysaccharides, oligosaccharides, and simple sugars ferment relatively quickly. In most meals, many forms of FODMAPs are present. Their effects are cumulative since they all produce distension in the same way until they reach the lower small intestine and colon. This indicates that the degree of intestinal distension can be determined by the overall quantity of FODMAPs taken rather than the amount of anyone FODMAP. Suppose someone who has trouble digesting lactose and absorbing fructose consumes a meal with some lactose. In that case, fructans, polyols, GOS, and fructose, the effect on the intestine will be $1 + 1 + 1 + 1 + 1 = 5$ times larger than if they ate the same quantity of simply one of that FODMAPs. As a result, we must take all FODMAPs into account while changing our diet.

FODMAPs are a group of naturally occurring sugars that are not absorbed in the small intestine; instead, they travel down the rest of the digestive tract and arrive into the large intestine, where bacteria are present (which is normal and healthy). These bacteria use the unabsorbed sugars (FODMAPs) as a food source. When the bacteria munch on the FODMAPs, they ferment them, and this results in the release of gas, which can lead to excessive flatulence, gassiness, bloating, and abdominal distension and pain. The FODMAPs can also change how quickly the bowels work, so can lead to constipation or diarrhea (or a combination of both) in susceptible people. So it is very clear how FODMAPs trigger symptoms of IBS.

All the recipes in this book use ingredients that are low in FODMAPs—that is, they exclude the ingredients known to be high in FODMAPs (see table on facing page).

FODMAP IS AN ACRONYM THAT STANDS FOR:

FERMENTABLE

These poorly absorbed sugars are fermented by bacteria in the large intestine (bowel).

OLIGOSACCHARIDES

Oligo means few, and saccharide means sugar. So these are individual sugars, joined together to make a chain.

The two main oligosaccharides that are FODMAPs are:

Fructans, made up of fructose sugars joined together to make a chain (with glucose at the very end).

Galacto-oligosaccharides (GOS), made up of galactose sugars joined together, with a fructose and glucose at the very end.

DISACCHARIDES

Di means two, and saccharide means sugar. So these are two individual sugars, joined together to make a double sugar.

The important FODMAP disaccharide is lactose, made up of an individual glucose sugar joined to an individual galactose sugar.

MONOSACCHARIDES

Mono means one, and saccharide means sugar. So these are individual sugars.

The important FODMAP monosaccharide is excess fructose. Not all fructose needs to be avoided. Only foods that contain more fructose than glucose (or "excess fructose" foods) need to be avoided on the low-FODMAP diet.

If a food contains more glucose than fructose, or if glucose and fructose are present in equal ("balanced") amounts, then it is suitable on the low-FODMAP diet.

If a food (for example, a piece of fruit) contains more glucose than fructose, or equal amounts of fructose and glucose, it is suitable to eat; however, only one piece of suitable fruit should be consumed at a time. This doesn't mean you can only have one piece of fruit per day! You can have several, but spread them out so that you only have one per sitting.

AND POLYOLS

A polyol is made up of a sugar molecule with an alcohol side-chain. Polyols are also known as sugar alcohols, but I promise they won't make you feel intoxicated!

The low-FODMAP diet

A diet low in FODMAPs is essentially a type of elimination diet. Other elimination diets include allergy elimination diet, keto, paleo, and autoimmune paleo (AIP). The goal of all elimination diets is to first reduce or eliminate specific foods or food groups that might be a culprit for certain reactions and symptoms. Later, you might reintroduce these foods or increase their intake to observe which ones impact you poorly or – in the case of many elimination diets – increase autoimmune markers and flare-ups.Often, a low FODMAP diet is implemented as a healing protocol for irritable bowel syndrome (IBS) or to treat small intestinal bacterial overgrowth (SIBO).

What to Choose (LOW-FODMAP)

Many foods are naturally low in FODMAPs. Here's a list of foods you can eat while following a low FODMAP diet (5Trusted Source, 6Trusted Source):

Proteins: beef, chicken, eggs, fish, lamb, pork, prawns, tempeh, and tofu

Whole grains and starches: white and brown rice, lentils, corn, oats, quinoa, cassava, and potatoes

Fruit: blueberries, raspberries, pineapple, honeydew melon, cantaloupe, kiwi, limes, guava, starfruit, grapes, and strawberries

Vegetables: bean sprouts, bell peppers, radishes, bok choy, carrots, celery, eggplant, kale, tomatoes, spinach, cucumber, pumpkin, and zucchini

Nuts: almonds (no more than 10 per sitting), macadamia nuts, peanuts, pecans, pine nuts, and walnuts

Seeds: pumpkin, sesame, and sunflower seeds, as well as linseeds

Dairy: lactose-free milk, Greek yogurt, and Parmesan, Colby, cheddar, and mozzarella cheeses

Oils: coconut and olive oils

Beverages: peppermint tea and water

Condiments: cumin, saffron, cinnamon, paprika, coriander, cardamom, soy sauce, fish sauce, some chile-based products, ginger, mustard, pepper, salt, white rice vinegar, and wasabi powder

While coffee and black and green teas are all low FODMAP foods, caffeinated beverages are usually discouraged a low FODMAP diet because caffeine tends to be a trigger for those with IBS.

What to lose (HIGH-FODMAP)

To ease IBS and SIBO symptoms, it's essential to avoid high FODMAP foods that aggravate the gut, including:

Dairy-based milk, yogurt and ice cream.

Wheat-based products such as cereal, bread and crackers.

Beans and lentils.

Some vegetables, such as artichokes, asparagus, onions and garlic.

Implementing Low-FODMAP Diet

If you've been diagnosed with IBS, or if you've had bloating and abdominal discomfort without a change in bowel habits, or if you and/or your doctor believe you should follow the low fodmap diet for another reason, your first step should be to contact a registered dietitian who specializes in gastrointestinal nutrition. That isn't to argue that following a low fodmap diet is impossible, but it will necessitate major dietary and lifestyle modifications. You'll need to understand your illness, which foods are appropriate, and what will happen if you don't stick to the diet. To keep your symptoms under control, we recommend sticking to the low fodmap diet for at least two months and avoiding any FODMAPs. Whether your symptoms have improved after this period, slowly reintroduce one FODMAP group at a time to determine if you can handle it. This is easiest to accomplish with the assistance of a qualified dietitian, who will examine your symptoms and recommend the best course of action, but for additional information on how to do it yourself and meal plans, go here.

At first, you may find certain components of the low fodmap diet to be overwhelming. Each morning, you'll have to ask yourself the following questions: What will I be doing today? Is it necessary for me to bring food? Should I eat something before I leave? Will there be something I can eat there? If you have to follow a specific diet, it can begin to control your thinking, and some individuals are better at dealing with this than others. Seek therapy or other assistance if you're having problems adapting. Here are some more considerations to keep in mind while creating a low fodmap diet to your specific needs:

Consider all the FODMAP groups. They all have the potential to cause bowel distension and other IBS symptoms.

No one can absorb fructans, GOS, or polyols well. This means you should always avoid them when first implementing the low fodmap diet.

Only some people have lactose or fructose malabsorption. A breath hydrogen test will tell you whether or not you need to limit lactose or excess fructose in your diet.

Some FODMAPs cause more trouble in some people than others. This depends on the proportions of each FODMAP in their diet, how well or poorly they absorb fructose and lactose, and how sensitive they are to each FODMAP, which could be related to which bacteria they have in their bowel. You'll learn which FODMAPs give you the most trouble through a combination of clinical tests and trials in your diet.

Chapter 2 Breakfast & Brunch Recipes

Hawaiian Toasted Sandwich

Servings:1

Cooking Time: 6 Minutes

Ingredients:

- 2 slices bread
- 1 tbsp butter
- 2 ½ tbsp pineapple chunks, drained
- 2 slices cheddar cheese
- 2 slices ham, cold cut
- 1 tbsp spring onion, tips finely chopped
- Pinch of black pepper

Directions:

1. Place a frying pan over medium heat.
2. Spread butter on the outside of each slice of bread.
3. Prepare the filling by grating the cheese, slicing the ham, rinsing the pineapple, and chopping the spring onion finely.
4. Put the sandwich together adding pepper to taste and ensuring the butter is on the outside.
5. Place in the frying pan and cook each side for 3 minutes. The bread should turn golden brown.
6. Serve warm.

Nutrition Info:

- 454g Calories, 26.5g Total fat, 9.9g Saturated fat, 33.7g Carbohydrates, 1.8 g Fiber, 19.9g Protein, 3g Sodium.

Pesto Noodles

Servings:2

Cooking Time: 10 Minutes

Ingredients:

- Pesto
- ¾ cup basil, fresh
- 2 tbsp garlic-infused oil
- ¼ cup pine nuts
- 2 tbsp olive oil
- Pinch of salt
- Pinch of pepper
- ½ cup Parmesan, grated
- Noodles
- 1 cup rice noodles

Directions:

1. In a food processor, mix basil, garlic oil, and pine nuts until coarsely chopped.
2. Add the olive oil, cheese, salt, and pepper to the processor and mix until the pesto is fully mixed and smooth.

3. Cook the noodles according to the instructions on the packet. Once cooked, toss the noodles in a bowl with 3 tablespoons pesto and mix until the noodles are covered.
4. Serve!

Nutrition Info:

- 569g Calories, 50g Total fat, 5.5g Saturated fat, 26g Carbohydrates, 3 g Fiber, 6g Protein, 1.5g Sodium.

Cranberry Almond Bowl

Servings:1

Cooking Time: 2 Minutes

Ingredients:

- 1 cup cranberries, frozen
- 1 tbsp almond butter
- ½ cup Greek yogurt
- 2 tbsp lactose-free milk
- ½ small banana, frozen
- 1 tbsp chia seeds
- ½ cup ice cubes
- Optional toppings, chopped nuts

Directions:

1. Blend together cranberries, butter, Greek yogurt, milk, banana, and chia seeds.
2. Add ice until the desired consistency is achieved.

Nutrition Info:

- 545g Calories, 30g Total fat, 9g Saturated fat, 65g Carbohydrates, 22 g Fiber, 13g Protein, 24g Sodium.

Feta, Chicken, And Pepper Sandwich

Servings:2

Cooking Time: 20 Minutes

Ingredients:

- 1 chicken breast fillet
- 1 tsp olive oil
- 4 slices gluten-free or spelt sourdough bread
- 1 cup feta cheese
- 1 large red capsicum, deseeded and cut into strips
- ¼ cup basil

Directions:

1. Cut the chicken in half to create thin fillets, drizzle olive oil over them, and season with salt and pepper. Place into a frying pan that has been heated over medium heat. Cook the fillets for 3 minutes on each side. Remove and cover with foil for 5 minutes before cutting into strips
2. Drizzle some oil onto one side of each slice of bread.

3. Assemble the sandwich by placing the feta, chicken, pepper, and basil, divided onto two slices of bread with the oil side down. Top with the other two slices of bread with the oil side facing up.

4. Cook the sandwiches in a frying pan for 3 minutes on each side until the bread is golden.

5. Remove from heat and serve.

Nutrition Info:

- 601g Calories, 27g Total fat, 12.5g Saturated fat, 40g Carbohydrates, 6 g Fiber, 46g Protein, 4g Sodium.

Spicy Scrambled Chickpeas

Servings:4

Cooking Time: 10 Minutes

Ingredients:

- 1 cup canned chickpeas, drained and rinsed
- ½ teaspoon paprika
- ½ teaspoon ground coriander
- ¼ teaspoon ground cumin
- ¼ teaspoon cayenne
- ¼ teaspoon freshly ground black pepper
- 2 tablespoons olive oil
- 1 red bell pepper, seeded and diced
- 1 yellow or orange bell pepper, seeded and diced
- 20 leaves Swiss chard, center ribs removed and leaves julienned
- ½ teaspoon salt
- 2 tablespoons chopped cilantro

Directions:

1. In a bowl, combine the chickpeas with the paprika, coriander, cumin, cayenne, and pepper. Toss until chickpeas are evenly coated with the spices.

2. Heat the oil in a large skillet over high heat. Add the bell peppers and chard. Cook, stirring frequently, until the vegetables begin to soften and brown on the edges, for about 5 minutes.

3. Add the chickpea mixture, salt, and about 1 tablespoon of water. Cook, stirring, for 5 minutes, until the chickpeas are heated through and the water has evaporated. Serve immediately, garnished with cilantro.

Nutrition Info:

- Calories: 275; Protein: 12g; Total Fat: 10g; Saturated Fat: 1g; Carbohydrates: 26g; Fiber: 11g; Sodium: 547mg;

Chicken Wrap

Servings:4

Cooking Time: 0 Minutes

Ingredients:

- 1 ½ cups chicken, cooked and chopped

- 3 cups lettuce, chopped
- 20 cherry tomatoes, halved
- ¼ cup Parmesan, grated
- Pinch of pepper
- 4 gluten-free wraps, can substitute with other low-FODMAP-approved wraps

Directions:

1. In a bowl, mix together all the ingredients, leaving the wraps to the side.

2. Lay the wraps out and place ¼ of the mixture onto the center. Roll up. If taking to eat on the go, use a toothpick to secure the wrap.

Nutrition Info:

- 392g Calories, 12.7g Total fat, 4.7g Saturated fat, 17.7g Carbohydrates, 5.5 g Fiber, 22.7g Protein, 3.5g Sodium.

Sweet Green Smoothie

Servings:2

Cooking Time: 0 Minutes

Ingredients:

- 3 cups fresh baby spinach
- 2 cup unsweetened almond milk
- 1 cup freshly squeezed orange juice
- 1 cup crushed ice
- 1 banana
- 1 packet stevia (optional), plus more as needed

Directions:

1. In a blender, combine the spinach, almond milk, orange juice, ice, banana, and stevia (if using).

2. Blend until smooth, and sweeten as desired.

Nutrition Info:

- Calories:159; Total Fat: 4g; Saturated Fat: 0g; Carbohydrates: 30g; Fiber: 4g; Sodium: 217mg; Protein: 4g

Pesto Toasted Sandwich

Servings:1

Cooking Time: 5 Minutes

Ingredients:

- 2 slices bread
- 1 tbsp butter
- 1 tbsp pesto, no garlic or onion
- in the mixture
- 4 cherry tomatoes, halved
- 1 slice mozzarella
- ½ cup chicken breast, cooked
- and cubed

Directions:

1. Place a frying pan over medium heat.

2. Butter the outside of each slice of bread.

3. Mix together the filling ingredients and place onto the bread. Ensure the butter is on the outside of the sandwich when assembling.

4. Place the sandwich in the pan and fry for 3 minutes on each side. The bread should be golden.

Nutrition Info:

- 555g Calories, 35g Total fat, 15g Saturated fat, 28g Carbohydrates, 3 g Fiber, 33g Protein, 3g Sodium.

Ginger-berry Rice Milk Smoothie

Servings:2

Cooking Time: None

Ingredients:

- 2 cups frozen strawberries, blueberries, or raspberries
- 1 cup unsweetened rice milk
- 2 tablespoons maple syrup
- 2 teaspoons finely grated fresh ginger
- 2 teaspoons lemon juice

Directions:

1. Place all of the ingredients in a blender and blend until smooth.

2. Serve immediately.

Nutrition Info:

- Calories: 162; Protein: 2g; Total Fat: 2g; Saturated Fat: 0g; Carbohydrates: 37g; Fiber: 8g;

Pumpkin Pie Pancakes

Servings:4

Cooking Time: 10 Minutes

Ingredients:

- 1 cup pumpkin purée
- 4 eggs, beaten
- 1 tablespoon ground flaxseed
- 1 tablespoon buckwheat flour
- 1 teaspoon baking powder
- 1 teaspoon pumpkin pie spice
- Pinch sea salt
- Nonstick cooking spray

Directions:

1. In a small bowl, whisk the pumpkin purée and eggs until well mixed.

2. In a medium bowl, whisk the flaxseed, buckwheat flour, baking powder, pumpkin pie spice, and salt.

3. Fold the wet ingredients into the dry ingredients until combined.

4. Spray a large nonstick skillet with cooking spray and place it over medium-high heat.

5. Spoon the batter in scant ¼-cup amounts onto the heated skillet. With the back of a spoon, spread the batter thin.

Cook for about 3 minutes, until bubbles form on the top. Flip and cook for about 3 minutes more, until browned on the other side.

Nutrition Info:

- Calories:102; Total Fat: 5g; Saturated Fat: 2g; Carbohydrates: 8g; Fiber: 3g; Sodium: 105mg; Protein: 7g

Melon And Berry Compote

Servings:2

Cooking Time: 0 Minutes

Ingredients:

- 2 cups chopped cantaloupe
- 2 cups fresh blueberries
- ¼ cup unsweetened coconut flakes
- 2 tablespoons flaxseed

Directions:

1. In a medium bowl, gently stir together the cantaloupe, blueberries, coconut flakes, and flaxseed.

Nutrition Info:

- Calories:196; Total Fat: 5g; Saturated Fat: 2g; Carbohydrates: 36g; Fiber: 7g; Sodium: 29mg; Protein: 4g

Sausage And Egg Omelet

Servings:2

Cooking Time: 8 Minutes

Ingredients:

- 6 eggs, beaten
- ¼ cup unsweetened almond milk
- ¼ teaspoon sea salt
- ¼ teaspoon freshly ground black pepper
- Nonstick cooking spray
- ½ pound cooked, hot Easy Breakfast Sausage, cut into small pieces
- ¼ cup grated Cheddar cheese

Directions:

1. In a large bowl, whisk the eggs, almond milk, salt, and pepper.

2. Spray a large nonstick skillet with cooking spray and place it over medium-high heat.

3. Add the eggs and cook for about 3 minutes until they start to solidify. With a spatula, gently pull the cooked eggs away from the edge of the pan. Tilt the pan so any uncooked egg flows into the spaces you've created. Continue cooking the eggs for about 3 minutes more.

4. Spread the sausage and cheese over half the omelet. Fold the other side over the filling. Cook for 1 to 2 minutes more to melt the cheese.

Nutrition Info:

- Calories:580; Total Fat: 36g; Saturated Fat: 17g; Carbohydrates: 2g; Fiber: 0g; Sodium: 470mg; Protein: 60g

Carrot Cake Porridge

Servings:4

Cooking Time: 20 Minutes

Ingredients:

- 1 cup oats
- 3 cups water
- 2 medium carrots, grated
- 1 tsp cinnamon
- 1 ½ tbsp flax seeds
- ¼ cup cranberries, dried
- ¼ cup walnuts
- ½ cup almond milk
- 1 tsp maple syrup

Directions:

1. Add the oats and water to a pot over medium heat. As it comes to a boil, turn the heat down and stir the carrots and cinnamon into the pot.

2. Cook for 10-12 minutes, until you reach the desired texture. Add the cranberries and nuts before serving.

Nutrition Info:

- 290g Calories, 9.6g Total fat, 2g Saturated fat, 29.5g Carbohydrates, 5.6 g Fiber, 9.6g Protein, 12.3g Sodium.

Cranberry Chocolate Chip Energy Bites

Servings:12

Cooking Time: 0 Minutes

Ingredients:

- ⅓ cup oats
- ½ cup cranberries, dried
- ⅓ cup peanut butter
- ¼ cup maple syrup
- 1 tbsp quinoa, puffed
- 2 tbsp mini dark chocolate chips

Directions:

1. Mix the oats in a blender or food processor until they are a flour-like consistency. Add the cranberries, peanut butter, and maple syrup, then blend until everything sticks together.

2. Add the quinoa and chocolate and mix until everything is evenly distributed.

3. Scoop a tablespoon at a time and roll into balls. Place in an airtight container and let rest in the fridge for at least 10 minutes. Store the remainder in the fridge until eaten.

4. It can be eaten for lunch or as a snack.

Nutrition Info:

- 111g Calories, 2.5g Total fat, 1g Saturated fat, 14.5g Carbohydrates, 1.6 g Fiber, 2.5g Protein, 5.5g Sodium.

Rhubarb Ginger Granola Bowl

Servings:4

Cooking Time: 30 Minutes

Ingredients:

- Yogurt
- 1 ½ cups chopped rhubarb
- 1 tbsp grated ginger
- ½ tbsp lemon juice
- 4 tbsp maple syrup
- Pinch of salt
- 2 cups Greek yogurt
- Granola
- ½ cup pumpkin seeds
- ¾ cup chopped nuts (low-FODMAP-approved)
- 2 tbsp melted coconut oil
- 1 tsp ground ginger
- ¼ tsp cinnamon
- Pinch of salt

Directions:

1. Preheat the oven to 350°F.

2. For the yogurt, in a small pot over medium heat, add chopped rhubarb, ginger, lemon juice, and 2 tablespoons of maple syrup. Stir the mixture occasionally until it begins to simmer, ensuring the bottom of the pot does not burn. Once the mixture has thickened to a purée consistency, mix in the other 2 tablespoons of maple syrup. Place the mixture into a bowl to cool.

3. Place the granola ingredients into a separate bowl and mix until the coconut oil coats everything. Move the mix onto a non-stick baking tray and place in the oven for 10-15 minutes, stirring halfway.

4. Once all components are ready, fold the rhubarb purée into the yogurt and sprinkle the granola over top. The yogurt can be stored in the fridge and the granola in a Tupperware.

5. Add a low-FODMAP-approved topping if desired.

Nutrition Info:

- 593g Calories, 4g Total fat, 1.5g Saturated fat, 32g Carbohydrates, 4 g Fiber, 20g Protein, 19g Sodium.

Melon And Yogurt Parfait

Servings:2

Cooking Time: 0 Minutes

Ingredients:

- 2 cups chopped honeydew melon, divided
- 2 cups plain, unsweetened, lactose-free yogurt
- ¼ cup macadamia nuts, chopped

Directions:

1. In each of two medium parfait glasses or bowls, place ½ cup honeydew melon.

2. Layer a ½ cup yogurt on top of the melon.
3. Top each with 2 tablespoons macadamia nuts.
4. Repeat with the remaining ingredients.

Nutrition Info:
- Calories:356; Total Fat: 16g; Saturated Fat: 5g; Carbohydrates: 35g; Fiber: 3g; Sodium: 203mg; Protein: 16g

Banana Toast

Servings:2
Cooking Time: 5 Minutes

Ingredients:
- 4 gluten-free sandwich bread slices
- 1 ripe banana
- ½ teaspoon ground cinnamon

Directions:
1. Toast the bread to your desired doneness.
2. In a small bowl, mash the banana with the cinnamon and spread it on the toast.

Nutrition Info:
- Calories:102; Total Fat: <1g; Saturated Fat: 0g; Carbohydrates: 23g; Fiber: 2g; Sodium: 123mg; Protein: 2g

Maple–brown Sugar Oatmeal

Servings:2
Cooking Time: 10 Minutes

Ingredients:
- 1 cup unsweetened almond milk
- ¼ cup packed brown sugar
- ¼ cup pure maple syrup
- 1 tablespoon unsalted butter
- Pinch sea salt
- 1 cup quick-cooking oatmeal (not instant)

Directions:
1. In a medium saucepan over medium-high heat, heat the almond milk, brown sugar, maple syrup, butter, and salt until it simmers.
2. Stir in the oats. Bring to a boil, stirring frequently.
3. Reduce the heat to medium. Cover and simmer for 5 minutes, until the oatmeal thickens.

Nutrition Info:
- Calories:399; Total Fat: 10g; Saturated Fat: 4g; Carbohydrates: 73g; Fiber: 5g; Sodium: 220mg; Protein: 6g

Orange-scented Overnight Oatmeal

Servings:4
Cooking Time: None

Ingredients:
- 1 cup gluten-free rolled oats
- 1¼ cups lactose-free milk, divided
- Juice of ½ orange

- ½ tablespoon chia seeds
- 1 tablespoon maple syrup, divided
- ¼ teaspoon cinnamon
- ½ teaspoon vanilla extract
- ¼ teaspoon orange extract
- ⅛ teaspoon ground ginger

Directions:
1. In a medium bowl, stir together the oats, 1 cup of the milk, orange juice, chia seeds, half of the maple syrup, cinnamon, vanilla and orange extracts, and ginger. Cover and refrigerate overnight.
2. To serve, stir in the remaining maple syrup, and serve chilled or warmed.

Nutrition Info:
- Calories: 231; Protein: 10g; Total Fat: 4g; Saturated Fat: 1g; Carbohydrates: 39g; Fiber: 6g; Sodium: 35mg;

Protein Smoothie

Servings:2
Cooking Time: 5 Minutes

Ingredients:
- ½ banana
- 1 cup vanilla protein powder
- 1 cup almond milk
- 1 ½ tbsp drinking chocolate
- 1 ½ cups ice cubes

Directions:
1. Add all the ingredients, except the ice, into a blender and mix together.
2. Add the ice slowly until the mixture is creamy.

Nutrition Info:
- 601g Calories, 14.5g Total fat, 2g Saturated fat, 78.5g Carbohydrates, 7.5 g Fiber, 40.5g Protein, 4g Sodium.

Pineapple-coconut Smoothie

Servings:2
Cooking Time: 0 Minutes

Ingredients:
- 2 cups crushed pineapple, fresh or canned in water and drained
- 1 cup canned full-fat coconut milk
- 1 cup unsweetened almond milk
- 1 cup crushed ice
- 2 tablespoons chia seeds or flaxseed

Directions:
1. In a blender, combine the pineapple, coconut milk, almond milk, ice, and chia seeds.
2. Blend until smooth.

Nutrition Info:

- Calories:415; Total Fat: 33g; Saturated Fat: 26g; Carbohydrates: 31g; Fiber: 7g; Sodium: 112mg; Protein: 5g

Strawberry Smoothie

Servings:1
Cooking Time: 3 Minutes
Ingredients:
- ½ cup FODMAP-approved milk (almond milk is recommended)
- ⅔ cup strawberries, fresh or frozen
- ¼ cup lactose-free yogurt or vegan yogurt
- 1 ½ tsp protein powder
- 1 tsp chia seeds
- ½ tbsp maple syrup
- 1 tsp lemon juice
- ¼ tsp vanilla extract
- 6 ice cubes (only when using fresh strawberries)

Directions:
1. Cut the strawberries into halves or quarters. If using frozen strawberries, it is recommended to cut them the day before.
2. Put ingredients into a blender and blend until smooth. If the mixture gets too thick, add a small amount of hot water and continue blending.
3. It is best drunk immediately.

Nutrition Info:
- 308g Calories, 10.3g Total fat, 1.4g Saturated fat, 1.4g Carbohydrates, 5.9 g Fiber, 5.4g Protein, 30.9g Sodium.

Basil Omelet With Smashed Tomato

Servings:2
Cooking Time: 10 Minutes
Ingredients:
- 2 tomatoes, halved
- 3 eggs
- 1 tbsp chives, chopped
- ¼ cup shredded mozzarella cheese (or other FODMAP-approved cheese)
- 1-2 basil leaves, chopped finely
- Pepper

Directions:
1. Break the eggs into a bowl and add a splash of water. Whisk the mixture with a fork and add the chives and a pinch of pepper. Set aside.
2. Place the halved tomatoes on til in a hot skillet on the stove or onto a hot grill on low to medium heat. Turn occasionally until they are starting to char, then remove them and place them on plates. Squish slightly so that the juices are released.

3. Take the egg mixture and whisk it slightly before pouring it into a hot pan on medium heat. Leave the mixture for a few seconds before gently stirring the uncooked egg until it is cooked but still slightly loose.
4. Place the cheese and a basil leaf on one half of the egg and then gently fold the omelet in half. Let it cook for another minute. Once it is cooked, cut the omelet in half and serve with the tomato.

Nutrition Info:
- 175.5g Calories, 10.5g Total fat, 48g Saturated fat, 6g Carbohydrates, 1.5 g Fiber, 14.5g Protein, 4g Sodium.

Quinoa Porridge

Servings:2
Cooking Time: 25 Minutes
Ingredients:
- ½ cup quinoa
- 1 tsp oil (FODMAP-approved)
- 1 cup water
- ¾ cup milk even vegetable milk(FODMAP-approved)
- ¼ tsp cinnamon
- 2 tbsp maple syrup
- 1 cup berries (FODMAP-approved)

Directions:
1. Rinse the quinoa under cold water for two minutes using a fine sieve and then transfer it to a medium saucepan with oil. Toast the quinoa until the water has evaporated.
2. Add water to the saucepan and bring to a boil. Once the water starts boiling, turn the heat down to the lowest setting and cover with a lid. Cook for 12-15 minutes until the quinoa is fluffy. Drain the excess water and place the quinoa back into the saucepan.
3. Mix the cinnamon, milk, and syrup into the quinoa. If the milk evaporates, add a small amount as needed. Let the mix simmer for 5 minutes or until the mixture is warmed through.
4. Serve the mixture in a bowl with berries on top.

Nutrition Info:
- 292g Calories, 8g Total fat, 1.5g Saturated fat, 50.5g Carbohydrates, 4.5 g Fiber, 7.5g Protein, 17g Sodium.

Sausage-stuffed Kabocha Squash

Servings:4
Cooking Time: 1 Hour
Ingredients:
- 2 small kabocha squash, halved and seeded
- 3 tablespoons olive oil, divided
- 1¼ teaspoons salt, divided
- 1 teaspoon freshly ground black pepper, divided
- ½ pound onion- and garlic-free pork sausage

- ¼ cup celery, finely diced
- ¼ teaspoon red pepper flakes
- 2 tablespoons Garlic Oil (here)
- 1 tablespoon chopped fresh thyme
- 1 tablespoon chopped fresh rosemary
- 2 cups cooked quinoa
- ¼ cup dried cranberries
- ¼ cup Parmesan cheese

Directions:

1. Preheat the oven to 400°F.
2. Arrange the squash halves cut-side up on a large baking sheet, drizzle them with 2 tablespoons of the olive oil, and season with ½ teaspoon each of the salt and pepper. Roast in the preheated oven for about 45 minutes, until tender.
3. Meanwhile, heat the remaining tablespoon of olive oil in a large skillet. Add the sausage and cook, breaking up with a spatula, for about 5 minutes, until browned. Add the celery, red pepper flakes, and the remainder of the salt and pepper. Cook for about 4 minutes more, until the vegetables are tender.
4. Stir in the Garlic Oil, thyme, and rosemary, then remove the skillet from the heat. Add the quinoa and cranberries, and stir to mix well.
5. Spoon the sausage mixture into the roasted squash halves and sprinkle with the cheese. Bake in the preheated oven for 10 minutes, until the cheese is melted and the filling is heated through. Serve immediately.

Nutrition Info:

- Calories: 577; Protein: 23g; Total Fat: 33g; Saturated Fat: 9g; Carbohydrates: 52g; Fiber: 7g; Sodium: 862mg;

Breakfast Tortillas

Servings:4
Cooking Time: 10 Minutes
Ingredients:

- 4 corn tortillas
- 4 eggs
- ¼ cup macadamia nuts
- 1 cup mozzarella cheese, grated
- 1 cup Greek yogurt
- 4 tomatoes, diced

Directions:

1. Boil the uncracked eggs in simmering water for 5 ½ minutes, then place in cold water to stop cooking. Peel when they have cooled.
2. Heat tortillas on both sides for 20 seconds in a pan over medium heat. Place in an airtight container and cover with a dry cloth while heating the rest of the tortillas.

3. Spread the yogurt over the tortillas and add the cheese and tomatoes. Cut the eggs in half before adding them to the tortilla. Season to taste.

Nutrition Info:

- 373g Calories, 19.5g Total fat, 9.75g Saturated fat, 19.75g Carbohydrates, 3.75 g Fiber, 19.5g Protein, 6g Sodium.

Breakfast Wrap

Servings:1
Cooking Time: 3 Minutes
Ingredients:

- Oil for frying pan (FODMAP-approved)
- 2 eggs
- 1 tsp garlic-infused oil (optional)
- 1 ½ tbsp chives, chopped
- 1 low-FODMAP wrap
- ¼ cup of spinach
- ½ sliced tomato
- 2 tbsp FODMAP-approved cheese (shredded)

Directions:

1. Grease a frying pan with oil and place on medium heat.
2. In a bowl, mix the eggs, garlic-infused oil, and chives before pouring into the pan. Once the mixture starts to set, carefully flip it to cook the other side.
3. Heat the wrap according to the instructions on the packaging, and then place it onto a plate. Put the egg mixture on the wrap with enough of the wrap open so it can be rolled. Add the spinach, tomato, and cheese on top of the egg and roll the wrap.

Nutrition Info:

- 247g Calories, 17g Total fat, 5g Saturated fat, 9.5g Carbohydrates, 2.5 g Fiber, 13.5g Protein, 1.5g Sodium.

Huevos Rancheros

Servings:4
Cooking Time: 20 Minutes
Ingredients:

- 8 small corn tortillas
- 1 tablespoon butter
- 4 eggs
- 2 tablespoons chopped cilantro
- FOR THE SAUCE
- 1 tablespoon olive oil
- 1 zucchini, diced
- 1 red, yellow, or green bell pepper, cored, seeded, diced
- 2 chopped jalapeños or 2 tablespoons roasted green chiles
- 2 plum tomatoes, peeled, seeded, and diced

- 1 teaspoon salt
- ½ teaspoon ground cumin
- ½ teaspoon gluten-free, onion- and garlic-free chili powder
- ½ teaspoon dried oregano
- 1 tablespoon Garlic Oil (here)

Directions:

1. Preheat the oven to 400°F.
2. Wrap the tortillas in aluminum foil and bake in the preheated oven for about 10 minutes.
3. While the tortillas are heating, make the sauce. Heat the olive oil in a large skillet over medium-high heat. Add the zucchini, bell pepper, and jalapeños. Cook, stirring frequently, until the vegetables are softened and beginning to brown, for about 5 minutes. Add the tomatoes along with the salt, cumin, chili powder, and oregano. Cook, stirring, for about another 5 minutes, until the tomatoes break down and become saucy. Stir in the Garlic Oil.
4. Heat the butter in another large skillet over medium heat. Add the eggs and fry to desired doneness.
5. To serve, arrange 2 tortillas on each of 4 serving plates, and top with a fried egg and a generous serving of sauce. Garnish with cilantro and serve immediately.

Nutrition Info:

- Calories: 257; Protein: 10g; Total Fat: 13g; Saturated Fat: 4g; Carbohydrates: 29g; Fiber: 5g; Sodium: 695mg;

Quiche In Ham Cups

Servings:6
Cooking Time: 20 Minutes

Ingredients:

- 6 slices ham, cold cut, rounded
- 1 small bell pepper, diced
- ½ cup spring onion, green tips only
- 4 eggs, beaten
- 2 tbsp rice flour
- 4 tbsp lactose-free milk, can be substituted with other approved milk
- Pinch of salt
- Pinch of pepper

Directions:

1. Preheat the oven to 350°F and line 6 muffin tins with the ham slices.
2. Mix together the flour and milk, whisking constantly.
3. Add in the eggs, salt, and pepper, mixing until smooth. Add the spring onion and bell pepper. Pour carefully into the ham cups.
4. Bake for 15-20 minutes. It's ready when the quiche is puffy and the ham is crispy.

5. Let cool for 10 minutes then use a knife to carefully lift the quiche out of the tins.

Nutrition Info:

- 190g Calories, 8.5g Total fat, 5.1g Saturated fat, 11.8g Carbohydrates, 1.6 g Fiber, 9.5g Protein, 1.6g Sodium.

Cheese, Ham, And Spinach Muffins

Servings:6
Cooking Time: 20-25 Minutes

Ingredients:

- 1 cup corn flour
- ¼ cup oats
- 2 ¼ tsp baking powder
- ½ tsp xanthan gum
- ½ cup thick Greek yogurt
- ⅔ cup lactose-free milk
- 2 large eggs
- 6 oz ham, lean
- ¼ cup chopped chives
- ½ cup cheddar cheese, grated (set 2 tbsp aside)
- ¼ cup baby spinach, chopped roughly
- ½ tsp paprika, smoked
- A drizzle of olive oil, used to grease the muffin tins

Directions:

1. Preheat the oven to 325°F and place a baking tray half-filled with water on the bottom shelf.
2. In a bowl, sift together the flour, baking powder, and xanthan gum, then stir in the oats.
3. In a smaller bowl, whisk the eggs, yogurt, and milk together, then add in the ham, chives, spinach, and cheese.
4. Make a well in the dry mix and pour the wet ingredients into it. Gently fold the ingredients together. The dough should be slightly wet but not liquid.
5. Grease the muffin tin and fill with the mixture. Wet your fingers and tap the top of the tin gently to settle the mixture.
6. Top with the remainder of the cheese and paprika.
7. Bake for 20-25 minutes.

Nutrition Info:

- 316g Calories, 11.9g Total fat, 6g Saturated fat, 35.7g Carbohydrates, 2.6 g Fiber, 16.8g Protein, 1.9g Sodium.

Banana Oatcakes

Servings:4
Cooking Time: 32 Minutes
Ingredients:
- 1 unripe banana
- 1 egg
- ½ cup rice milk
- 1 tbsp Greek yogurt
- 1 ½ cups rolled oats
- ⅓ cup oat flour
- 2 tsp cinnamon
- Pinch of salt

Directions:
1. Mash the banana in a bowl and add the egg, milk, and yogurt, whisking after each ingredient. Next, add the dry ingredients, making sure to mix thoroughly.
2. Let the mixture rest for 15-30 minutes.
3. Grease a pan with low-FODMAP-approved oil and place it on medium heat.
4. Pour ¼ of the batter into the pan and flip when it begins bubbling. Remove the oatcake when it is golden brown on both sides.
5. Repeat 3 more times until you have 4 oatcakes.
6. Add a low-FODMAP-approved topping if desired.
Nutrition Info:
- 530g Calories, 12.5g Total fat, 2.75g Saturated fat, 80g Carbohydrates, 14.5 g Fiber, 21.25g Protein, 5.5g Sodium.

Easy Breakfast Sausage

Servings:4
Cooking Time: 8 Minutes
Ingredients:
- 1 pound ground pork
- 1 teaspoon ground sage
- ½ teaspoon sea salt
- ⅛ teaspoon red pepper flakes
- ⅛ teaspoon freshly ground black pepper
- Nonstick cooking spray

Directions:
1. In a large bowl, mix the pork, sage, salt, red pepper flakes, and pepper. Form the mixture into 8 patties.
2. Spray a large nonstick skillet with cooking spray and place it over medium-high heat.
3. Add the sausage patties and cook for about 4 minutes per side, until browned on both sides.
Nutrition Info:
- Calories:163; Total Fat: 4g; Saturated Fat: 1g; Carbohydrates: <1g; Fiber: 0g; Sodium: 299mg; Protein: 30g

Fried Eggs With Potato Hash

Servings:2
Cooking Time: 26 Minutes
Ingredients:
- 2 tablespoons Garlic Oil, plus more as needed
- 2 russet potatoes, cut into ½-inch cubes
- 3 scallions, green parts only, chopped
- ½ teaspoon sea salt, plus more for seasoning the eggs
- ¼ teaspoon freshly ground black pepper, plus more for seasoning the eggs
- 4 eggs

Directions:
1. In a large skillet over medium-high heat, heat the garlic oil until it shimmers.
2. Add the potatoes. Cook for about 20 minutes, stirring occasionally, until soft and browned.
3. Add the scallions, salt, and pepper. Cook for 1 minute more, stirring frequently. Spoon the potatoes onto two plates.
4. Return the skillet to medium heat. If the pan is dry, add a little more garlic oil and swirl it to coat the skillet (see Tip).
5. Carefully crack the eggs into the skillet and season them with a pinch of salt and pepper. Cook undisturbed for 3 to 4 minutes, until the whites solidify.
6. Turn off the heat and carefully flip the eggs so you do not break the yolk. Leave the eggs in the hot pan for 60 to 90 seconds until the surface is cooked but the yolks remain runny.
7. Serve the potatoes topped with the eggs.
Nutrition Info:
- Calories:401; Total Fat: 23g; Saturated Fat: 5g; Carbohydrates: 36g; Fiber: 6g; Sodium: 608mg; Protein: 15g

French Toast Casserole

Servings:8
Cooking Time: 1 Hour
Ingredients:
- 1 banana
- ¼ cup maple syrup
- ½ cup chickpea water (drained from canned chickpeas in water)
- ¾ cup almond milk
- 1 tsp vanilla extract
- 1 tsp cinnamon
- 8 servings gluten-free bread, cut into 1-inch squares
- 2 cups mixed berries

Directions:
1. Mash the banana in a bowl and stir in the maple syrup.
2. In a separate bowl, whip the chickpea water into soft peaks with a hand mixer.

3. Mix the banana, vanilla extract, and cinnamon into the whipped chickpea water.

4. Grease a casserole dish and add the bread chunks. Pour the banana mixture over it while gently tossing it to cover all the bread.

5. Scatter the berries over the top and place in the fridge overnight

6. In the morning, place the mixture into an oven preheated to 350°F and bake for 50-60 minutes.

Nutrition Info:

- 208g Calories, 2.75g Total fat, 0.8g Saturated fat, 41.6g Carbohydrates, 2.25 g Fiber, 3g Protein, 9.75g Sodium.

Green Smoothie

Servings:1

Cooking Time: 0 Minutes

Ingredients:

- ½ cup fresh pineapple, chopped and then frozen
- 2 tablespoons baby spinach
- ¼ cup Greek yogurt
- 1 tbsp shredded coconut
- 2 tsp chia seeds
- ¼ cup almond milk
- 6 ice cubes

Directions:

1. Blend all the ingredients, except for the ice and milk.
2. Add the ice and blend.
3. Add the milk and continue blending until smooth.

Nutrition Info:

- 347g Calories, 24g Total fat, 16g Saturated fat, 31g Carbohydrates, 10 g Fiber, 8g Protein, 17g Sodium.

Tomato And Green Bean Salad

Servings:6

Cooking Time: 5 Minutes

Ingredients:

- 1 cup green beans
- ½ cup mayonnaise
- ½ cup Greek yogurt
- 1 tbsp chopped basil
- 2 tbsp chopped parsley
- Pinch of salt
- Pinch of pepper
- 2 tbsp lactose-free or another FODMAP-approved milk
- 1 tbsp Dijon mustard
- 2 tomatoes
- 2 spring onions, green part only
- 1 ½ cups lettuce

Directions:

1. In a bowl, mix mayonnaise, yogurt, milk, mustard, basil, parsley, salt, and pepper.

2. Wash the green beans, lettuce, and spring onions, then drain the water and chop the green onions. Shred the lettuce into a separate bowl and mix in the green beans and spring onions.

3. Cut the tomatoes into quarters and mix into the bowl. Put the dressing into a serving jug and serve.

Nutrition Info:

- 125g Calories, 8.8g Total fat, 2g Saturated fat, 10.8g Carbohydrates, 1.8 g Fiber, 2.5g Protein, 4.5g Sodium.

Tropical Fruit Salad

Servings:4

Cooking Time: 0 Minutes

Ingredients:

- 2 bananas, sliced
- 1 papaya, peeled, seeded, and cut into bite-size cubes
- 1 cup pineapple chunks, fresh or canned, drained
- 2 tablespoons unsweetened shredded coconut

Directions:

1. In a medium bowl, gently stir together the bananas, papaya, pineapple chunks, and coconut.

Nutrition Info:

- Calories:116; Total Fat: 1g; Saturated Fat: <1g; Carbohydrates: 28g; Fiber: 4g; Sodium: 8m; Protein: 1g

Pb&j Smoothie

Servings:2

Cooking Time: 0 Minutes

Ingredients:

- 3 cups unsweetened almond milk
- 1 cup sliced strawberries, fresh or frozen
- 1 cup crushed ice
- ¼ cup sugar-free natural peanut butter
- 3 tablespoons chia seeds or ground flaxseed
- 1 packet stevia (optional)

Directions:

1. In a blender, combine the almond milk, strawberries, ice, peanut butter, chia seeds or flaxseed, and stevia (if using).
2. Blend until smooth.

Nutrition Info:

- Calories:328; Total Fat: 25g; Saturated Fat: 4g; Carbohydrates: 18g; Fiber: 8g; Sodium: 422mg; Protein: 12g

Rice & Zucchini Slice

Servings: 4
Cooking Time: 55 Minutes
Ingredients:

- ⅔ cup rice
- (brown, white, or basmati)
- ⅔ cup water
- 1 cup grated zucchini
- ½ cup grated carrot
- 3 eggs, beaten lightly
- 1 cup grated cheddar cheese

Directions:

1. Preheat the oven to 350°F. Line the base and sides of a loaf pan with parchment paper, leaving space for overhang.
2. Add rice and water to a saucepan and cook according to instructions on the packet.
3. In a bowl, add the zucchini, eggs, ½ cup cheese, rice, and carrot and mix well. Spread evenly over the bottom of the pan. Spread the remainder of the cheese over the top.
4. Bake for 30-35 minutes. When it's finished, the top should appear golden. Let cool before cutting into quarters. Place into a microwaveable, airtight Tupperware and put into the fridge within 2 hours of baking.

Nutrition Info:

- 201g Calories, 14g Total fat, 9.8g Saturated fat, 7.8g Carbohydrates, 2 g Fiber, 11.9g Protein, 3.5g Sodium.

Kale, Ginger, And Pineapple Smoothie

Servings: 1
Cooking Time: 2 Minutes
Ingredients:

- 1 cup FODMAP-approved milk (lactose-free or coconut)
- ½ peeled orange
- ¾ cup pineapple, fresh or frozen
- 1 cup raw kale
- Pinch of ground ginger
- 1 cup ice

Directions:

1. Place ingredients in a blender and blend until smooth.

Nutrition Info:

- 215g Calories, 4g Total fat, 1g Saturated fat, 37g Carbohydrates, 7 g Fiber, 10g Protein, 19g Sodium.

Basic Smoothie Base

Servings: 1
Cooking Time: 3 Minutes
Ingredients:

- Base *
- 1 banana, sliced and frozen
- ¾ cup Greek yogurt
- 2 tbsp almond milk
- ¼ tsp vanilla extract
- ¼ cup ice, optional
- Flavoring variations
- Choconut *
- 1 tbsp peanut butter
- 1 tbsp cocoa powder
- Pinch of salt
- Berry *
- ½ cup strawberries, can be replaced with any other approved berry or a mixture
- 5 mint leaves
- Pinch of salt
- Tropical *
- 1 cup papaya, peeled and diced
- 1 tbsp lime juice
- Pinch of salt

Directions:

1. In a blender, add the base ingredients and one of the flavor combinations.
2. If ice is added, drink immediately or cover and put in the fridge.

Nutrition Info:

- 334g Calories, 17g Total fat, 10g Saturated fat, 36g Carbohydrates, 3 g Fiber, 9g Protein, 23g Sodium.

Peanut Butter Bowl

Servings: 2
Cooking Time: 5 Minutes
Ingredients:

- 2 bananas, chopped and frozen
- 1 ½ cups Greek yogurt
- 2 tbsp peanut butter
- ¼ cup chopped nuts

Directions:

1. In a blender, mix the bananas, yogurt, and peanut butter.
2. When the mixture is a smooth consistency, pour it into a bowl and top with chopped nuts.
3. Simple!

Nutrition Info:

- 519g Calories, 35g Total fat, 13.5g Saturated fat, 5.5g Carbohydrates, 5.5 g Fiber, 15.5g Protein, 25g Sodium.

Tropical Smoothie

Servings:1
Cooking Time: 3 Minutes
Ingredients:
- ¾ cup frozen pineapple
- 1 cup baby spinach
- ½ tbsp lime juice
- ¾ cup ginger, ground
- ½ cup oat milk
- ½ cup coconut milk
- 1 tbsp flaxseed
- Pinch of salt

Directions:
1. Once the mixture has a smooth consistency, enjoy!

Nutrition Info:
- 434g Calories, 28g Total fat, 22g Saturated fat, 44g Carbohydrates, 7 g Fiber, 7g Protein, 20g Sodium.

Crepes And Berries

Servings:4
Cooking Time: 8 Minutes
Ingredients:
- Crepes
- ½ cup oat flour
- 1 tsp brown sugar
- 1 tsp white sugar
- 2 eggs
- 1 ½ tbsp melted butter
- 1 tsp vanilla extract
- Filling
- ½ cup berry mix
- Pinch of brown sugar
- Pinch of cinnamon
- 2 tbsp Greek yogurt

Directions:
1. In a blender, place the crepe ingredients and blend for two minutes. Set aside to rest for 15 minutes.
2. Mix the brown sugar and cinnamon with the berries.
3. After the crepe mix has rested, place a non-stick pan, greased with oil, over medium heat. Add ¼ cup of the crepe batter to the pan. Gently move the pan to cover the bottom of the pan with a thin layer of batter. Cook for a minute and gently flip.
4. Once the crepes are cooked, place them on a plate and top with a small amount of yogurt, fold, and place the berries on top.

Nutrition Info:
- 277g Calories, 10.5g Total fat, 4.5g Saturated fat, 25g Carbohydrates, 3.5 g Fiber, 8g Protein, 6g Sodium.

Banana Porridge

Servings:1
Cooking Time: 5 Minutes
Ingredients:
- ½ cup rolled oats
- ½ cup almond milk
- ⅓ cup banana, sliced
- 2 tsp sunflower oil
- 2 tsp maple syrup
- ¼ tsp vanilla extract
- Pinch of cinnamon

Directions:
1. Cook the oats according to the instructions and use almond milk.
2. Combine oil, syrup, cinnamon, and vanilla in a saucepan over medium heat. Let the mixture bubble for a minute and add the banana. Cook for 3 minutes. The banana should look plump.
3. Serve the oats with the banana on top.

Nutrition Info:
- 450g Calories, 14.7g Total fat, 1.4g Saturated fat, 73.3g Carbohydrates, 7.6 g Fiber, 7.8g Protein, 25.4g Sodium.

Gluten-free Eggs Benedict

Servings:4
Cooking Time: 30 Minutes
Ingredients:
- Olive oil for preparing the pan and brushing the polenta slices
- 8 (½-inch-thick) slices precooked polenta (from an 18-ounce tube)
- 8 eggs
- 8 slices ham or Canadian bacon
- FOR THE SAUCE
- 1 large egg yolk
- 1½ teaspoons lemon juice
- ½ teaspoon salt
- 4 tablespoons (½ stick) unsalted butter, melted

Directions:
1. Preheat the oven to 375°F.
2. Oil a large baking sheet, arrange the polenta slices on the prepared sheet, and brush the tops with olive oil. Bake the polenta rounds in the preheated oven for 18 to 20 minutes, until they are golden brown and crisp.

3. Meanwhile, make the sauce. In a blender, add the egg yolk, lemon juice, and salt, and blend for about 5 seconds, until just combined.

4. Set the blender to high, and add the butter to the yolk mixture in a thin stream until the sauce is thick and smooth, which will happen almost immediately. If the sauce thickens too much, add 1 or 2 teaspoons of warm water.

5. To poach the eggs, bring a pan of water about 3 inches deep to a boil over high heat. Reduce the heat to low, carefully break the eggs into the water, and simmer for 4 minutes.

6. While the eggs cook, heat a large skillet over medium-high heat. Add the ham or Canadian bacon slices in a single layer and cook until they begin to brown, for about 3 minutes. Turn over and cook on the other side until hot and just beginning to brown, for about 1 minute.

7. To serve, arrange 2 polenta slices on each of 4 serving plates. Top each round with a slice of ham or Canadian bacon, a poached egg, and a drizzle of the Hollandaise sauce. Serve immediately.

Nutrition Info:
- Calories: 550; Protein: 26g; Total Fat: 28g; Saturated Fat: 12g; Carbohydrates: 49g; Fiber: 2g; Sodium: 1231mg;

Bacon And Sweet Potato Hash

Servings:4
Cooking Time: 25 Minutes
Ingredients:
- 2 cups peeled and diced sweet potatoes
- 3 tablespoons olive oil, divided
- ½ teaspoon salt
- 4 slices thick-cut bacon, diced
- 1 large red bell pepper, chopped
- 4 sliced scallions (green parts only)
- 2 teaspoons smoked paprika
- 2 tablespoons chopped fresh parsley

Directions:
1. Preheat the oven to 400°F.
2. On a large baking sheet, toss the sweet potatoes with 2 tablespoons of the olive oil and sprinkle with the salt. Roast in the preheated oven until tender, about 15 minutes.
3. While the potatoes are roasting, heat the remaining tablespoon of olive oil in a large skillet over medium-high heat. Add the bacon and reduce the heat to medium. Cook until the bacon begins to crisp, for 6 to 8 minutes. Add the bell pepper, scallions, and paprika. Cook for about 4 minutes, until the vegetables begin to soften.
4. Once the sweet potatoes are finished roasting, add them to the skillet and cook until they begin to brown, for about 8 minutes. Serve hot, garnished with parsley.

Nutrition Info:
- Calories: 267; Protein: 9g; Total Fat: 19g; Saturated Fat: 4g; Carbohydrates: 17g; Fiber: 4g; Sodium: 682mg;

Quinoa Breakfast Bowl With Basil "hollandaise" Sauce

Servings:4
Cooking Time: 15 Minutes
Ingredients:
- 1 cup uncooked quinoa
- 12 ounces green beans, trimmed and cut into 1-inch pieces
- 1½ cups water
- ½ teaspoon salt
- Basil "Hollandaise" Sauce (here)

Directions:
1. In a medium saucepan, stir together the quinoa, green beans, water, and salt. Bring to a boil over medium-high heat. Reduce the heat to low, cover, and simmer for about 15 minutes, until the quinoa is tender.
2. To serve, spoon the quinoa mixture into bowls and drizzle the sauce over the top.

Nutrition Info:
- Calories: 415; Protein: 9g; Total Fat: 28g; Saturated Fat: 3g; Carbohydrates: 36g; Fiber: 6g; Sodium: 605mg;

Fruit Salad Smoothie

Servings:2
Cooking Time: 5 Minutes
Ingredients:
- 1 cup canned fruit salad, frozen
- 2 tbsp lactose-free yogurt
- 2 tbsp coconut milk
- 2 tsp coconut, shredded
- 2 tsp walnuts, chopped finely
- 1 tsp lemon zest, optional
- ½ cup water to thin out the mixture

Directions:
1. Blend together fruit, yogurt, milk, water, and lemon zest until smooth.
2. Add water to thin out the consistency, if desired.
3. Top with shredded coconut and walnuts.

Nutrition Info:
- 129.5g Calories, 8g Total fat, 3g Saturated fat, 15.5g Carbohydrates, 2.5 g Fiber, 2g Protein, 11g Sodium.

Tomato Omelet

Servings:2

Cooking Time: 5 Minutes

Ingredients:

- 4 fresh tomatoes
- 4 eggs
- ¼ cup water
- ½ tsp chopped basil
- Pinch of salt
- Pinch of pepper
- 2 tbsp olive oil (or other approved oil)

Directions:

1. Place a pot of water on the stove and bring to a boil. Mark each tomato with an 'x' in the skin and place them in the water. Leave the tomatoes in the water for 30 seconds before removing them with a draining spoon and placing them into cold water.

2. Peel the skin off the tomatoes and cut them in half. Remove the core and seeds and slice into strips. Set them aside.

3. Break the eggs into a bowl and whisk together while adding the basil, salt, and pepper. Stop whisking when the mixture is frothy. Place the mixture into a hot pan that has been greased with oil.

4. Gently stir the mixture while cooking over medium heat. When the mixture starts to get firm, spread the tomato over it. Do not continue stirring the mixture. When the tomatoes are warmed through, remove from the pan and enjoy.

Nutrition Info:

- 311.5g Calories, 24g Total fat, 5g Saturated fat, 10.5g Carbohydrates, 3 g Fiber, 15g Protein, 7g Sodium.

Potato Pancakes

Servings:4

Cooking Time: 10 Minutes

Ingredients:

- 3 medium potatoes, peeled and quartered
- 2 eggs
- 2 tablespoons rice flour
- ½ teaspoon salt
- ¼ teaspoon freshly ground pepper
- 2 tablespoons coconut or grapeseed oil

Directions:

1. In a blender or food processor, pulse the potatoes until they are finely chopped.

2. In a medium bowl, whisk the eggs, and then add the flour, salt, pepper, and the finely chopped potatoes, and stir to mix well.

3. Heat the oil in a large skillet over medium-high heat. Add the potato mixture about ¼ cup at a time, using the back of a spoon or scoop to flatten into pancakes about 3 inches in diameter. Cook for 3 to 4 minutes per side, until the pancakes are golden brown and crisp. Serve hot.

Nutrition Info:

- Calories: 169; Protein: 6g; Total Fat: 3g; Saturated Fat: 2g; Carbohydrates: 30g; Fiber: 4g; Sodium: 332mg;

Thai Pumpkin Noodle Soup

Servings:6

Cooking Time: 55 Minutes

Ingredients:

- Roast vegetables
- 3 ¼ cups pumpkin, peeled, deseeded, and cubed
- 1 cup carrots, peeled and cubed
- 1 tsp cumin, ground
- 2 tsp olive oil
- Pinch of salt
- Pinch of pepper
- Soup
- 2 cups vegetable stock, without garlic or onion
- 1 cup spring onions, green part only, chopped finely
- 1 tsp ginger, crushed
- ½ tsp lemon zest
- 2 tsp soy sauce
- Pinch of chili flakes, to taste
- 1 ½ cups coconut milk, canned
- 1 cup thin rice noodles
- ¼ cup cilantro

Directions:

1. Preheat the oven to 350°F. Place the peeled and cubed pumpkin and carrots onto a roasting tray. Use the oil to coat the vegetables and season with cumin, salt, and pepper. Bake for 20-30 minutes, turning halfway. Remove when the vegetables are soft and golden.

2. Set the vegetables aside to cool for 10 minutes, and then blend them together with the stock until smooth.

3. Over medium heat, heat a saucepan, add some oil, and fry the spring onion for 3 minutes. Add the ginger. Let cook for another minute before adding the pumpkin and coconut milk.

4. Stir in the lemon zest, soy sauce, and chili flakes. Allow the soup to simmer for 10 minutes on low heat. Add water if the soup seems too thick.

5. Cook the noodles according to the instructions on the packet while the soup cooks. When cooked, stir the noodles into the soup with cilantro and serve.

Nutrition Info:

- 373g Calories, 16.3g Total fat, 12.3g Saturated fat, 52.6g Carbohydrates, 7.7 g Fiber, 7.4g Protein, 8.1g Sodium.

Egg Wraps

Servings:4
Cooking Time: 5 Minutes
Ingredients:
- Oil to grease the pan (from the approved food list: avocado, olive, or sunflower)
- 4-8 eggs
- Pinch of salt
- Pepper

Directions:
1. Grease a non-stick pan with oil then place over medium heat to warm.
2. Whisk the egg in a bowl and pour it into the pan, ensuring it is spread evenly. Add in salt and pepper to taste.
3. Cook for 30-60 seconds on each side; gently flip when the edges on the first side are cooked.
4. Place on a plate to cool and repeat with the remainder of the eggs.

Nutrition Info:
- 414g Calories, 33g Total fat, 8g Saturated fat, 2g Carbohydrates, 0 g Fiber, 25g Protein, 2g Sodium.

Mixed Berry & Yogurt Granola Bar

Servings:12
Cooking Time: 30 Minutes
Ingredients:
- 2 cups rolled oats
- 3 tbsp shredded coconut
- 2 tbsp macadamia nut meal
- 4 tbsp chia seeds
- 1 egg (whites only)
- ⅓ cup peanut oil
- ¼ cup maple syrup
- 1 cup mixed berries
- 1 ½ cups Greek yogurt
- 3 tbsp white chocolate, melted

Directions:
1. Preheat the oven to 375°F. Line a baking tray with parchment paper.
2. Mix the ingredients in a bowl, and then press into the pan. Bake for 30 minutes.
3. Allow to cool, then drizzle with chocolate and serve.

Nutrition Info:
- 784g Calories, 9.5g Total fat, 3.2g Saturated fat, 18.5g Carbohydrates, 2.8 g Fiber, 3.9g Protein, 6.4g Sodium.

Cucumber Salad

Servings:4
Cooking Time: -
Ingredients:
- ¾ cup cucumber
- 2 tbsp chives, fresh
- ½ cup Greek yogurt
- ¼ cup white vinegar

Directions:
1. Slice the cucumber thinly and place it into salad bowls along with the yogurt.
2. Chop the chives and mix them into the cucumber along with the vinegar.
3. Refrigerate until you are ready to eat.

Nutrition Info:
- 46.5g Calories, 3g Total fat, 1.75g Saturated fat, 3.5g Carbohydrates, 0.5 g Fiber, 1.75g Protein, 2.25g Sodium.

Raspberry Smoothie

Servings:2
Cooking Time: 0 Minutes
Ingredients:
- 2 cups unsweetened almond milk
- 1 cup crushed ice
- 1 cup fresh raspberries
- 3 tablespoons ground flaxseed
- 1 packet stevia (optional)
- ½ teaspoon vanilla extract

Directions:
1. In a blender, combine the almond milk, ice, raspberries, flaxseed, stevia (if using), and vanilla.
2. Blend until smooth.

Nutrition Info:
- Calories:177; Total Fat: 9g; Saturated Fat: <1g; Carbohydrates: 20g; Fiber: 7g; Sodium: 181mg; Protein: 5g

Peanut Butter Pancakes

Servings:4
Cooking Time: 10 Minutes
Ingredients:
- 4 eggs
- 1 cup creamy sugar-free natural peanut butter
- ¼ cup cottage cheese
- 2 tablespoons pure maple syrup
- 1 teaspoon vanilla extract
- 1 cup sliced fresh strawberries
- Nonstick cooking spray

Directions:
1. Heat a skillet over medium-high heat.

2. In a blender or food processor, combine the eggs, peanut butter, cottage cheese, maple syrup, and vanilla. Blend until smooth.

3. In 2-tablespoon amounts, pour the batter onto the heated skillet, 3 pancakes at a time, leaving room for each to spread. Cook for 2 to 3 minutes, until bubbles form on the surface. Flip each pancake and cook the other side for 2 to 3 minutes until browned at the edges.

4. Transfer to a plate, and serve topped with the sliced strawberries.

Nutrition Info:

- Calories:495; Total Fat: 37g; Saturated Fat: 8g; Carbohydrates: 23g; Fiber: 5g; Sodium: 417mg; Protein: 24g

Scrambled Tofu

Servings:1
Cooking Time: 5 Minutes
Ingredients:

- ½ cup medium-firm tofu
- ¼ cup water
- 1 tbsp soy sauce (gluten-free)
- ¼ tsp turmeric, ground
- ½ cup grated carrot and zucchini
- Oil for greasing the pan
- 1 slice FODMAP-approved bread

Directions:

1. In a bowl, thoroughly mix together the water, soy sauce, and turmeric. Once mixed, add the vegetables and crumble the tofu into the bowl.

2. Place an oil-greased pan onto medium heat and place the mixture in it. Fry the mixture for 5 minutes or until it is golden brown.

3. Serve with a slice of FODMAP-approved toast.

Nutrition Info:

- 82g Calories, 5g Total fat, 0.5g Saturated fat, 4g Carbohydrates, 0.5 g Fiber, 5g Protein, 2g Sodium.

Everything-free Pancakes

Servings:4
Cooking Time: 10 Minutes
Ingredients:

- ⅓ cup warm water
- 2 tablespoons chia-seed meal
- ¼ cup maple syrup
- 5 tablespoons coconut oil, melted, divided
- 2 teaspoons vanilla extract
- 2 cups gluten-free flour (see Ingredient Tip)
- ½ teaspoon salt
- ¾ teaspoon baking powder

- ½ teaspoon baking soda

Directions:

1. In a large bowl, combine the warm water and chia-seed meal. Let it sit for about 3 minutes, until the mixture is thickened. Stir in the maple syrup, 3 tablespoons of the coconut oil, vanilla extract, and gluten-free flour, and whisk to combine. Add the salt, baking powder, and baking soda, and whisk to incorporate.

2. Heat 1 tablespoon of the coconut oil in a large skillet over medium-high heat.

3. Ladle the batter, ¼ cup at a time, into the heated skillet. Cook until bubbles appear on the tops of the pancakes, about 2 to 3 minutes. Flip over and cook until the second side is golden brown, about 1 to 2 minutes more. Repeat with the remaining batter, adding more oil to the pan as needed. Serve hot, topped with fresh fruit, if desired.

Nutrition Info:

- Calories: 528; Protein: 7g; Total Fat: 19g; Saturated Fat: 15g; Carbohydrates: 82g; Fiber: 3g; Sodium: 472mg;

Ham Salad

Servings:2
Cooking Time: 5 Minutes
Ingredients:

- Salad
- 2 cups baby spinach and arugula
- 25 blueberries
- 6 slices ham, cold cut, cut into small pieces
- 15 macadamia nuts, halved
- 1 cup feta cheese
- Pinch of salt
- Pinch of pepper
- Dressing
- 1 tbsp rice vinegar
- 1 tbsp olive oil
- 1 tbsp maple syrup

Directions:

1. Place the salad ingredients, except for the feta and black pepper, into a bowl and set aside.

2. Mix the dressing ingredients in a small bowl, then pour over the salad. Cover the salad and shake until the dressing covers everything evenly. Crumble the feta into the bowl and add the pepper.

Nutrition Info:

- 576g Calories, 48g Total fat, 24g Saturated fat, 5.5g Carbohydrates, 2 g Fiber, 31.5g Protein, 2.5g Sodium.

Peanut Butter Granola

Servings:4

Cooking Time: 10 Minutes

Ingredients:

- Coconut oil for preparing the baking sheet
- ¼ cup creamy peanut butter
- ¼ cup maple syrup
- ½ teaspoon cinnamon
- ½ teaspoon vanilla extract
- 1 cup gluten-free oats
- ½ cup pumpkin seeds
- 2 tablespoons sunflower seeds

Directions:

1. Preheat the oven to 325°F.
2. Oil a large, rimmed baking sheet with coconut oil.
3. In the top of a double boiler set over simmering water, stir together the peanut butter and maple syrup until the peanut butter melts and the mixture is well combined, for about 2 minutes. Stir in the cinnamon and vanilla.
4. In a medium bowl, combine the peanut butter mixture with the oats, pumpkin seeds, and sunflower seeds and stir until the oats and seeds are well coated.
5. Spread the oat mixture onto the prepared baking sheet and bake in the preheated oven for about 8 minutes, until lightly browned. Remove from the oven and let the granola cool. It will become crisp as it cools. Serve at room temperature.

Nutrition Info:

- Calories: 340; Protein: 12g; Total Fat: 19g; Saturated Fat: 3g; Carbohydrates: 36g; Fiber: 4g; Sodium: 79mg;

Chia Seed Carrot Cake Pudding

Servings:2

Cooking Time: None

Ingredients:

- ¾ cup unsweetened rice milk
- ½ cup chopped carrots
- 3 tablespoons chia seeds, divided
- 2 tablespoons maple syrup
- ½ teaspoon vanilla
- ½ teaspoon cinnamon
- ¼ teaspoon ground ginger
- ⅛ teaspoon ground cloves
- Pinch nutmeg

Directions:

1. Place the rice milk, carrots, 2 tablespoons of the chia seeds, maple syrup, vanilla, cinnamon, ginger, cloves, and nutmeg in a blender and blend until smooth. Add the remaining tablespoon of chia seeds and pulse just to incorporate.
2. Pour the mixture into two custard cups or bowls, cover, and refrigerate overnight. Serve chilled.

Nutrition Info:

- Calories: 135; Protein: 3g; Total Fat: 5g; Saturated Fat: 0g; Carbohydrates: 26g; Fiber: 8g; Sodium: 88mg;

Carrot And Walnut Salad

Servings:4

Cooking Time: 5 Minutes

Ingredients:

- ½ cup lettuce
- 3 carrots, peeled
- ¼ cup walnuts, chopped
- ¼ cup orange juice
- Pinch of salt

Directions:

1. Wash the lettuce and carrots, and then shred the lettuce into a bowl. Shave the carrots into strips and mix with the lettuce.
2. Place a greased pan over medium heat. Add the walnuts and fry quickly (2 minutes), stirring often to prevent the walnuts from burning. Remove the walnuts from the pan and place onto a paper towel. Sprinkle with salt.
3. Mix the lettuce and carrots in a bowl. Add the orange juice and the walnuts before serving.

Nutrition Info:

- 277g Calories, 2.4g Total fat, 0.2g Saturated fat, 7.5g Carbohydrates, 2.9 g Fiber, 1.7g Protein, 5g Sodium.

Strawberry-kiwi Smoothie With Chia Seeds

Servings:2

Cooking Time: None

Ingredients:

- ¾ cup orange juice
- ¾ cup unsweetened rice milk
- 1 ripe banana, peeled and sliced
- 2 kiwifruit, peeled and sliced
- 10 frozen strawberries
- 2 tablespoons maple syrup
- 2 tablespoons chia seeds

Directions:

1. Place all of the ingredients in a blender and blend until smooth.
2. Serve immediately.

Nutrition Info:

- Calories: 294; Protein: 4g; Total Fat: 5g; Saturated Fat: 0g; Carbohydrates: 63g; Fiber: 8g; Sodium: 43mg;

Pineapple, Strawberry, Raspberry Smoothie

Servings:2

Cooking Time: 3 Minutes

Ingredients:

- 1 banana, frozen and sliced
- ½ cup strawberries, fresh or frozen
- ¼ cup pineapple, fresh
- ½ cup raspberries, frozen
- 1 cup almond milk, can substitute other approved milk

Directions:

1. Add more milk to create a thinner consistency.

Nutrition Info:

- 110g Calories, 2.5g Total fat, 0g Saturated fat, 23g Carbohydrates, 5 g Fiber, 2g Protein, 12.5g Sodium.

Corn Salad

Servings:2

Cooking Time: 5 Minutes

Ingredients:

- 1 can (15 oz) corn
- 1 cup cherry tomatoes
- 1 cup cucumber
- 2 spring onions, green parts only
- 1 red capsicum
- 2 tbsp mayonnaise (even vegan or gluten free)

Directions:

1. Slice the tomatoes in half.
2. Cut the cucumber into slices and then quarters. Chop the green part of the spring onion finely.
3. Thinly slice the capsicum.
4. Mix all the ingredients with the mayonnaise in a bowl and serve.

Nutrition Info:

- 189g Calories, 8g Total fat, 1.5g Saturated fat, 17g Carbohydrates, 5 g Fiber, 5g Protein, 10.5g Sodium.

Smoothie Bowl

Servings:2

Cooking Time: 5 Minutes

Ingredients:

- 1 cup coconut yogurt
- ½ cup coconut milk, canned or fresh
- 4 bananas, cut into slices and frozen
- 2 cups frozen mixed berries
- 2 tsp lemon juice

- ½ cup mixed nuts, chopped
- 2 mint leaves, torn

Directions:

1. In a blender, mix yogurt, milk, bananas, frozen berries, and lemon juice.
2. Pour the mix into bowls and top with nuts and mint.

Nutrition Info:

- 324g Calories, 17g Total fat, 10g Saturated fat, 36g Carbohydrates, 3 g Fiber, 9g Protein, 23g Sodium.

Summer Berry Smoothie

Servings:4

Cooking Time: -

Ingredients:

- 1 large banana, unripe
- ¼ cup blueberries
- 1 ¼ cups lactose-free milk, even vegetable milk (no oat milk for gluten-free)
- 1 cup Greek yogurt
- Ice

Directions:

1. Place ingredients in a blender and mix until smooth.

Nutrition Info:

- 406g Calories, 3.3g Total fat, 1.6g Saturated fat, 10.7g Carbohydrates, 0.8 g Fiber, 5.8g Protein, 10.7g Sodium.

Blueberry Lime Smoothie

Servings:1

Cooking Time: 3 Minutes

Ingredients:

- ½ cup blueberries, fresh or frozen
- 2 tbsp coconut flakes
- 2 tbsp lime juice, fresh
- ½ cup Greek or lactose-free yogurt
- 1 tsp chia seeds
- 2 tbsp water
- Ice (only if using fresh blueberries and if you want a thicker consistency)

Directions:

1. Place ingredients in a blender and mix until it starts to look frothy.

Nutrition Info:

- 319g Calories, 23g Total fat, 7g Saturated fat, 26g Carbohydrates, 6 g Fiber, 7g Protein, 15g Sodium.

Blueberry, Lime, And Coconut Smoothie

Servings:2

Cooking Time: 5 Minutes

Ingredients:

- ½ cup blueberries, fresh or frozen
- 2 tbsp coconut flakes
- 2 tbsp lime juice
- ⅔ cup FODMAP-approved yogurt or vegan yogurt
- 1 tsp chia seeds
- 2 tbsp water
- Ice, when using fresh blueberries (Approximately 6 cubes, depending on the desired texture)

Directions:

1. Blend all ingredients together until frothy.

Nutrition Info:

- 186g Calories, 13.5g Total fat, 5g Saturated fat, 14g Carbohydrates, 3 g Fiber, 4.5g Protein, 8.5g Sodium.

Oven-baked Zucchini And Carrot Fritters With Ginger-lime Sauce

Servings:4

Cooking Time: 40 Minutes

Ingredients:

- Oil for preparing the baking sheet
- 2 large zucchini
- 1 teaspoon salt
- 2 large carrots
- 1 cup chopped cilantro, plus additional for garnish
- 2 eggs, lightly beaten
- 1 tablespoon gluten-free, onion- and garlic-free curry powder
- 2 teaspoons gluten-free, onion- and garlic-free chili powder
- 2 teaspoons cumin
- ½ cup brown-rice flour
- 1 cup coconut milk
- 2 tablespoons lemon juice
- 1 tablespoon lime juice
- 1 teaspoon cornstarch
- 1 teaspoon sugar
- ¾ teaspoon ground ginger

Directions:

1. Preheat the oven to 400°F.
2. Line a large baking sheet with parchment paper and lightly oil the parchment.
3. In a food processor, pulse the zucchini to chop it finely. Transfer the chopped zucchini to a colander set over the sink and sprinkle generously with salt. Let sit for about 15 minutes.
4. Finely chop the carrots and cilantro in the food processor, then combine with the zucchini in a large mixing bowl. Add the eggs, curry powder, chili powder, and cumin. Stir to mix.
5. Add the flour, ¼ cup at a time, stirring to incorporate it.
6. Drop the batter onto the prepared baking sheet by heaping tablespoons, flattening the fritters with the back of the spoon.
7. Bake in the preheated oven for 25 minutes. Turn the fritters over and continue to bake for another 15 to 20 minutes, until the fritters are crisp and golden brown.
8. While the fritters are in the oven, make the sauce. In a small bowl, stir together the coconut milk, lemon juice, lime juice, cornstarch, sugar, and ginger.
9. Serve the fritters hot, with a drizzle of the sauce and a sprinkling of cilantro.

Nutrition Info:

- Calories: 296; Protein: 8g; Total Fat: 18g; Saturated Fat: 14g; Carbohydrates: 30g; Fiber: 5g; Sodium: 88mg;

Savory Muffins

Servings:12

Cooking Time: 25 Minutes

Ingredients:

- ¼ cup quinoa, boiled in ½ cup water
- 1 cup oat flour
- ¼ cup corn flour
- ¼ tsp cinnamon
- Pinch of salt
- Pinch of pepper
- 3 eggs
- ½ cup lactose-free or Greek yogurt
- 2 cups zucchini, grated
- ⅓ cup baby spinach, chopped
- A few sprigs of rosemary
- ¼ cup walnuts, chopped
- ½ lemon, zested

Directions:

1. Preheat the oven to 350°F and grease a 12-hole muffin pan.
2. In a saucepan, cook the quinoa in water for 15 minutes, then drain the excess water and let cool.
3. In a bowl, mix the dry ingredients together.
4. In a larger bowl, whisk the eggs and yogurt together, then add in the zucchini, spinach, nuts, spices, lemon zest, and quinoa slowly.

5. Add the bowl of dry ingredients to the larger bowl and mix well. Spoon the batter into muffin tins and bake for 25 minutes.

Nutrition Info:

- 120g Calories, 4g Total fat, 0.8g Saturated fat, 15g Carbohydrates, 1.5 g Fiber, 4.9g Protein, 0.5g Sodium.

French Toast

Servings:2

Cooking Time: 10 Minutes

Ingredients:

- 4 eggs, beaten
- 1 cup unsweetened almond milk
- 1 teaspoon vanilla extract
- 1 teaspoon grated orange zest
- 1 packet stevia
- ½ teaspoon ground nutmeg
- 4 gluten-free bread slices
- Nonstick cooking spray

Directions:

1. In a medium bowl, whisk together the eggs, almond milk, vanilla, orange zest, stevia, and nutmeg.
2. Soak the bread slices in the mixture for about 5 minutes.
3. Spray a large nonstick skillet with cooking spray and place it over medium-high heat.
4. Add the soaked bread. Cook for about 5 minutes, until browned on one side. Flip and cook for 3 to 4 more minutes on the other side.

Nutrition Info:

- Calories:206; Total Fat: 12g; Saturated Fat: 3g; Carbohydrates: 12g; Fiber: 1g; Sodium: 336mg; Protein: 13g

Breakfast Ratatouille With Poached Eggs

Servings:4

Cooking Time: 40 Minutes

Ingredients:

- 2 tablespoons butter
- 1 medium eggplant, diced
- 4 medium tomatoes, peeled, seeded, and diced
- 1 red bell pepper, diced
- 1 green bell pepper, diced
- 2 medium zucchini, diced
- ½ cup halved artichoke hearts
- 1 jalapeño, diced
- 2 tablespoons chopped fresh thyme
- 1 tablespoon chopped fresh oregano
- ¼ cup chopped parsley
- ½ cup homemade (onion- and garlic-free) chicken or vegetable broth
- 1 teaspoon salt
- ½ teaspoon freshly ground pepper
- 4 eggs
- 2 ounces freshly grated Parmesan cheese

Directions:

1. Heat the butter in a large skillet over medium-high heat. Add the eggplant and cook, stirring occasionally, for about 10 minutes, until the eggplant is tender. Add the tomatoes and cook for about 5 minutes, until the tomatoes have begun to break down.
2. Add the bell peppers, zucchini, artichoke hearts, jalapeño, thyme, oregano, and parsley. Stir to mix. Add the broth, salt, and pepper, and bring to a boil. Cover, reduce the heat to low, and simmer for about 20 minutes, until the liquid has evaporated and the vegetables are tender.
3. While the vegetables are cooking, poach the eggs. Bring a pan of water about 3 inches deep to a boil over high heat. Reduce the heat to low, carefully break the eggs into the water, and simmer for 4 minutes.
4. To serve, ladle the vegetable mixture into 4 serving bowls, top each with a poached egg, and sprinkle the cheese over the top. Serve hot.

Nutrition Info:

- Calories: 292; Protein: 21g; Total Fat: 15g; Saturated Fat: 7g; Carbohydrates: 24g; Fiber: 10g; Sodium: 819mg;

Chapter 3 Meat Recipes

Snapper With Tropical Salsa

Servings:4
Cooking Time: 8 Minutes
Ingredients:

- 2 tablespoons extra-virgin olive oil
- 1 pound snapper, quartered
- 1 teaspoon sea salt, divided
- ⅛ teaspoon freshly ground black pepper
- 1 papaya, chopped
- 1 cup chopped pineapple
- 1 jalapeño pepper, seeded and minced
- 1 tablespoon chopped fresh cilantro leaves
- Juice of 1 lime

Directions:

1. In a large nonstick skillet over medium-high heat, heat the olive oil until it shimmers.
2. Season the snapper with ½ teaspoon salt and the pepper. Add it to the skillet and cook for about 4 minutes per side, until the fish is opaque.
3. In a medium bowl, gently stir together the papaya, pineapple, jalapeño, cilantro, lime juice, and remaining ½ teaspoon salt.
4. Serve the salsa on top of the snapper.

Nutrition Info:

- Calories:236; Total Fat: 8g; Saturated Fat: 1g; Carbohydrates: 14g; Fiber: 2g; Sodium: 565mg; Protein: 27g

Pork Tenderloin Chops With Potatoes And Pan Sauce

Servings:4
Cooking Time: 20 Minutes
Ingredients:

- 4 tablespoons garlic oil, divided
- 2 cups chopped Yukon Gold potatoes
- 1 teaspoon sea salt, divided
- 1 pound pork tenderloin, cut into 8 slices
- ½ teaspoon black pepper
- 1 cup low-FODMAP poultry broth
- 3 tablespoons very cold butter, cut into pieces
- ¼ cup flat-leafed parsley leaves

Directions:

1. In a large skillet, heat 2 tablespoons of the garlic oil on medium-high until they shimmer.
2. Add the potatoes and ½ teaspoon of the sea salt and cook, stirring occasionally, until they are soft and browned,

about 10 minutes. Remove and set aside tented with foil to keep warm.
3. In the same pot, add the remaining 2 tablespoons of garlic oil. Season the pork tenderloin pieces with the remaining ½ teaspoon of sea salt and the pepper. Add to the hot oil and cook without moving until well browned on both sides, about 5 minutes per side.
4. Set aside tented with foil.
5. Add the poultry broth to the pan, using the side of the spoon to scrape any browned bits from the bottom of the pan. Reduce the heat to medium-low. Simmer until the liquid reduces by half.
6. Whisk in the butter one piece at a time until it is melted. Spoon the sauce over the potatoes and the meat. Garnish with the parsley leaves.

Nutrition Info:

- Calories:422; Total Fat: 27g; Saturated Fat: 9g; Carbohydrates: 12g; Fiber: 2g; Sodium: 791mg; Protein: 32g

Chili-rubbed Pork Chops With Raspberry Sauce

Servings:4
Cooking Time: 10 Minutes
Ingredients:

- 2 teaspoons gluten-free, onion- and garlic-free chili powder
- ½ teaspoon salt
- 1 teaspoon chopped fresh thyme
- 4 (6-ounce) bone-in, center-cut pork chops (about ½-inch thick)
- 2 tablespoons olive oil
- ¼ cup homemade (onion- and garlic-free) chicken broth
- 2 tablespoons seedless raspberry preserves

Directions:

1. In a small bowl, combine the chili powder, salt, and thyme. Coat the pork chops all over with the spice mixture.
2. Heat the oil in a large skillet over medium-high heat. Cook the chops for about 3 minutes per side, until they are browned and cooked through. Transfer the cooked chops to a large plate or serving platter, tent loosely with foil, and keep warm.
3. Add the broth to the skillet and cook, stirring and scraping up any browned bits from the bottom of the pan, for about 30 seconds. Add the preserves and cook, stirring constantly, for 1 minute or until the sauce thickens.
4. Serve the pork chops brushed with the glaze.

Nutrition Info:

- Calories: 286; Protein: 35g; Total Fat: 14g; Saturated Fat: 3g; Carbohydrates: 7g; Fiber: 0g; Sodium: 657mg;

Ginger-orange Braised Short Ribs

Servings:4
Cooking Time: 3 Hours, 20 Minutes

Ingredients:

- 5 pounds beef short ribs, cut into 4-ounce pieces
- 1 cup gluten-free soy sauce
- ½ cup light-brown sugar
- ¼ cup rice vinegar
- 1 to 2 tablespoons onion- and garlic-free chili paste
- 1 tablespoon dark sesame oil
- 2 tablespoons minced fresh ginger
- ¾ teaspoon red-pepper flakes
- 4 tablespoons orange juice, divided
- 4 cups water
- 2 tablespoons lemon juice

Directions:

1. Preheat the oven to 350°F.
2. Place the ribs, soy sauce, brown sugar, vinegar, chili paste, sesame oil, ginger, red-pepper flakes, 2 tablespoons of the orange juice, and water in a large Dutch oven. Cover the pot and cook in the preheated oven for 3 hours, until the meat is very tender and falling apart. Take the pot out of the oven and carefully transfer the ribs to a plate. Set aside.
3. Raise the oven temperature to 425°F.
4. Skim the fat off the top of the cooking liquid. Bring the liquid to a boil over medium-high heat, and cook until it is reduced to about 1¼ cups, for about 10 minutes. Strain the liquid through a fine-meshed sieve and discard the solids. Return the liquid to the pot and stir in the remaining 2 tablespoons of the orange juice and the lemon juice.
5. Return the ribs to the pot in the oven. Cook for about 10 minutes, until the liquid becomes a thick glaze. Serve hot.

Nutrition Info:

- Calories: 577; Protein: 17g; Total Fat: 45g; Saturated Fat: 18g; Carbohydrates: 23g; Fiber: 0g; Sodium: 283mg;

Baked Atlantic Salmon On Soft Blue Cheese Polenta

Servings:4
Cooking Time:x

Ingredients:

- Olive oil
- Four 5½-ounce (160 g) Atlantic salmon fillets, skin on, pin bones removed
- 3 cups (750 ml) low-fat milk, lactose-free milk, or suitable plant-based milk
- 2 garlic cloves, peeled and halved
- ⅔ cup (110 g) coarse cornmeal (instant polenta)
- ⅔ cup (90 g) strong blue cheese (or to taste)
- Salt and freshly ground black pepper
- Green salad or vegetables, for serving

Directions:

1. Preheat the oven to 350°F (180°C). Brush a baking sheet lightly with olive oil.
2. Place the salmon fillets on the baking sheet, brush with olive oil, and bake for 10 to 12 minutes, until cooked to your preferred doneness.
3. Meanwhile, combine the milk and garlic in a medium saucepan over medium heat and bring to just below a boil. Remove the garlic with a slotted spoon and discard. Add the cornmeal to the milk and stir until the polenta comes to a boil. Reduce the heat to low and cook, stirring constantly, for 3 to 5 minutes more. The polenta should be the texture of smooth mashed potatoes. Stir in the blue cheese and allow to melt. Season to taste with salt and pepper.
4. Spoon the polenta onto warmed plates, top with the salmon fillets, and serve with your choice of salad or vegetables.

Nutrition Info:

- 556 calories; 44 g protein; 29 g total fat; 9 g saturated fat; 27 g carbohydrates; 2 g fiber; 490 mg sodium

Chicken Tenders

Servings:4
Cooking Time: 15 Minutes

Ingredients:

- 1 cup gluten-free bread crumbs
- 1 teaspoon dried thyme
- ½ teaspoon sea salt
- ⅛ teaspoon freshly ground black pepper
- 2 eggs, beaten
- 1 tablespoon Dijon mustard
- 1 pound boneless skinless chicken breast, cut into strips

Directions:

1. Preheat the oven to 425°F.
2. In a medium bowl, mix the bread crumbs, thyme, salt, and pepper.
3. In a small bowl, whisk the eggs and mustard.
4. Dip the chicken strips into the egg mixture and into the bread crumb mixture to coat. Place them on a nonstick rimmed baking sheet.
5. Bake for 15 to 20 minutes, until the breading is golden and the juices run clear.

Nutrition Info:

- Calories:183; Total Fat: 5g; Saturated Fat: 2g; Carbohydrates: 20g; Fiber: 2g; Sodium: 526mg; Protein: 13g

Spicy Pulled Pork

Servings:8
Cooking Time: 6 Hours
Ingredients:
- FOR THE PORK
- 3 tablespoons paprika
- 1 tablespoon brown sugar
- 1 tablespoon dry mustard
- 3 tablespoons salt
- 1 pork shoulder or butt roast (about 5 pounds)
- FOR THE SAUCE
- 1½ cups white-wine vinegar
- 1 cup onion- and garlic-free mustard
- ⅓ cup onion- and garlic-free tomato sauce
- ½ cup packed brown sugar
- 1 tablespoon Garlic Oil (here)
- 1 teaspoon salt
- 1 teaspoon cayenne
- ½ teaspoon freshly ground black pepper

Directions:
1. To prepare the roast, in a small bowl, combine the paprika, brown sugar, dry mustard, and salt.
2. Rub the spice blend all over the pork. Cover and refrigerate for at least 1 hour or as long as overnight.
3. Preheat the oven to 300°F.
4. Roast the pork in a roasting pan in the preheated oven for 6 hours, until the meat is falling apart (a meat thermometer should read about 170°F).
5. While the pork is in the oven, prepare the sauce. In a medium saucepan, combine the vinegar, mustard, tomato sauce, brown sugar, Garlic Oil, salt, cayenne, and black pepper, and bring to a simmer over medium heat. Cook, stirring occasionally, until the sugar is completely dissolved, for about 10 minutes. Remove from the heat.
6. When the pork is done, remove it from the oven and let it rest for about 10 minutes. While the pork is still warm, shred the meat using two forks. Place the shredded meat in a large bowl and mix in half of the sauce.
7. Serve warm, topped with additional sauce.

Nutrition Info:
- Calories: 988; Protein: 72g; Total Fat: 67g; Saturated Fat: 23g; Carbohydrates: 20g; Fiber: 4g; Sodium: 3167mg;

Easy Shepherd's Pie

Servings:4
Cooking Time: 10 Minutes

Ingredients:
- 2 tablespoons Garlic Oil
- 1 pound ground lamb
- 2 carrots, chopped
- ¼ cup Low-FODMAP Poultry Broth
- 1 tablespoon chopped fresh rosemary leaves
- ½ teaspoon sea salt
- ¼ teaspoon freshly ground black pepper
- 1 recipe Mashed Potatoes, hot
- ½ cup grated Cheddar cheese

Directions:
1. Heat the broiler to high.
2. In a large nonstick skillet over medium-high heat, heat the garlic oil until it shimmers.
3. Add the lamb and carrots. Cook for about 5 minutes, stirring, until the lamb is browned.
4. Stir in the broth, rosemary, salt, and pepper. Cook for 2 minutes more. Spoon the mixture into a 9-inch-square casserole.
5. Spread the mashed potatoes over the top and sprinkle with the cheese.
6. Broil the pie for about 3 minutes, watching closely, until the cheese melts.

Nutrition Info:
- Calories:577; Total Fat: 30g; Saturated Fat: 14; Carbohydrates: 38g; Fiber: 7g; Sodium: 490mg; Protein: 40g

Sesame-crusted Cod

Servings:4
Cooking Time: 15 Minutes
Ingredients:
- 2 eggs, beaten
- 1 tablespoon Garlic Oil
- 1 tablespoon peeled and grated fresh ginger
- 1 teaspoon sesame oil
- ½ teaspoon Chinese hot mustard powder
- ½ cup sesame seeds
- ½ teaspoon sea salt
- ⅛ teaspoon freshly ground black pepper
- 1 pound cod, quartered

Directions:
1. Preheat the oven to 400°F.
2. In a small bowl, whisk together the eggs, garlic oil, ginger, sesame oil, and Chinese hot mustard powder.
3. In another small bowl, mix the sesame seeds, salt, and pepper.
4. Dip the cod into the egg mixture and into the seasoned sesame seeds to coat. Place it on a rimmed baking sheet. Bake for 15 minutes, until opaque.

Crunchy Homemade Fish Sticks

Servings:4
Cooking Time: 15 Minutes
Ingredients:
- 3½ cups gluten-free cornflakes
- ⅓ cup rice flour
- 1 egg
- 2 tablespoons lactose-free milk
- 1 pound firm whitefish fillets, such as snapper, skin removed, cut into 1-by-3-inch pieces
- 1 teaspoon salt
- Cooking spray

Directions:
1. Preheat the oven to 400°F.
2. Line a large, rimmed baking sheet with parchment paper.
3. In a food processor, pulse the cornflakes to make fine crumbs, and place the crumbs in a wide, shallow bowl. Next, place the rice flour in another wide, shallow bowl. In a separate wide, shallow bowl, beat together the egg and milk.
4. Season the fish all over with salt and dredge each piece in the flour. Next, dip each piece of fish in the egg mixture and then into the cornflake crumbs. Arrange the fish pieces on the prepared baking sheet. Spray the fish lightly with cooking spray and bake in the preheated oven for about 15 minutes, until golden brown and crisp. Serve hot.

Nutrition Info:
- Calories: 310; Protein: 34g; Total Fat: 4g; Saturated Fat: 1g; Carbohydrates: 33g; Fiber: 1g; Sodium: 842mg;

Chicken With Macadamia Spinach Pesto

Servings:4
Cooking Time: 10 Minutes
Ingredients:
- 4 (4- to 6-ounce) boneless, skinless chicken breast halves, pounded to ½-inch thickness (see Tip)
- ½ teaspoon sea salt
- ⅛ teaspoon freshly ground black pepper
- 2 tablespoons extra-virgin olive oil
- ½ cup Macadamia Spinach Pesto

Directions:
1. Season the chicken breast with salt and pepper.
2. In a large nonstick skillet over medium-high heat, heat the olive oil until it shimmers.
3. Add the chicken and cook for about 4 minutes per side, until the juices run clear.
4. Serve with the pesto spooned over the top.

Tuna And Pineapple Burgers

Servings:4
Cooking Time: 10 Minutes
Ingredients:
- 1 pound canned tuna, flaked
- ½ cup gluten-free bread crumbs
- 1 egg, beaten
- ¼ cup plus 2 tablespoons Low-FODMAP Mayonnaise, divided
- Zest of 1 lemon
- ½ teaspoon sea salt
- ⅛ teaspoon freshly ground black pepper
- 2 tablespoons Garlic Oil
- 3 tablespoons Teriyaki Sauce
- 4 canned pineapple slices, packed in water, drained
- 4 gluten-free hamburger buns

Directions:
1. In a large bowl, mix the tuna, bread crumbs, egg, 2 tablespoons mayonnaise, lemon zest, salt, and pepper until thoroughly combined. Form the tuna mixture into 4 patties.
2. In a large nonstick skillet over medium-high heat, heat the garlic oil until it shimmers.
3. Add the patties and cook for 5 minutes per side.
4. While the burgers cook, in a small bowl, whisk together the teriyaki sauce and remaining ¼ cup mayonnaise. Spread the sauce on the buns.
5. Place 1 cooked burger in each bun and top with 1 pineapple slice.

Nutrition Info:
- Calories:495; Total Fat: 18g; Saturated Fat: 4g; Carbohydrates: 42g; Fiber: 2g; Sodium: 1,270mg; Protein: 39g

Beef Rolls With Horseradish Cream

Servings:4
Cooking Time:x
Ingredients:
- Nonstick cooking spray
- 1½ pounds (675 g) flank, sirloin, or top round steak, trimmed of fat and cut into 4 pieces
- 2 ounces (60 g) baby spinach leaves (2 cups), rinsed, dried, and finely chopped
- 2 heaping tablespoons finely chopped pitted black olives
- ¼ cup plus 1 tablespoon (75 g) reduced-fat cream cheese, at room temperature

- Salt and freshly ground black pepper
- 1 heaping tablespoon freshly grated horseradish
- Squeeze of fresh lemon juice
- ¼ cup (60 ml) light cream
- 2 heaping tablespoons finely chopped flat-leaf parsley
- Salt and freshly ground black pepper
- Green salad or vegetables, for serving

Directions:

1. Preheat the oven to 350°F (180°C). Grease a baking dish with nonstick cooking spray.

2. Place each steak between two sheets of parchment or waxed paper and flatten with a meat tenderizer or rolling pin until the steak is about a third of its original thickness. Cut each steak in half to make 8 thin steaks. Set aside.

3. Mix together the spinach, olives, and cream cheese and season with salt and pepper. Place about 1 tablespoon of the cream cheese filling across the center of each steak portion and roll up to enclose the filling. Secure with a toothpick.

4. Place the rolls in the baking dish and bake for 10 minutes. Cover with foil and bake for 5 minutes more or until cooked through.

5. Meanwhile, to make the horseradish cream, combine all the ingredients in a small saucepan and simmer gently over medium-low heat for 5 to 8 minutes, until thickened slightly. (Don't let it boil.)

6. Serve 2 beef rolls per person with the horseradish cream and your choice of salad or vegetables.

Nutrition Info:

- 479 calories; 35 g protein; 36 g total fat; 16 g saturated fat; 3 g carbohydrates; 1 g fiber; 391 mg sodium

Turkey And Sweet Potato Chili

Servings:4
Cooking Time: 30 Minutes

Ingredients:

- 2 tablespoons Garlic Oil (here)
- 1¼ pounds ground turkey
- 1 red bell pepper, chopped
- 1 teaspoon salt
- ½ teaspoon ground cumin
- ¼ teaspoon gluten-, onion-, and garlic-free chili powder
- ¼ teaspoon paprika
- 1 bay leaf
- 1 (14½-ounce) can onion- and garlic-free diced tomatoes with juice
- 1 (4-ounce) can diced green chiles
- 1 cup canned corn, drained and rinsed
- 1 cup onion- and garlic-free tomato sauce
- ¾ cup water

- 1 sweet potato, peeled and diced into ½-inch cubes
- 2 tablespoons chopped fresh cilantro

Directions:

1. Heat the Garlic Oil in a large skillet over medium-high heat. Add the turkey and cook, stirring and breaking up the meat with a spatula, until it is browned, for about 5 minutes. Add the bell pepper and cook until it begins to soften, about 3 minutes more.

2. Add the salt, cumin, chili powder, paprika, and bay leaf and cook, stirring, for 1 minute. Add the tomatoes with their juice, chiles, corn, tomato sauce, water, and sweet potato, and bring to a boil. Reduce the heat to low, cover, and simmer for about 25 minutes, stirring occasionally, until the sweet potatoes are tender.

3. Serve hot, garnished with cilantro.

Nutrition Info:

- Calories: 390; Protein: 44g; Total Fat: 16g; Saturated Fat: 3g; Carbohydrates: 29g; Fiber: 6g; Sodium: 1326mg;

Chile Chicken Stir-fry

Servings:4
Cooking Time:x

Ingredients:

- 2 tablespoons plus 2 teaspoons sesame oil
- 1 pound 5 ounces (600 g) boneless, skinless chicken breasts or thighs, cut into thin strips
- 1 small red chile pepper, seeded and finely chopped, or ½ teaspoon cayenne pepper
- 1 bunch bok choy, leaves separated, cut if large, rinsed, and drained
- 5 ounces (125 g) green beans, trimmed and halved (1 heaping cup)
- 1 heaping cup (150 g) baby corn (about two thirds of a 15-ounce/425 g can, drained)
- 1 cup (80 g) bean sprouts
- One 8-ounce (225 g) can bamboo shoots, drained
- 1 heaping tablespoon cornstarch
- 2 tablespoons plus 2 teaspoons gluten-free soy sauce
- 1 cup (250 ml) gluten-free, onion-free chicken or vegetable stock*
- Steamed rice or prepared rice noodles, for serving

Directions:

1. Heat the sesame oil in a wok over medium heat. Add the chicken and chile pepper and stir-fry for 4 to 5 minutes, until the chicken is nicely browned. Increase the heat to medium-high, add the bok choy, green beans, baby corn, bean sprouts, and bamboo shoots and stir-fry for another 2 to 3 minutes, until the vegetables are tender.

2. Blend the cornstarch with the soy sauce and 2 tablespoons of the stock in a small bowl to form a paste. Slowly add the remaining stock, whisking to remove any lumps.

3. Pour the sauce over the chicken and vegetables and toss until heated through and thickened. Serve immediately over rice or rice noodles.

Nutrition Info:
- 340 calories; 41 g protein; 12 g total fat; 2 g saturated fat; 16 g carbohydrates; 6 g fiber; 1082 mg sodium

Grilled Carne Asada Tacos With Chimichurri Sauce

Servings:4
Cooking Time: 10 Minutes
Ingredients:
- 3 tablespoons olive oil, divided
- 2 tablespoons fresh lime juice, divided
- 1 teaspoon ground chipotle pepper
- 1 teaspoon salt
- 1 pound skirt steak
- 8 corn tortillas
- Chimichurri Sauce (here)
- ¼ cup chopped fresh cilantro, for garnish

Directions:
1. In a large bowl or resealable plastic bag, combine the olive oil, lime juice, ground chipotle, and salt. Add the steak and turn to coat. Marinate at room temperature for 30 minutes.

2. Heat a grill or grill pan to medium-high heat.

3. Grill the skirt steak to desired doneness, for 4 to 5 minutes per side for medium-rare. Remove the steak from the grill, tent it loosely with aluminum foil, and let rest for 10 minutes. Then slice it against the grain in ⅛-inch-thick slices.

4. Reduce the heat of the grill and set the tortillas on it to warm them, for about 1 minute.

5. Arrange 2 tortillas on each serving plate and top with several slices of the steak. Spoon the Chimichurri Sauce over the steak, garnish with cilantro, and serve immediately.

Nutrition Info:
- Calories: 559; Protein: 34g; Total Fat: 36g; Saturated Fat: 8g; Carbohydrates: 26g; Fiber: 4g; Sodium: 994mg;

Ginger-sesame Grilled Flank Steak

Servings:4
Cooking Time: 10 Minutes
Ingredients:
- 1 (5-inch) piece fresh ginger, minced

- 3 tablespoons dark sesame oil
- 2 tablespoons Garlic Oil (here)
- 2 teaspoons lime juice
- 1 tablespoon brown sugar
- 2 teaspoons salt
- 1 teaspoon pepper
- 1½ pounds flank steak
- Oil for preparing the grill or grill pan

Directions:
1. In large bowl or resealable plastic bag, combine the ginger, sesame oil, Garlic Oil, lime juice, brown sugar, salt, and pepper. Add the steak and turn to coat. Marinate the meat at room temperature for 30 minutes.

2. To cook the steak, oil a grill or grill pan, and heat to medium-high heat. Remove the steak from the marinade and cook on the grill for 4 to 5 minutes per side for medium-rare (cook a minute or two longer per side for medium, and even longer for well-done).

3. Tent the cooked steak loosely with aluminum foil and let rest for 10 minutes before slicing.

4. To serve, slice the steak across the grain into ⅛-inch-thick slices and serve immediately.

Nutrition Info:
- Calories: 460; Protein: 48g; Total Fat: 25g; Saturated Fat: 8g; Carbohydrates: 9g; Fiber: 1g; Sodium: 1262mg;

Chili-lime Shrimp And Bell Peppers

Servings:4
Cooking Time: 10 Minutes
Ingredients:
- 3 tablespoons Garlic Oil
- 1 red bell pepper, chopped
- 1 pound shrimp, peeled and deveined
- Juice of 1 lime
- 1 teaspoon chili powder
- ½ teaspoon sea salt
- ⅛ teaspoon cayenne pepper
- ⅛ teaspoon freshly ground black pepper

Directions:
1. In a large nonstick skillet over medium-high heat, heat the garlic oil until it shimmers.

2. Add the bell pepper. Cook for 3 minutes, stirring.

3. Add the shrimp. Cook for about 5 minutes, stirring occasionally, until it is pink.

4. Stir in the lime juice, chili powder, salt, cayenne, and pepper. Cook for 2 minutes.

Nutrition Info:
- Calories:360; Total Fat: 11g; Saturated Fat: 2g; Carbohydrates: 38g; Fiber: 2g; Sodium: 494mg; Protein: 28g

Green Chile-stuffed Turkey Burgers

Servings:4

Cooking Time: 15 Minutes

Ingredients:

- 1¼ pounds ground turkey
- 2 (4-ounce) cans diced green chiles
- 2 scallions (green part only), thinly sliced
- ½ cup chopped fresh cilantro
- 2 teaspoons ground cumin
- 1 teaspoon gluten-, onion-, and garlic-free chili powder
- 1 teaspoon gluten-free soy sauce
- 1 teaspoon salt
- 4 gluten-free hamburger buns
- 4 leaves crisp lettuce, such as romaine
- 1 large tomato, sliced
- 2 tablespoons Dijon mustard
- Oil, for preparing the grill

Directions:

1. In a medium bowl, combine the turkey, chiles, scallions, cilantro, cumin, chili powder, soy sauce, and salt.
2. Form the mixture into 4 patties, about 4 inches across.
3. Oil a grill or grill pan and heat to medium-high heat.
4. Grill the burgers for 5 to 6 minutes per side, until grill marks appear and the burgers are cooked through.
5. Serve the burgers on gluten-free buns with lettuce, tomato slices, and Dijon mustard.

Nutrition Info:

- Calories: 501; Protein: 45g; Total Fat: 21g; Saturated Fat: 3g; Carbohydrates: 40g; Fiber: 6g; Sodium: 1481mg;

Red Snapper With Sweet Potato Crust And Cilantro-lime Sauce

Servings:4

Cooking Time: 15 Minutes

Ingredients:

- FOR THE SAUCE
- 1 cup chopped fresh cilantro
- Juice of 2 limes
- ½ cup olive oil
- 1 tablespoon Garlic Oil (here)
- 1 teaspoon salt
- ½ teaspoon freshly ground black pepper
- ½ teaspoon sugar
- FOR THE FISH
- ½ cup gluten-free all-purpose flour
- 1 egg plus 2 egg whites
- 4 (6-ounce) snapper fillets
- 1 teaspoon salt

- ½ teaspoon freshly ground black pepper
- 1 tablespoon grapeseed oil
- 2 tablespoons butter
- 2 sweet potatoes, peeled and shredded

Directions:

1. To make the sauce, combine the cilantro, lime juice, olive oil, Garlic Oil, salt, pepper, and sugar in a blender or food processor and process until smooth.
2. Preheat the oven to 375°F. Place the flour in a wide, shallow bowl. Beat together the egg and egg whites in a second wide, shallow bowl. Season the fish on both sides with salt and pepper.
3. To prepare the fish, heat the oil and butter in a large, oven-safe skillet over medium-high heat. Place a handful of sweet potatoes in the skillet, making a bed roughly the size and shape of each fish fillet. Dredge the fish fillets in the flour, then the egg, and set on top of the sweet potatoes. Cook until the sweet potatoes are crisp and golden brown, for about 4 minutes. Using a spatula, lift the crusted fish out of the pan, and use your other hand to create another bed of sweet potatoes. Flip the fish over onto the new sweet potato bed. Repeat with the other pieces of fish. Place the skillet in the preheated oven and cook for 5 to 7 minutes more, until the bottom crust is crisp and golden brown and the fish is cooked through.
4. Serve hot, with the sauce drizzled over the top.

Nutrition Info:

- Calories: 653; Protein: 49g; Total Fat: 39g; Saturated Fat: 8g; Carbohydrates: 26g; Fiber: 4g; Sodium: 1357mg;

Lemon-dill Cod On A Bed Of Spinach

Servings:4

Cooking Time: 15 Minutes

Ingredients:

- 3 tablespoons Garlic Oil
- 1 pound cod, quartered
- ½ teaspoon sea salt
- ⅛ teaspoon freshly ground black pepper
- Juice of 1 lemon
- 2 tablespoons chopped fresh dill
- 3 cups fresh baby spinach

Directions:

1. In a large nonstick skillet over medium-high heat, heat the garlic oil until it shimmers.
2. Season the cod with salt and pepper. Add it to the skillet and cook for about 4 minutes per side, until opaque.
3. Sprinkle on the lemon juice and dill. Cook for 2 minutes more, spooning the sauce over the fish. With tongs, transfer

the fish to a plate and tent with aluminum foil to keep warm. Return the skillet to the heat.

4. Add the spinach to the pan. Cook for about 3 minutes, stirring occasionally, until wilted.

5. Serve the cod on top of the spinach.

Nutrition Info:

- Calories:222; Total Fat: 12g; Saturated Fat: 2g; Carbohydrates: 2g; Fiber: <1g; Sodium: 347mg; Protein: 27g

20-minute Pulled Pork

Servings:4

Cooking Time: 20 Minutes

Ingredients:

- 1 recipe Homemade Barbecue Sauce
- 1 pound pork tenderloin, cut into 5 pieces

Directions:

1. In a large pot over medium-high heat, heat the barbecue sauce until it simmers.

2. Add the pork and cook for 20 minutes.

3. With two forks, carefully shred the pork and mix it with the barbecue sauce.

Nutrition Info:

- Calories:244; Total Fat: 11g; Saturated Fat: 2; Carbohydrates: 4g; Fiber: 1g; Sodium: 318mg; Protein: 31g

Spaghetti And Meat Sauce

Servings:4

Cooking Time: 10 Minutes

Ingredients:

- 2 tablespoons Garlic Oil
- 1 pound ground beef
- 1 cup tomato sauce
- 1 teaspoon dried oregano
- 1 cup Low-FODMAP Poultry Broth
- 1 tablespoon cornstarch
- ½ teaspoon sea salt
- Pinch red pepper flakes
- ¼ cup chopped fresh basil leaves
- 8 ounces gluten-free spaghetti, cooked according to the package directions and drained

Directions:

1. In a large nonstick skillet over medium-high heat, heat the garlic oil until it shimmers.

2. Add the ground beef and cook for about 6 minutes, crumbling it with the back of a spoon, until browned.

3. Stir in the tomato sauce and oregano.

4. In a small bowl, whisk together the broth, cornstarch, salt, and red pepper flakes. Add this to the skillet and cook

for about 2 minutes, stirring, until the sauce begins to thicken.

5. Stir in the basil.

6. Toss with the hot spaghetti.

Nutrition Info:

- Calories:468; Total Fat: 16g; Saturated Fat: 4g; Carbohydrates: 37g; Fiber: 1g; Sodium: 835mg; Protein: 43g

Fish With Thai Red Curry Sauce

Servings:4

Cooking Time: 30 Minutes

Ingredients:

- 1 tablespoon grapeseed oil
- ¼ cup Thai Red Curry Paste (here)
- 2½ cups coconut milk
- 2 tablespoons fish sauce
- 2 Kaffir lime leaves
- 1 sweet potato, peeled and diced
- 1 zucchini, diced
- 1 cup green beans, cut into 1-inch pieces
- 1½ pounds fish fillet
- ¼ cup crushed toasted peanuts
- ¼ cup chopped fresh cilantro

Directions:

1. Heat the oil in a large saucepan over medium-high heat. Add the curry paste and cook, stirring, for about 1 minute. Stir in the coconut milk, fish sauce, and lime leaves, and bring to a boil.

2. Add the sweet potato, reduce the heat to low, and simmer for 10 minutes. Stir in the zucchini and green beans, and continue to cook for about 10 minutes more, until the vegetables are tender.

3. Add the fish and cook for 7 to 9 minutes more, until the fish is cooked through. Serve hot, garnished with peanuts and cilantro.

Nutrition Info:

- Calories: 571; Protein: 23g; Total Fat: 35g; Saturated Fat: 7g; Carbohydrates: 44g; Fiber: 5g; Sodium: 2261mg;

Chicken Pockets

Servings:4

Cooking Time:x

Ingredients:

- Four 6-ounce (170 g) boneless, skinless chicken breasts
- ⅔ cup (100 g) sun-dried tomatoes, drained (if packed in oil) and finely chopped
- 1 cup (150 g) cooked white rice
- 3½ ounces (100 g) feta, finely diced (about ⅔ cup)
- 1 heaping tablespoon finely grated lemon zest

- 1 large egg white
- 2 heaping tablespoons fresh oregano
- Salt and freshly ground black pepper
- 2 teaspoons garlic-infused olive oil
- 3 tablespoons olive oil
- 1 teaspoon fresh oregano
- 1 teaspoon finely grated lemon zest
- 6 ounces (170 g) mashed sweet potato (from about 1 small sweet potato)
- 1 cup (150 g) cooked white rice
- 1 teaspoon ground cumin
- 1 large egg white
- Salt and freshly ground black pepper
- 2 teaspoons garlic-infused olive oil
- 3 tablespoons olive oil
- 1 teaspoon ground cumin
- 2 heaping tablespoons Basil Pesto
- 1 cup (150 g) cooked white rice
- 1 large egg white
- Salt and freshly ground black pepper
- 2 teaspoons garlic-infused olive oil
- 3 tablespoons olive oil
- 1 teaspoon Basil Pesto
- Small basil leaves, for garnish (optional)
- Green salad or vegetables, for serving

Directions:

1. Preheat the oven to 350°F (180°C).
2. Using a small sharp knife, insert the blade into the middle of the chicken breast and work to form a pocket (you want to cut to about ⅓ inch/1 cm from the internal edge).
3. Combine all the ingredients for your choice of filling in a medium bowl and mix well.
4. Spoon the filling into the chicken pockets, pressing it in firmly and making sure it is evenly spread. Seal the ends with a toothpick.
5. Place the chicken breasts on a baking sheet. Whisk together all the ingredients for your choice of basting liquid and brush it over the chicken. Bake for 15 minutes, or until golden brown, then cover with foil and bake for 5 to 10 minutes more, until cooked through (no longer pink inside). Let rest for 5 to 10 minutes.
6. Cut into thick slices, garnish with basil leaves (if desired), and serve with your choice of salad or vegetables.

Nutrition Info:
- 393 calories; 42 g protein; 19 g total fat; 3 g saturated fat; 12 g carbohydrates; 0 g fiber; 309 mg sodium

Beef Stir-fry With Chinese Broccoli And Green Beans

Servings:4
Cooking Time:x
Ingredients:
- 1 heaping tablespoon grated ginger
- 2 teaspoons garlic-infused olive oil
- 2 teaspoons olive oil
- ¼ cup (60 ml) sesame oil
- 1 pound (450 g) beef sirloin or top round steak, very thinly sliced
- 1 bunch Chinese broccoli, cut into 1-inch (3 cm) lengths
- 7 ounces (200 g) green beans, trimmed (1¾ cups)
- 1 cup (80 g) bean sprouts
- 1 tablespoon gluten-free, onion-free, garlic-free oyster sauce
- ¼ teaspoon cayenne pepper
- Steamed rice or prepared rice noodles, for serving

Directions:

1. Combine the ginger, garlic-infused oil, olive oil, and 2 tablespoons of the sesame oil in a bowl. Add the beef and toss to coat. Cover and refrigerate for 2 to 3 hours.
2. Heat the remaining 2 tablespoons of sesame oil in a wok over medium-high heat. Add the beef and cook for 2 minutes, or until lightly browned. Add the Chinese broccoli, green beans, and bean sprouts and stir-fry for 2 to 4 minutes, until the ingredients are tender. Pour in the oyster sauce and cayenne pepper and stir-fry for 1 to 2 minutes, until the sauce is warmed through and the beef and vegetables are coated.
3. Serve over rice or rice noodles.

Nutrition Info:
- 437 calories; 24 g protein; 34 g total fat; 6 g saturated fat; 7 g carbohydrates; 3 g fiber; 92 mg sodium

Turkey And Red Pepper Burgers

Servings:4
Cooking Time: 10 Minutes
Ingredients:
- 1 pound ground turkey
- ½ teaspoon sea salt
- ⅛ teaspoon freshly ground black pepper
- 2 tablespoons extra-virgin olive oil
- ¼ cup Low-FODMAP Mayonnaise
- 2 jarred roasted red peppers, minced
- 4 gluten-free hamburger buns

Directions:

1. Form the turkey into 4 patties and season them with salt and pepper.

2. In a large nonstick skillet over medium-high heat, heat the olive oil until it shimmers.

3. Add the burgers and cook for about 5 minutes per side, until browned.

4. In a small bowl, whisk the mayonnaise and red peppers. Spread the mixture on the buns and add the cooked patties.

Nutrition Info:

- Calories:468; Total Fat: 26g; Saturated Fat: 4g; Carbohydrates: 27g; Fiber: 1g; Sodium: 753mg; Protein: 36g

Asian-style Pork Meatballs

Servings:4

Cooking Time: 40 Minutes

Ingredients:

- Oil for preparing the baking sheet
- 1¼ pounds ground pork
- ¼ cup finely chopped fresh basil
- 1 tablespoon Garlic Oil (here)
- 2 scallions, green parts only, thinly sliced
- 1 tablespoon fish sauce
- 1 teaspoon onion- and garlic-free chili paste
- 1 tablespoon sugar
- 2 teaspoons cornstarch
- 1 teaspoon salt
- 1 teaspoon freshly ground black pepper

Directions:

1. Preheat the oven to 350°F.

2. Line a large, rimmed baking sheet with lightly oiled parchment paper. In a large bowl, combine the pork, basil, Garlic Oil, scallions, fish sauce, chili paste, sugar, cornstarch, salt, and pepper, and mix to combine. With wet hands, form the mixture into 2-inch balls. Place the meatballs on the prepared baking sheet as they are formed.

3. Bake the meatballs in the preheated oven for about 40 minutes, until they are browned and cooked through. Serve hot.

Nutrition Info:

- Calories: 232; Protein: 38g; Total Fat: 5g; Saturated Fat: 2g; Carbohydrates: 7g; Fiber: 0g; Sodium: 1027mg;

Swiss Chicken With Mustard Sauce

Servings:4

Cooking Time:x

Ingredients:

- Four 6-ounce (170 g) boneless, skinless chicken breasts
- 2 slices Swiss cheese, halved

- 2 slices gluten-free smoked or double-smoked ham, halved
- ¼ cup (35 g) cornstarch
- 2 large eggs
- 1 cup (120 g) dried gluten-free, soy-free bread crumbs*
- ¼ cup (60 ml) canola oil
- ¼ cup (60 ml) light cream
- ¼ cup (75 g) gluten-free mayonnaise
- 2 to 3 teaspoons gluten-free smooth mild mustard
- Green salad or vegetables, for serving

Directions:

1. Cut each chicken breast nearly in half horizontally without cutting all the way through. Open out like a book. Place a piece of cheese and a piece of ham on each, fold the top over the filling, and secure with a toothpick.

2. Set out 3 shallow bowls. Fill one with the cornstarch, one with the eggs, and one with the bread crumbs. Beat the eggs lightly. Coat the chicken breasts in the cornstarch, shaking off any excess, then dip in the egg, and finally toss in the bread crumbs. Make sure the chicken breasts stay closed, enclosing the filling.

3. Heat the canola oil in a large nonstick pan over medium-low heat. Add the chicken and cook for 4 to 5 minutes on each side, until golden brown and cooked through.

4. Meanwhile, to make the mustard sauce, combine the cream, mayonnaise, and mustard in a small saucepan. Stir over medium heat for 3 to 5 minutes, until the sauce has thickened slightly.

5. Divide the chicken among four plates, drizzle with the sauce, and serve with your choice of salad or vegetables.

Nutrition Info:

- 580 calories; 52 g protein; 30 g total fat; 9 g saturated fat; 21 g carbohydrates; 0 g fiber; 622 mg sodium

Soy-infused Roast Chicken

Servings:4

Cooking Time:x

Ingredients:

- ½ cup (125 ml) gluten-free soy sauce
- 2 tablespoons plus 2 teaspoons sesame oil
- 2 heaping tablespoons light brown sugar
- 2 teaspoons grated ginger
- 3 star anise (or 2 teaspoons ground star anise)
- ½ teaspoon ground cinnamon
- One 4-pound (1.8 kg) whole chicken, excess fat removed
- 2 cups (500 ml) gluten-free, onion-free chicken stock*
- Vegetables, for serving

Directions:

1. Combine the soy sauce, sesame oil, brown sugar, ginger, star anise, and cinnamon in a bowl and stir until the sugar has dissolved. Place the chicken, breast up, in a baking dish. Pour the marinade over it and use a pastry brush to ensure the entire chicken is well coated. Cover and refrigerate for 3 to 4 hours, brushing the chicken with the marinade every 1 to 2 hours.

2. Preheat the oven to 350°F (180°C).

3. Uncover the chicken, pour the stock into the baking dish, and roast for 30 minutes. Cover loosely with foil and roast for 20 to 30 minutes more, until the juices run clear when you piece the chicken with a toothpick in the thickest part of the thigh. Let rest for a few minutes before carving.

4. Serve with the pan juices and your choice of vegetables.

Nutrition Info:

- 304 calories; 40 g protein; 12 g total fat; 2 g saturated fat; 6 g carbohydrates; 0 g fiber; 1485 mg sodium

Grilled Steak With Pesto And Potato Wedges

Servings:4
Cooking Time:x

Ingredients:

- 8 skin-on new potatoes, scrubbed
- 2 heaping tablespoons cornstarch
- 1 heaping tablespoon minced herbs (such as rosemary and/or oregano)
- ½ teaspoon salt
- 2 tablespoons olive oil
- 2 pounds (900 g) beef sirloin or top round steaks, or beef fillet
- Basil Pesto

Directions:

1. Preheat the oven to 400°F (200°C). Line a baking sheet with parchment paper.

2. Cut the potatoes in half, then into ½-inch (1.5 cm) wedges. Combine the cornstarch, herbs, and salt in a resealable plastic bag. Add the potato wedges, seal, and toss to coat. Transfer to a colander and shake off any excess coating; the potatoes should only be lightly coated. Place the wedges in a single layer on the baking sheet, brush with the oil, and bake for 10 minutes. Reduce the oven temperature to 350°F (180°C) and bake for 20 minutes more, turning the wedges halfway through, until crisp and golden brown.

3. Preheat the broiler or a grill to medium-high, or place a ridged grill pan or cast-iron skillet over medium-high heat, and cook the steaks to your preferred doneness. Cover and let rest for a few minutes.

4. Serve the steaks and potato wedges with a dollop of pesto.

Nutrition Info:

- 711 calories; 52 g protein; 46 g total fat; 15 g saturated fat; 22 g carbohydrates; 9 g fiber; 498 mg sodium

Lamb And Vegetable Pilaf

Servings:4
Cooking Time:x

Ingredients:

- 2 tablespoons olive oil
- 2 teaspoons garlic-infused olive oil
- 2½ teaspoons grated ginger
- 2 teaspoons ground cinnamon
- 6 whole cloves
- ½ teaspoon cayenne pepper
- 2 teaspoons ground cumin
- 1¼ pounds (500 g) boneless lamb loin, sliced
- 1½ cups (300 g) white basmati rice
- 1 small sweet potato, chopped
- 2½ cups (625 ml) gluten-free, onion-free beef or vegetable stock*
- ⅔ cup (65 g) slivered almonds
- 1 large eggplant, trimmed and sliced
- 2 medium zucchini, halved lengthwise and thickly sliced
- Salt and freshly ground black pepper
- ¼ cup (5 g) roughly chopped cilantro
- 3 tablespoons roughly chopped flat-leaf parsley

Directions:

1. Heat 1 tablespoon plus 2 teaspoons of the olive oil and the 2 teaspoons garlic-infused oil in a large saucepan or Dutch oven over medium heat. Add the ginger, cinnamon, cloves, cayenne, and cumin and cook for 1 to 2 minutes, until fragrant. Add the lamb and toss until browned.

2. Add the rice, sweet potato, and eggplant to the pan and cook, stirring, for 2 to 3 minutes, until the rice is well coated in the spiced oil. Pour in the stock and bring to a boil, then reduce the heat to low and simmer, covered, for 10 minutes.

3. Meanwhile, heat the remaining 1 teaspoon of olive oil in a small frying pan over medium heat. Add the almonds and cook, stirring, until golden. Drain on paper towels.

4. Add the zucchini to the rice mixture and cook for 5 minutes more, or until all the liquid has been absorbed and the rice is tender. Remove and discard the whole cloves. Season with salt and pepper, then stir in the almonds, cilantro, and parsley. Serve hot.

Nutrition Info:

- 630 calories; 24 g protein; 34 g total fat; 11 g saturated fat; 54 g carbohydrates; 7 g fiber; 318 mg sodium

Quick Shepherd's Pie

Servings:4
Cooking Time: 25 Minutes
Ingredients:
- 2 pounds potatoes, peeled and cubed
- 2 teaspoons salt, divided, plus additional if needed
- 2 tablespoons softened cream cheese
- ½ cup heavy cream
- 1 tablespoon olive oil
- 1¾ pounds ground beef or lamb
- 2 teaspoons freshly ground black pepper
- 1 carrot, diced
- 2 tablespoons butter
- 2 tablespoons gluten-free, low-FODMAP all-purpose flour (such as King Arthur's)
- 1 cup homemade (onion- and garlic-free) beef stock or broth
- 1 tablespoon Low-FODMAP Worcestershire Sauce (here) or gluten-free soy sauce
- 1 cup fresh or frozen green beans, cut into 1-inch pieces
- 1 tablespoon minced fresh thyme
- 1 tablespoon Garlic Oil (here)
- 2 tablespoons chopped fresh parsley, for garnish

Directions:
1. Place the potatoes in a large saucepan and cover with water. Add 1 teaspoon of the salt and bring to a boil over high heat. Reduce the heat to medium, and simmer until the potatoes are tender, for about 12 minutes.
2. While the potatoes are cooking, heat the oil in a large skillet over medium-high heat. Add the meat, the remaining salt, and pepper. Cook, stirring and breaking up with a spatula, until the meat is browned, for about 4 minutes. Drain the excess fat from the pan. Add the carrot and cook, stirring occasionally, for another 5 minutes.
3. Drain the potatoes and transfer them to a large bowl. Add the cream cheese and cream, and mash with a potato masher until smooth. Taste and add more salt if needed.
4. In a small saucepan over medium heat, melt the butter. Add the flour and cook, whisking constantly, for 2 minutes. Whisk in the beef broth and Low-FODMAP Worcestershire Sauce or soy sauce, and cook until thickened, for about 1 more minute. Add the sauce to the meat mixture and stir in the green beans and thyme.
5. Preheat the broiler on high.
6. Transfer the meat mixture to a baking dish. Spoon the potato mixture over the top and spread out evenly. Broil for

3 to 4 minutes, until the potatoes are nicely browned. Remove from the oven and drizzle the Garlic Oil over the top. Serve hot, garnished with parsley.
Nutrition Info:
- Calories: 692; Protein: 67g; Total Fat: 26g; Saturated Fat: 12g; Carbohydrates: 45g; Fiber: 7g; Sodium: 1780mg;

Risotto With Smoked Salmon And Dill

Servings:4
Cooking Time: 30 Minutes
Ingredients:
- 6 cups homemade (onion- and garlic-free) vegetable broth
- 3 tablespoons butter
- 1 medium leek (green part only), halved lengthwise and thinly sliced
- 1½ cups Arborio rice
- ½ cup dry white wine
- 1 teaspoon salt
- 1 tablespoon minced fresh dill
- ¾ cup freshly grated Parmesan cheese, divided
- 8 ounces smoked salmon

Directions:
1. In a large saucepan, heat the broth to a simmer over medium-high heat. Reduce the heat to low and keep warm.
2. In a stockpot or Dutch oven, melt the butter over medium-high heat. Add the leek and cook, stirring, until softened, for about 5 minutes. Add the rice and cook, stirring, for about 2 minutes, until all of the grains of rice are well coated in butter. Add the wine and cook, stirring and scraping up any browned bits on the bottom of the pan, until the liquid has been absorbed. Add the salt and a ladleful of stock.
3. Cook, stirring, until the liquid has mostly evaporated. Continue to add broth a ladleful at a time and cook, stirring frequently, after each addition until most of the liquid has been absorbed. Cook for about 25 minutes total, until all of the broth has been used up and the rice is tender.
4. Stir in the dill and ½ cup of the cheese. Just before serving, stir in the salmon. Serve hot, garnished with the remaining cheese.
Nutrition Info:
- Calories: 634; Protein: 37g; Total Fat: 23g; Saturated Fat: 13g; Carbohydrates: 64g; Fiber: 2g; Sodium: 3329mg;

Grilled Fish With Coconut-lime Rice

Servings:4
Cooking Time:x
Ingredients:

- 1 tablespoon plus 1 teaspoon fresh lemon juice
- 1 tablespoon plus 1 teaspoon sesame oil
- 1 teaspoon garlic-infused olive oil
- ¼ small red chile pepper, seeded and finely chopped (optional)
- Freshly ground black pepper
- 4 large boneless, skinless firm white fish fillets (such as snapper or cod; 5½ ounces/160 g each)
- 1½ cups (300 g) jasmine rice
- 3 kaffir lime leaves, very thinly sliced
- ½ cup (125 ml) coconut milk
- Garlic-infused olive oil

Directions:

1. Place all the ingredients for the marinade in a large glass or ceramic bowl and stir to combine well. Add the fish fillets and toss gently to coat. Cover and place in the refrigerator for 2 to 3 hours, turning every hour to ensure even marinating.
2. Bring a large pot of water to a boil over high heat. Reduce the heat to medium, add the rice and one third of the lime leaves, and cook, stirring occasionally, for 10 minutes, or until the rice is tender. Drain and rinse under hot water.
3. Place the rinsed rice in a bowl and stir in the coconut milk and remaining lime leaves. Cover and keep warm.
4. Brush a ridged grill pan or cast-iron skillet with the garlic-infused oil and heat over medium-high heat. Drain the fish fillets and cook for 2 to 3 minutes on each side, until cooked to your preferred doneness.
5. Serve with the coconut-lime rice.

Nutrition Info:

- 475 calories; 33 g protein; 11g total fat; 6 g saturated fat; 59 g carbohydrates; 2 g fiber; 92 mg sodium

Spanish Meatloaf With Garlic Mashed Potatoes

Servings:6
Cooking Time:x
Ingredients:

- Nonstick cooking spray
- 1½ pounds (700 g) extra-lean ground beef
- ½ cup (125 ml) tomato paste
- ¾ cup (90 g) dried gluten-free, soy-free bread crumbs*
- 2 large eggs, lightly beaten
- 2 teaspoons garlic-infused olive oil
- 2 teaspoons olive oil
- Small handful of flat-leaf parsley leaves, roughly chopped
- ¾ teaspoon ground ginger
- 1 teaspoon chili powder
- 1½ teaspoons cayenne pepper
- 1½ teaspoons sweet paprika
- Salt and freshly ground black pepper
- 4 potatoes, peeled (if desired) and quartered
- 1 tablespoon garlic-infused olive oil
- 2 tablespoons (30 g) salted butter
- ⅓ cup (80 ml) low-fat milk, lactose-free milk, or suitable plant-based milk
- Salt and freshly ground black pepper
- Green salad or vegetables, for serving

Directions:

1. Preheat the oven to 350°F (180°C). Line an 8½ x 4½-inch (25 x 11.5 cm) loaf pan with foil and spray with cooking spray.
2. Combine the beef, tomato paste, bread crumbs, eggs, garlic-infused oil, olive oil, parsley, ginger, chili powder, cayenne, paprika, salt, and pepper in a large bowl. Mix well with your hands. Press into the loaf pan.
3. Bake for 40 to 45 minutes, until cooked through. (The juices will run clear when you pierce the center with a small knife.) Let rest for at least 5 minutes before serving.
4. Meanwhile, to make the garlic mashed potatoes, cook the potatoes in a saucepan of boiling water until very tender, about 10 minutes. Drain. Mash with a potato masher. Stir in the garlic-infused oil, butter, and milk and season with salt and pepper. Adjust the ingredients for taste or texture if needed.
5. Cut the meatloaf into thick slices and serve with a generous spoonful (or two) of mashed potatoes and your choice of salad or vegetables.

Nutrition Info:

- 437 calories; 29 g protein; 23 g total fat; 8 g saturated fat; 28 g carbohydrates; 3 g fiber; 370 mg sodium

Orange-ginger Salmon

Servings:4
Cooking Time: 12 Minutes
Ingredients:

- ¼ cup Garlic Oil
- Juice of 2 oranges
- 2 tablespoons gluten-free soy sauce
- 1 tablespoon peeled and grated fresh ginger
- 1 pound salmon fillet, quartered

Directions:

1. Preheat the oven to 450°F.

2. In a shallow baking dish, whisk together the garlic oil, orange juice, soy sauce, and ginger.

3. Place the salmon, flesh-side down, in the marinade. Marinate for 10 minutes.

4. Place the salmon, skin-side up, on a rimmed baking sheet. Bake for 12 to 15 minutes, until opaque.

Nutrition Info:

- Calories:282; Total Fat: 20g; Saturated Fat: 3g; Carbohydrates: 5g; Fiber: 0g; Sodium: 553mg; Protein: 23g

Red Snapper With Creole Sauce

Servings:4

Cooking Time: 20 Minutes

Ingredients:

- 1 tablespoon olive oil
- 1 tablespoon Garlic Oil (here)
- ½ medium green bell pepper, diced
- 1 (14½-ounce) can onion- and garlic-free diced tomatoes with juice
- 2 scallions (green part only), thinly sliced
- 1 tablespoon red-wine vinegar
- 1 teaspoon gluten-free soy sauce or coconut aminos
- ½ teaspoon dried basil
- ½ teaspoon salt
- ½ teaspoon freshly ground black pepper
- Dash of hot-pepper sauce
- 4 (6-ounce) red-snapper fillets
- ¼ cup chopped fresh basil

Directions:

1. Heat the olive oil and Garlic Oil in a large skillet over medium-high heat. Add the bell pepper and cook, stirring, until softened, for about 5 minutes. Add the tomatoes with their juice, scallions, vinegar, soy sauce, basil, salt, pepper, and hot sauce and bring to a boil.

2. Reduce the heat to low, add the fish, and spoon the saucy tomato mixture over the top. Cover the pan and cook until the fish is cooked through and flakes easily with a fork, for about 10 minutes. Serve immediately, with sauce spooned over the top and garnished with basil.

Nutrition Info:

- Calories: 281; Protein: 46g; Total Fat: 7g; Saturated Fat: 1g; Carbohydrates: 7g; Fiber: 2g; Sodium: 588mg;

Dijon-roasted Pork Tenderloin

Servings:8

Cooking Time: 60 Minutes

Ingredients:

- 1 pork loin roast (about 4 pounds), trimmed of excess fat
- 1 teaspoon salt
- ½ teaspoon pepper
- ¼ cup whole-grain Dijon mustard
- ¼ cup brown sugar

Directions:

1. Preheat the oven to 425°F.

2. Season the roast all over with the salt and pepper, place it on a roasting rack in a roasting pan, and roast in the preheated oven for 30 minutes.

3. Brush the mustard over the entire roast, then sprinkle the brown sugar over it, pressing the sugar into the mustard.

4. Lower the oven heat to 375°F and continue roasting, basting now and then with the drippings, for about 30 minutes more, until a meat thermometer inserted into the center of the roast reads 145°F. Remove the roast from the oven, tent loosely with aluminum foil, and let rest for 10 minutes before slicing.

5. To serve, slice the roast into ½-inch-thick slices, and spoon a bit of the drippings over them.

Nutrition Info:

- Calories: 499; Protein: 65g; Total Fat: 22g; Saturated Fat: 8g; Carbohydrates: 5g; Fiber: 0g; Sodium: 604mg;

Herb-crusted Halibut

Servings:4

Cooking Time: 15 Minutes

Ingredients:

- 1 pound halibut, quartered
- ½ cup finely chopped fresh parsley leaves
- 2 tablespoons Dijon mustard
- 2 tablespoons Garlic Oil
- 2 teaspoons dried thyme
- ½ teaspoon sea salt
- ⅛ teaspoon freshly ground black pepper

Directions:

1. Preheat the oven to 450°F.

2. Place the halibut fillets on a nonstick rimmed baking sheet.

3. In a small bowl, whisk the parsley with the mustard, garlic oil, thyme, salt, and pepper. Spread the mustard mixture over the halibut.

4. Bake the halibut for about 15 minutes, until opaque.

Nutrition Info:

- Calories:189; Total Fat: 8g; Saturated Fat: 1g; Carbohydrates: 1g; Fiber: <1g; Sodium: 416mg; Protein: 27g

Grilled Chicken With Maple-mustard Glaze

Servings:4
Cooking Time: 20 Minutes
Ingredients:

- ½ cup onion- and garlic-free spicy brown mustard
- 2 tablespoons brown sugar
- 3 tablespoons maple syrup
- 1 tablespoon white-wine vinegar
- 2 teaspoons gluten-free soy sauce
- ½ teaspoon pepper
- 1 tablespoon Garlic Oil (here)
- 8 skinless, bone-in chicken thighs
- Cooking spray
- ½ teaspoon salt

Directions:

1. In a small bowl, stir together the mustard, brown sugar, maple syrup, vinegar, soy sauce, pepper, and Garlic Oil. Place the chicken pieces in a resealable plastic bag, and add half of the mustard mixture.
2. Seal the bag and shake to coat the chicken pieces well. Marinate for at least 30 minutes (or up to 2 hours).
3. Spray a grill or grill pan with cooking spray, and heat to medium-high.
4. Remove the chicken pieces from the marinade, discarding the marinade, and sprinkle them with salt. Cook the chicken on the grill until grill marks appear and the chicken is thoroughly cooked, for about 8 minutes per side. Serve immediately, drizzled with the reserved mustard mixture.

Nutrition Info:

- Calories: 357; Protein: 51g; Total Fat: 8g; Saturated Fat: 3g; Carbohydrates: 16g; Fiber: 0g; Sodium: 879mg;

Pork Sausages With Cheesy Potato Rösti

Servings:4
Cooking Time:x
Ingredients:

- 3 or 4 medium russet potatoes (1 pound 10 ounces/750 g), peeled
- 3 tablespoons (45 g) salted butter, melted
- Salt and freshly ground black pepper
- Nonstick cooking spray
- Four 2½-ounce (70 g) gluten-free, onion-free pork sausages
- Four 1-ounce (28 g) Jarlsberg cheese slices
- Gluten-free mustard (optional)
- Green salad or vegetables, for serving

Directions:

1. Place the potatoes in a medium saucepan and cover with cold water. Bring to a boil over high heat. Reduce the heat to medium-high and boil for 12 to 15 minutes. Test for doneness by inserting a toothpick into the middle of a potato; there should be no resistance. Drain and set aside to cool completely.
2. If making individual rösti, preheat the oven to 250°F (120°C).
3. Grate the potatoes into a large bowl and add the butter and salt and pepper to taste. Toss well to combine.
4. Grease a small frying pan with cooking spray and heat over medium heat. Add one quarter of the potatoes and press down firmly. Cook for 15 minutes or until the bottom is golden brown and crisp. Using a spatula, slide the rösti out of the pan onto a cutting board or large plate. Flip it over and return it to the pan. Cook for 10 minutes more, or until cooked through and golden brown. Transfer to a baking sheet and keep warm in the oven while you make the remaining rösti. (Alternatively, make one large rösti in a large frying pan and cut into wedges to serve.)
5. Meanwhile, preheat a ridged grill pan, cast-iron skillet, frying pan, or grill to medium-high and cook the sausages to your desired doneness.
6. Top each rösti with a slice of Jarlsberg cheese and broil until the cheese has melted. Serve with the sausages, a spoonful of mustard (if desired), and your choice of salad or vegetables.

Nutrition Info:

- 662 calories; 22 g protein; 51 g total fat; 23 g saturated fat; 27 g carbohydrates; 4 g fiber; 757 mg sodium

Chicken And Vegetable Curry

Servings:4
Cooking Time:x
Ingredients:

- 2 teaspoons garlic-infused olive oil
- 2 tablespoons olive oil
- 1 heaping tablespoon garam masala
- 1 heaping tablespoon ground cumin
- 2 teaspoons ground turmeric
- ½ teaspoon cayenne pepper (or to taste)
- 1 tablespoon sesame oil
- Four 7-ounce (200 g) boneless, skinless chicken thighs, trimmed of fat
- 3 Roma (plum) tomatoes, chopped
- 1 zucchini, halved lengthwise and sliced
- 1¾ cups (180 g) trimmed and halved green beans

- 9 ounces (250 g) kabocha or other suitable winter squash, peeled, seeded, and cut into ¾-inch (2 cm) pieces
- ¼ cup (55 g) packed light brown sugar
- Steamed rice, for serving

Directions:

1. Heat the garlic-infused oil and olive oil in a large heavy-bottomed saucepan or Dutch oven over medium heat. Add the garam masala, cumin, turmeric, cayenne, and sesame oil, and cook for 1 to 2 minutes, until fragrant.

2. Add the chicken, tomatoes, zucchini, green beans, squash, brown sugar, and ½ cup (125 ml) water. Reduce the heat to medium-low, then cover and cook, stirring occasionally, until the chicken and vegetables are tender and the sauce has thickened.

3. Serve with steamed rice.

Nutrition Info:

- 496 calories; 43 g protein; 21 g total fat; 4 g saturated fat; 32 g carbohydrates; 6 g fiber; 193 mg sodium

Chicken And Rice With Peanut Sauce

Servings:4
Cooking Time: 10 Minutes

Ingredients:

- 2 tablespoons Garlic Oil
- 1 pound boneless skinless chicken thigh meat, cut into strips
- ½ cup sugar-free natural peanut butter
- ½ cup coconut milk
- 2 tablespoons gluten-free soy sauce
- 1 tablespoon peeled and grated fresh ginger
- Juice of 1 lime
- 2 cups cooked brown rice

Directions:

1. In a large nonstick skillet over medium-high heat, heat the garlic oil until it shimmers.

2. Add the chicken and cook for about 6 minutes, stirring occasionally, until browned.

3. In a small bowl, whisk the peanut butter, coconut milk, soy sauce, ginger, and lime juice. Add this to the chicken.

4. Mix in the rice. Cook for 3 minutes more, stirring.

Nutrition Info:

- Calories:718; Total Fat: 40g; Saturated Fat: 13g; Carbohydrates: 46g; Fiber: 5g; Sodium: 757mg; Protein: 46g

Quick Steak Tacos

Servings:4
Cooking Time: 15 Minutes

Ingredients:

- 2 tablespoons Garlic Oil
- 1 pound flat iron steak
- ½ teaspoon sea salt
- ⅛ teaspoon freshly ground black pepper
- 1 teaspoon chili powder
- 6 scallions, green parts only, finely chopped
- ¼ cup freshly squeezed lime juice
- 8 corn tortillas
- ½ cup grated Cheddar cheese

Directions:

1. In a large nonstick skillet over medium-high heat, heat the garlic oil until it shimmers.

2. Season the steak with the salt, pepper, and chili powder. Add it to the hot skillet and cook for about 5 minutes per side, or until your desired doneness. Transfer the steak to a cutting board and cut it against the grain into strips. Return the skillet to the heat.

3. Return the steak strips to the hot pan, and add the scallions and lime juice. Cook for 2 minutes.

4. Serve on the corn tortillas topped with the cheese.

Nutrition Info:

- Calories:460; Total Fat: 19g; Saturated Fat: 6; Carbohydrates: 24g; Fiber: 4g; Sodium: 408mg; Protein: 48g

Sweet-and-sour Turkey Meatballs

Servings:4
Cooking Time: 12 Minutes

Ingredients:

- 1 pound ground turkey
- ½ cup gluten-free bread crumbs
- ¼ cup chopped fresh cilantro leaves
- 1 egg, beaten
- 2 tablespoons peeled and grated fresh ginger
- 1 teaspoon sea salt
- ½ teaspoon freshly ground black pepper
- 2 tablespoons Garlic Oil
- 1 recipe Sweet-and-Sour Sauce

Directions:

1. In a large bowl, mix the turkey, bread crumbs, cilantro, egg, ginger, salt, and pepper. Form the turkey mixture into about 16 (1-inch) meatballs.

2. In a large nonstick skillet over medium-high heat, heat the garlic oil until it shimmers.

3. Add the meatballs and cook, turning, for about 8 minutes, or until the juices run clear and the meatballs are browned.

4. Stir in the sweet-and-sour sauce. Cook for 2 minutes more, stirring to coat the meatballs in the sauce.

Nutrition Info:

- Calories:396; Total Fat: 15g; Saturated Fat: 3g; Carbohydrates: 32g; Fiber: 2g; Sodium: 1,041mg; Protein: 36g

Mexican-style Ground Beef And Rice

Servings:4

Cooking Time: 15 Minutes

Ingredients:
- 2 tablespoons Garlic Oil
- 1 pound 85 percent lean ground beef (see Tip)
- 6 scallions, green parts only, chopped
- ½ cup water
- 1 tablespoon chili powder
- 1 teaspoon dried cumin
- ½ teaspoon sea salt
- ⅛ teaspoon freshly ground black pepper
- 2 cups cooked brown rice
- ¼ cup chopped fresh cilantro leaves

Directions:

1. In a large nonstick skillet over medium-high heat, heat the garlic oil until it shimmers.

2. Add the ground beef and scallions. Cook for about 6 minutes, crumbling the beef with the back of a spoon, until it is browned.

3. Stir in the water, chili powder, cumin, salt, and pepper. Cook for 2 minutes more, stirring, until the spices are mixed in.

4. Stir in the brown rice and cilantro. Cook for 2 minutes more to heat.

Nutrition Info:
- Calories:458; Total Fat: 16g; Saturated Fat: 4g; Carbohydrates: 39g; Fiber: 3g; Sodium: 335mg; Protein: 39g

Lime Pork Stir-fry With Rice Noodles

Servings:4

Cooking Time:x

Ingredients:
- 1 heaping tablespoon finely grated ginger
- 6 kaffir lime leaves, shredded, or 1½ heaping tablespoons grated lime zest
- 1 small red chile pepper, seeded and thinly sliced
- 2 tablespoons plus 2 teaspoons fresh lime juice
- ¼ cup (55 g) brown sugar
- ⅓ cup (80 ml) gluten-free soy sauce
- 3 tablespoons sesame oil
- 1 pound 5 ounces (600 g) lean pork, cut into ⅛-inch (3 to 4 mm) strips
- 8 ounces (225 g) rice noodles

- 1 bunch bok choy, leaves separated, cut if large, rinsed, and drained
- 1 red bell pepper, seeded and cut into thin strips
- 1½ cups (150 g) broccoli florets
- ¼ cup (5 g) roughly chopped cilantro

Directions:

1. Combine the ginger, lime leaves, chile pepper, lime juice, brown sugar, 1 tablespoon of the soy sauce, and 1 tablespoon of the sesame oil in a bowl. Add the pork and toss to coat, then cover and refrigerate for 3 to 4 hours or overnight.

2. Shortly before you're ready to eat, soak the noodles in boiling water for 5 minutes or until tender. Drain and set aside until needed.

3. Heat the remaining 2 tablespoons of sesame oil in a wok, add the pork strips and stir-fry until just cooked.

4. Add the bok choy, bell pepper, broccoli, and the remaining soy sauce and cook until the vegetables are just tender.

5. Add the noodles and toss to combine. Sprinkle with the cilantro and serve.

Nutrition Info:
- 613 calories; 38 g protein; 20 g total fat; 4 g saturated fat; 72 g carbohydrates; 5 g fiber; 1091 mg sodium

Thai Sweet Chili Broiled Salmon

Servings:4

Cooking Time: 10 Minutes

Ingredients:
- 6 tablespoons homemade Thai Sweet Chili Sauce (here)
- 3 tablespoons gluten-free soy sauce
- 1 tablespoon finely grated fresh ginger
- 4 (6-ounce) salmon fillets
- 2 scallions (green part only), thinly sliced
- 1 tablespoon chopped fresh cilantro
- 1½ teaspoons toasted sesame seeds

Directions:

1. In a large bowl, combine the chili sauce, soy sauce, and ginger, and mix well. Add the fish, turning until evenly coated. Cover the bowl and marinate fish in the refrigerator for 30 minutes.

2. To cook the fish, heat the broiler to high and line a rimmed baking sheet with foil.

3. Arrange the salmon fillets skin-side down on the prepared baking sheet. Brush some of the marinade over the fish, coating generously. Broil for about 8 to 10 minutes, until just cooked through. Serve immediately, garnished with scallions, cilantro, and sesame seeds.

Nutrition Info:

- Calories: 291; Protein: 34g; Total Fat: 11g; Saturated Fat: 2g; Carbohydrates: 13g; Fiber: 1g; Sodium: 812mg;

Steamed Mussels With Saffron-infused Cream

Servings:4
Cooking Time: 15 Minutes
Ingredients:
- 2 tablespoons olive oil
- 1 tablespoon Garlic Oil (here)
- 1 large bulb fennel, thinly sliced
- 1 cup dry white wine
- Large pinch saffron threads
- ¾ teaspoon salt
- ¾ cup heavy cream
- ¼ teaspoon freshly ground pepper
- 4 pounds cultivated mussels, rinsed well
- 2 tablespoons chopped fresh flat-leaf parsley

Directions:
1. Heat the olive oil and Garlic Oil in a stockpot over medium heat.
2. Add the fennel and cook, stirring frequently, until softened, for about 5 minutes. Add the wine, saffron, and salt, and bring to a boil. Stir in the cream, pepper, and mussels.
3. Cover the pot and cook for about 6 minutes or until all of the mussels have opened (discard any mussels that don't open after 8 minutes of cooking). Serve the mussels and broth in bowls, garnished with the parsley.

Nutrition Info:
- Calories: 599; Protein: 55g; Total Fat: 26g; Saturated Fat: 8g; Carbohydrates: 24g; Fiber: 2g; Sodium: 1779mg;

Tarragon Chicken Terrine

Servings:8
Cooking Time:x
Ingredients:
- 2 teaspoons garlic-infused olive oil
- 2 tablespoons olive oil
- 2 tablespoons (30 g) salted butter
- ¼ cup (60 ml) dry white wine
- 14 ounces (400 g) boneless, skinless chicken thighs, excess fat removed, finely chopped
- 12 ounces (340 g) ground white meat chicken
- Nine 1-ounce (28 g) slices gluten-free, soy-free bread, crusts removed, crumbled into coarse crumbs
- 1 large egg, lightly beaten
- ½ cup (125 ml) light cream
- Small handful of flat-leaf parsley leaves, chopped

- Small handful of tarragon leaves, chopped
- Salt and freshly ground black pepper
- 14 long, thin prosciutto slices (about 12 ounces/340 g total)
- Boiling water
- Green salad, for serving

Directions:
1. Preheat the oven to 350°F (180°C).
2. Heat the garlic-infused oil, olive oil, and butter in a small heavy-bottomed frying pan over medium heat until the butter has melted. Stir in the wine and set aside.
3. Place the chicken thigh meat, ground chicken, bread crumbs, egg, cream, parsley, and tarragon in a large bowl, pour in the wine mixture, and mix together well. Season with the salt and pepper.
4. Line a deep 8 x 4-inch (20 x 10 cm) loaf pan with overlapping slices of prosciutto, leaving a little overhang on both long sides. Spoon the chicken mixture into the pan and smooth the surface. Fold in the overhanging prosciutto to enclose the filling. Cover the pan with foil and place in a large baking dish. Pour enough boiling water into the dish to come two thirds of the way up the side of the pan.
5. Bake for 1 hour, or until the juices run clear when a toothpick is inserted into the center of the terrine. Set aside to cool to room temperature.
6. Remove the foil and invert the pan onto a wire rack over the baking dish to allow the juices to drain away. After the juices stop running, turn the pan upright and cover again with foil. Top with another loaf pan containing two or three heavy cans, to compress the terrine. Place in the refrigerator for a few hours or overnight.
7. To serve, remove the weights, extra pan, and foil, turn out the terrine onto a cutting board, and pat dry with paper towel. Cut into thick slices and serve with your favorite salad.

Nutrition Info:
- 439 calories; 32 g protein; 27 g total fat; 5 g saturated fat; 15 g carbohydrates; 1 g fiber; 922 mg sodium

Roasted Chicken, Potatoes, And Kale

Servings:8
Cooking Time: 50 Minutes
Ingredients:
- 1½ pounds Yukon Gold potatoes, cut into ¼-inch-thick slices
- 1½ pounds kale, stems and inner ribs removed
- ¼ cup olive oil
- 2 teaspoons salt, divided
- ½ teaspoon freshly ground black pepper

52

- 8 chicken drumsticks
- 8 chicken thighs
- 1 teaspoon paprika
- Juice of 1 lemon

Directions:

1. Preheat the oven to 450°F.
2. In a large roasting pan, combine the potatoes and kale, and toss with the olive oil. Spread the vegetables out in an even layer and sprinkle with the pepper and 1 teaspoon of the salt.
3. Season the chicken pieces all over with the remaining teaspoon of salt and arrange them on top of the vegetables in the roasting pan. Sprinkle the paprika over the top, and cover the roasting pan with aluminum foil.
4. Roast the chicken in the preheated oven for 20 minutes. Remove the foil and continue to cook for another 30 minutes, until the chicken is thoroughly cooked and the potatoes are tender. Remove from the oven and let rest for a few minutes before serving.
5. Just before serving, squeeze the lemon over the chicken and vegetables. Serve immediately.

Nutrition Info:

- Calories: 458; Protein: 36g; Total Fat: 25g; Saturated Fat: 6g; Carbohydrates: 24g; Fiber: 3g; Sodium: 884mg;

Turkey Dijon

Servings:4

Cooking Time: 15 Minutes

Ingredients:

- 2 tablespoons Garlic Oil
- 4 (4-ounce) turkey cutlets, pounded to ¼-inch thickness
- 2 tablespoons Dijon mustard
- 1 cup Low-FODMAP Poultry Broth
- 1 tablespoon cornstarch
- ½ teaspoon sea salt
- ⅛ teaspoon freshly ground black pepper

Directions:

1. In a large nonstick skillet over medium-high heat, heat the garlic oil until it shimmers.
2. Add the turkey and cook for about 4 minutes per side, until the juices run clear. Transfer the turkey to a plate and tent with aluminum foil to keep warm. Return the skillet to the heat.
3. In a small bowl, whisk the broth, cornstarch, salt, and pepper. Whisk this into the hot skillet and cook for 1 to 2 minutes, whisking until the sauce thickens.
4. Serve the turkey with the sauce spooned over the top.

Nutrition Info:

- Calories:270; Total Fat: 13g; Saturated Fat: 3g; Carbohydrates: 3g; Fiber: 0g; Sodium: 420mg; Protein: 34g

Teriyaki Salmon

Servings:4

Cooking Time: 10 Minutes

Ingredients:

- 1 pound salmon, quartered
- ¼ cup Teriyaki Sauce

Directions:

1. Preheat the oven to 425°F.
2. Place the salmon on a nonstick rimmed baking sheet.
3. Brush the salmon with the sauce and bake for about 10 minutes, until opaque.

Nutrition Info:

- Calories:166; Total Fat: 7g; Saturated Fat: 1g; Carbohydrates: 3g; Fiber: 0g; Sodium: 740mg; Protein: 23g

Roasted Lamb Racks On Buttered Mashed Rutabaga

Servings:4

Cooking Time:x

Ingredients:

- 2 tablespoons (30 g) salted butter, at room temperature
- 1 teaspoon ground cumin
- Salt and freshly ground black pepper
- 2 lamb racks (8 chops each, about 3 pounds/1360 g total), trimmed of fat
- 2 large rutabagas (1¾ pounds/800 g total), peeled and cut into 2-inch (5 cm) chunks
- 1 tablespoon (15 g) salted butter, at room temperature
- Salt and freshly ground black pepper

Directions:

1. Preheat the oven to 350°F (180°C).
2. Combine the butter, cumin, salt, and pepper in a small bowl. Rub over the lamb racks. Place the lamb in a baking dish and roast for 30 minutes or until the lamb is cooked but still pink in the middle. Remove from the oven and let rest for a few minutes.
3. Meanwhile, to make the mashed rutabagas, cook the rutabagas in boiling water for 8 to 10 minutes, until tender. Drain, then mash with a potato masher. Stir in the butter while still hot, and season well with salt and pepper.
4. Cut each rack of lamb in half or in quarters and serve on a bed of mashed rutabagas.

Nutrition Info:

- 448 calories; 26 g protein; 31 g total fat; 14 g saturated fat; 16 g carbohydrates; 5 g fiber; 650 mg sodium

Stuffed Rolled Roast Beef With Popovers And Gravy

Servings:8
Cooking Time:x
Ingredients:
- ½ cup (65 g) superfine white rice flour
- ⅓ cup (50 g) cornstarch
- 1 teaspoon salt
- 2 large eggs
- ½ cup (125 ml) skim milk, lactose-free milk, or suitable plant-based milk
- ⅔ cup (80 g) dried gluten-free, soy-free bread crumbs*
- 1 large egg
- ¼ cup (60 ml) gluten-free whole grain mustard
- 3 to 4 heaping tablespoons roughly chopped flat-leaf parsley
- 1 heaping tablespoon tomato paste or puree
- ¼ teaspoon salt
- ¼ teaspoon freshly ground black pepper
- 2 teaspoons paprika
- 2 pounds 10 ounces (1.2 kg) beef tenderloin
- 1 tablespoon olive oil
- 2 teaspoons salt
- 2 tablespoons vegetable oil
- About 1 cup (250 ml) boiling water
- ¼ cup (85 g) gluten-free, onion-free gravy mix*
- Roasted vegetables, for serving

Directions:
1. Preheat the oven to 400°F (200°C).
2. To make the popovers, sift the rice flour, cornstarch, and salt three times into a large bowl (or whisk in the bowl until well combined). Make a well in the middle and add the eggs and one third of the milk. Using a wooden spoon, mix the batter from the center out—first mixing the eggs and milk together, and then gradually working in the flour from the sides. Beat the batter until smooth and shiny. Stir in the remaining milk and let stand for 1 hour.
3. To make the stuffing, combine all the ingredients in a bowl. Set aside.
4. Place the beef on a cutting board and slice horizontally through the thickest part to open out the meat like a book. Press the stuffing along the center. Carefully roll up the beef to enclose the stuffing and secure with kitchen string at ¾-inch (2 cm) intervals.
5. Place the rolled beef in a metal baking dish, seam-side down, brush with the olive oil, and sprinkle with the salt. Roast for 40 to 45 minutes for medium-rare, or until your desired doneness. Remove from the oven and increase the

oven temperature to 425°F (220°C). Transfer the beef to a cutting board and let rest, covered loosely with foil, while you make the popovers.
6. To make the popovers, put ½ teaspoon of vegetable oil into each cup of a 12-cup muffin pan. Place on the top shelf of the oven for 5 minutes to heat the oil. Carefully pour the batter into each cup. Reduce the heat to 375°F (190°C) and bake for 6 to 8 minutes, until the popovers are risen and golden brown.
7. To make the gravy, combine the pan juices with enough boiling water to equal 1 cup (250 ml) liquid. Return to the baking dish and whisk in the gravy mix. Cook over medium heat, whisking constantly, until thickened and well combined.
8. Remove the string from the beef and slice carefully so you don't disturb the stuffing. Serve with the popovers, gravy, and your choice of roasted vegetables.

Nutrition Info:
- 578 calories; 31 g protein; 40 g total fat; 15 g saturated fat; 22 g carbohydrates; 0 g fiber; 1205 mg sodium

Moroccan Fish Stew With Cod, Fennel, Potatoes, And Tomatoes

Servings:4
Cooking Time: 15 Minutes
Ingredients:
- 1 tablespoon olive oil
- 1 tablespoon minced fresh ginger
- 1 teaspoon ground cumin
- 1 teaspoon ground turmeric
- 1 cinnamon stick
- ⅛ teaspoon cayenne
- 1 (14½-ounce) can onion- and garlic-free diced tomatoes with juice
- 1 large fennel bulb, cored and thinly sliced
- 1 pound new potatoes, halved or quartered
- 1 cup water
- 1 teaspoon salt
- ½ teaspoon freshly ground black pepper
- 1¼ pounds cod fillets, cut into 2-inch chunks
- 2 tablespoons Garlic Oil (here)
- 2 tablespoons chopped fresh parsley

Directions:
1. Heat the olive oil in a large skillet over medium heat.
2. Add the ginger, cumin, turmeric, cinnamon stick, and cayenne and cook, stirring, for 1 minute. Stir in the tomatoes with their juice, fennel, potatoes, water, salt, and pepper. Cook, stirring frequently, for about 10 minutes, until the potatoes are tender.

3. Add the fish and cook until the fish is cooked through, for about 5 minutes. Remove and discard the cinnamon stick.

4. Serve hot, garnished with a drizzle of Garlic Oil and a sprinkling of parsley.

Nutrition Info:

- Calories: 306; Protein: 28g; Total Fat: 6g; Saturated Fat: 1g; Carbohydrates: 33g; Fiber: 5g; Sodium: 636mg;

Flanken-style Beef Ribs With Quick Slaw

Servings:4

Cooking Time: 8 Minutes

Ingredients:

- 1 pound flanken-style beef ribs
- ½ teaspoon sea salt
- ⅛ teaspoon freshly ground black pepper
- 2 tablespoons Garlic Oil
- 2 cups shredded cabbage
- 6 scallions, green parts only, chopped
- ¼ cup Lemon-Dill Vinaigrette

Directions:

1. Season the ribs with salt and pepper.

2. In a large nonstick skillet over medium-high heat, heat the garlic oil until it shimmers.

3. Add the ribs and cook for about 4 minutes per side, or until browned.

4. In a large bowl, combine the cabbage, scallions, and vinaigrette. Toss to combine.

Nutrition Info:

- Calories:357; Total Fat: 22g; Saturated Fat: 5; Carbohydrates: 4g; Fiber: 2g; Sodium: 319mg; Protein: 35g

Creamy Smoked Salmon Pasta

Servings:4

Cooking Time: 9 Minutes

Ingredients:

- 2 tablespoons Garlic Oil
- 6 scallions, green parts only, chopped
- 2 tablespoons capers, drained
- 12 ounces smoked salmon, flaked
- ¾ cup unsweetened almond milk
- 2 tablespoons chopped fresh dill
- ⅛ teaspoon freshly ground black pepper
- 8 ounces gluten-free pasta, cooked according to the package directions and drained

Directions:

1. In a large nonstick skillet over medium-high heat, heat the garlic oil until it shimmers.

2. Add the scallions and capers. Cook for 2 minutes, stirring.

3. Add the salmon and cook for 2 minutes more.

4. Stir in the almond milk, dill, and pepper. Simmer for 3 minutes.

5. Toss with the hot pasta.

Nutrition Info:

- Calories:287; Total Fat: 6g; Saturated Fat: 1g; Carbohydrates: 35g; Fiber: 1g; Sodium: 1,920mg; Protein: 23g

Spicy Salmon Burgers With Cilantro-lime Mayo

Servings:4

Cooking Time: 5 Minutes

Ingredients:

- FOR THE MAYO
- ¼ cup mayonnaise
- 1 tablespoon chopped fresh cilantro
- Zest and juice of 1 lime
- ⅛ teaspoon salt
- ⅛ teaspoon freshly ground black pepper
- FOR THE BURGERS
- 1 pound salmon fillet, skinned and cut into pieces
- ¼ cup gluten-free plain bread crumbs
- 2 tablespoons chopped fresh cilantro
- 1 small jalapeño chile, seeded and diced
- 2 tablespoons lime juice
- ½ teaspoon salt
- ¼ teaspoon freshly ground black pepper
- Cooking spray
- TO SERVE
- 4 gluten-free hamburger buns, toasted
- ½ medium cucumber, thinly sliced
- 1 large tomato, sliced
- 4 lettuce leaves

Directions:

1. To make the mayo, combine the mayonnaise, cilantro, lime zest and juice, and salt and pepper in a small bowl, and stir to mix well. Cover and refrigerate until ready to use.

2. To make the burgers, pulse the salmon in a food processor until coarsely chopped. Add the bread crumbs, cilantro, jalapeño, lime juice, salt, and pepper, and pulse until well combined. Form the mixture into 4 (¾-inch-thick) patties.

3. Coat a grill or grill pan with cooking spray and heat over medium-high heat. Cook the salmon burgers for about 2 minutes per side, until browned and cooked through.

4. To serve, spread some of the cilantro-lime mayo onto the bottom half of each burger bun. Top with a salmon patty,

a few slices of cucumber, a tomato slice, a lettuce leaf, and the top half of the bun. Serve immediately.

Nutrition Info:

- Calories: 455; Protein: 29g; Total Fat: 19g; Saturated Fat: 3g; Carbohydrates: 48g; Fiber: 6g; Sodium: 841mg;

Sirloin Chimichurri

Servings:4
Cooking Time: 10 Minutes

Ingredients:

- 1 pound sirloin steak
- ½ teaspoon sea salt
- ⅛ teaspoon freshly ground black pepper
- ½ cup Chimichurri Sauce

Directions:

1. Preheat the broiler to high.
2. Season the sirloin with salt and pepper and place it on a broiling pan.
3. Broil the steak for about 4 minutes per side, or until your desired doneness.
4. Slice the steak into 1-inch-thick slices and serve topped with the chimichurri.

Nutrition Info:

- Calories:331; Total Fat: 19g; Saturated Fat: 4; Carbohydrates: 2g; Fiber: 4g; Sodium: 499mg; Protein: 35g

Arroz Con Pollo With Olives, Raisins, And Pine Nuts

Servings:6
Cooking Time: 60 Minutes

Ingredients:

- FOR THE CHICKEN
- 2 tablespoons orange juice
- 2 tablespoons lime juice
- 1½ teaspoons salt
- ¾ teaspoon freshly ground black pepper
- 1 whole chicken (about 3½ to 4½ pounds), cut into 8 serving pieces
- 1 tablespoon vegetable oil
- 1 tablespoon unsalted butter
- FOR THE RICE
- 2 green bell peppers, diced
- ¼ teaspoon saffron threads, soaked in ¼ cup warm water
- 2 teaspoons ground cumin
- 2 teaspoons salt
- 1 bay leaf
- 1 (14½-ounce) can diced onion- and garlic-free tomatoes with juice
- 1½ cups homemade (onion- and garlic-free) chicken broth
- 1¼ cups water
- 1½ cups long-grain white rice
- ½ cup golden raisins
- ½ cup small pimiento-stuffed green olives, rinsed
- ¼ cup toasted pine nuts (optional)

Directions:

1. To prepare the chicken, combine the orange juice, lime juice, salt, and pepper in a large bowl. Add the chicken and turn to coat. Cover and marinate in the refrigerator for at least 1 hour.
2. Remove the chicken from the marinade, reserving the marinade. Pat the chicken pieces dry with paper towels.
3. Heat the oil and butter in a large Dutch oven or stockpot over medium-high heat. Brown the chicken in batches for about 6 minutes per batch, until the chicken is browned on both sides. Transfer the browned chicken pieces to a large plate.
4. To make the rice, begin by preheating the oven to 350°F.
5. Add the bell peppers to the Dutch oven and sauté over medium-high heat, stirring occasionally, until the vegetables soften, for about 8 minutes. Add the saffron along with its soaking liquid, the cumin, salt, bay leaf, tomatoes along with their juice, broth, water, and the reserved marinade. Bring to a boil. Add the chicken pieces except for the breasts. Reduce the heat to low, cover, and simmer for 10 minutes. Stir in the rice and add the chicken breasts, skin-side up, on top of the rice and vegetables. Cover and transfer to the preheated oven. Cook for 20 minutes, until the rice is tender and the liquid has been absorbed.
6. Remove the pot from the oven and sprinkle the raisins, olives, and pine nuts (if using) over the top. Cover the pot with a clean dish towel and let rest for 5 to 10 minutes. Discard the bay leaf.

Nutrition Info:

- Calories: 651; Protein: 55g; Total Fat: 23g; Saturated Fat: 5g; Carbohydrates: 53g; Fiber: 3g; Sodium: 1725mg;

Italian-herbed Chicken Meatballs In Broth

Servings:4
Cooking Time: 25 Minutes

Ingredients:

- FOR THE MEATBALLS
- Oil for preparing the baking sheet
- 1 pound ground chicken
- ¾ cup cooked rice
- ½ cup chopped fresh basil

56

- 1½ ounces freshly grated Parmesan cheese, plus more for garnish
- 1 tablespoon Garlic Oil (here)
- 1 egg, lightly beaten
- 1¼ teaspoons salt
- ½ teaspoon freshly ground black pepper
- FOR THE BROTH
- 1 tablespoon olive oil
- 1 tablespoon Garlic Oil (here)
- 1 large carrot, thinly sliced
- 5 cups homemade (onion- and garlic-free) chicken broth
- 4 cups baby spinach
- ½ cup chopped fresh basil

Directions:

1. Preheat the oven to 400°F.
2. Line a large, rimmed baking sheet with parchment paper lightly coated with oil.
3. In a large bowl, combine the chicken, rice, basil, cheese, Garlic Oil, egg, salt, and pepper, and mix well. Form the mixture into 1-inch balls and arrange them on the prepared baking sheet. Bake in the preheated oven for about 25 minutes, until the meatballs are browned and cooked through.
4. Meanwhile, make the broth. Heat the olive oil and Garlic Oil in a stockpot over medium-high heat. Add the carrots and cook, stirring, for 3 minutes, then add the broth and bring to a boil. Reduce the heat to low and simmer, uncovered, for about 10 minutes, until the carrots are tender. Stir in the spinach and basil, and cook just until wilted, for about 3 minutes.
5. To serve, place several meatballs in a serving bowl, and ladle the broth and vegetables over the top. Serve immediately, garnished with additional Parmesan cheese if desired.

Nutrition Info:

- Calories: 493; Protein: 48g; Total Fat: 17g; Saturated Fat: 5g; Carbohydrates: 33g; Fiber: 2g; Sodium: 1933mg;

Pan-seared Scallops With Sautéed Kale

Servings:4
Cooking Time: 15 Minutes

Ingredients:

- 2 tablespoons extra-virgin olive oil
- 1 pound sea scallops
- ½ teaspoon sea salt
- ⅛ teaspoon freshly ground black pepper
- 3 cups stemmed, chopped kale leaves
- Juice of 1 orange
- Zest of 1 orange

Directions:

1. In a large nonstick skillet over medium-high heat, heat the olive oil until it shimmers. Swirl the pan to coat it with the oil.
2. Season the scallops with salt and pepper. Add them to the hot skillet and cook for about 3 minutes per side. Transfer the scallops to a platter and tent with foil to keep warm. Return the skillet to the heat.
3. Add the kale to the skillet. Cook for about 5 minutes, stirring.
4. Add the orange juice and zest. Cook for 3 minutes more.
5. Serve the scallops on top of the sautéed kale.

Nutrition Info:

- Calories:199; Total Fat: 8g; Saturated Fat: 1g; Carbohydrates: 11g; Fiber: <1g; Sodium: 439mg; Protein: 21g

Pork Tenderloin On Creamy Garlic Polenta With Cranberry Sauce

Servings:4
Cooking Time:x

Ingredients:

- 1 teaspoon garlic-infused olive oil
- 1 tablespoon plus 1 teaspoon olive oil
- 1 tablespoon plus 1 teaspoon fresh lemon juice
- Salt and freshly ground black pepper
- 1 pound (450 g) pork tenderloin
- ⅓ cup (80 g) whole berry cranberry sauce
- 3 cups (750 ml) low-fat milk, lactose-free milk, or suitable plant-based milk
- 2 garlic cloves, peeled and halved
- ⅔ cup (135 g) coarse cornmeal (instant polenta)
- Salt and freshly ground black pepper
- Green salad or vegetables, for serving

Directions:

1. Combine the garlic-infused oil, olive oil, lemon juice, salt, and pepper in a baking dish. Add the pork and brush the marinade all over. Cover and refrigerate for at least 3 hours.
2. Preheat the oven to 350°F (180°C).
3. Remove the pork from the fridge and bake, uncovered, for 30 minutes, or until your desired doneness.
4. Meanwhile, for the polenta, combine the milk and garlic in a medium saucepan over medium heat and bring to just below a boil. Remove the garlic with a slotted spoon and discard. Add the cornmeal and stir until the polenta comes to a boil. Reduce the heat to low and cook, stirring constantly, for 3 to 5 minutes more, until the polenta is the texture of smooth mashed potatoes. Season to taste with salt and pepper.

5. Remove the pork from the baking dish and carefully pour the cooking juices into a small frying pan. Return the pork to the dish and cover with foil to keep warm while you prepare the sauce.

6. Add the cranberry sauce to the cooking juices in the frying pan and cook, stirring, until warmed through and well combined.

7. Cut the pork into thick slices. Spoon the polenta onto warmed plates and top with the pork and a good spoonful of cranberry sauce. Finish with a grinding of pepper and serve with your choice of salad or vegetables.

Nutrition Info:
- 389 calories; 31 g protein; 15 g total fat; 3 g saturated fat; 33 g carbohydrates; 2 g fiber; 306 mg sodium

Chicken Parmigiana

Servings:4
Cooking Time:x
Ingredients:
- One 14.5-ounce (425 g) can crushed tomatoes
- 2 heaping tablespoons chopped flat-leaf parsley
- 1 teaspoon sweet paprika
- 2 teaspoons sugar
- ½ cup (80 g) sliced black olives
- ½ cup (75 g) cornstarch
- 2 large eggs
- 1 cup (120 g) dried gluten-free, soy-free bread crumbs*
- Salt and freshly ground black pepper
- Four 6-ounce (170 g) boneless, skinless chicken breasts
- 1 tablespoon olive oil
- ⅔ cup (80 g) grated reduced-fat Parmesan or cheddar
- Green salad or vegetables, for serving

Directions:
1. Preheat the oven to 350°F (180°C).
2. To make the sauce, combine the tomatoes, parsley, paprika, sugar, and olives in a small frying pan and cook over medium-low heat for 15 minutes, stirring occasionally.
3. Set out three shallow bowls and fill one with the cornstarch, one with the eggs, and one with the bread crumbs mixed with the salt and pepper. Beat the eggs lightly. Coat the chicken breasts in the cornstarch, shaking off any excess, then dip in the egg, and finally toss in the bread crumbs until well coated.
4. Heat the olive oil in a large frying pan over medium-low heat. Add the chicken and cook for 3 to 4 minutes on each side, until golden brown and cooked through.
5. Place the chicken breasts in a baking dish, spoon the sauce over them, and top with the cheddar. Cover and bake for 15 minutes, or until the cheese is golden and melted.

6. Serve with your choice of salad or vegetables.

Nutrition Info:
- 516 calories; 50 g protein; 16 g total fat; 5 g saturated fat; 37 g carbohydrates; 2 g fiber; 805 mg sodium

Chicken With Olives, Sun-dried Tomato, And Basil With Mediterranean Vegetables

Servings:4
Cooking Time:x
Ingredients:
- 2 heaping tablespoons pitted black or kalamata olives
- ½ cup (75 g) sun-dried tomatoes, drained (if packed in oil)
- Small handful of basil leaves
- 2 tablespoons olive oil
- Salt and freshly ground black pepper
- Four 6-ounce (170 g) boneless, skinless chicken breasts
- Nonstick cooking spray
- 2 small zucchini, thinly sliced lengthwise
- 1 small (80 g) eggplant, thinly sliced lengthwise
- ½ cup (80 g) kalamata olives, pitted
- 2 tablespoons plus 2 teaspoons balsamic vinegar

Directions:
1. Preheat the oven to 325°F (170°C). Line a baking sheet with parchment paper.
2. Using a mortar and pestle, crush the black olives, sun-dried tomatoes, basil, 1 tablespoon of the olive oil, and salt and pepper to taste into an even paste (it can be as smooth or chunky as you like). If you don't have a mortar and pestle, use a blender or mini food processor.
3. Heat the remaining 1 tablespoon of olive oil in a large frying pan over medium-low heat. Add the chicken breasts and pan-fry for 5 minutes on each side, until lightly browned and cooked through.
4. Transfer the chicken to the prepared baking sheet and spoon the olive paste over the top. Cover with foil and bake for 10 to 15 minutes.
5. Meanwhile, to make the Mediterranean vegetables, spray a ridged grill pan or cast-iron skillet with cooking spray and heat over medium heat. Add the zucchini and eggplant (in batches, if necessary) and cook for 3 to 4 minutes on each side, until tender. Add the kalamata olives and warm through.
6. Lightly drizzle both the chicken and the vegetables with balsamic vinegar and serve together.

Nutrition Info:
- 363 calories; 41 g protein; 16 g total fat; 2 g saturated fat; 13 g carbohydrates; 4 g fiber; 505 mg sodium

Chimichurri Chicken Drumsticks

Servings:4

Cooking Time: 30 Minutes

Ingredients:

- 8 chicken drumsticks
- 1 cup Chimichurri Sauce, divided

Directions:

1. In a gallon-size zip-top bag, combine the drumsticks with ½ cup chimichurri sauce. Seal the bag and shake to coat. Refrigerate for 8 hours.
2. Preheat the oven to 375°F.
3. Line a rimmed baking sheet with parchment paper.
4. Remove the drumsticks from the bag, pat the marinade off with a paper towel (a little will be left, which is okay), and place them on the prepared baking sheet. Bake for about 30 minutes, or until the juices run clear.
5. Serve with the remaining ½ cup chimichurri sauce on the side.

Nutrition Info:

- Calories:401; Total Fat: 11g; Saturated Fat: 3g; Carbohydrates: 39g; Fiber: 3g; Sodium: 968mg; Protein: 35g

Rosemary-lemon Chicken Thighs

Servings:4

Cooking Time: 30 Minutes

Ingredients:

- 8 chicken thighs
- 1 tablespoon chopped fresh rosemary leaves
- 1 teaspoon sea salt
- Zest of 1 lemon
- ¼ teaspoon freshly ground black pepper

Directions:

1. Preheat the oven to 375°F.
2. Line a rimmed baking sheet with parchment paper and place the chicken thighs, skin-side up, on the sheet.
3. In a small bowl, mix the rosemary, salt, lemon zest, and pepper. Sprinkle this over the thighs.
4. Bake for about 30 minutes, or until the juices run clear.

Nutrition Info:

- Calories:535; Total Fat: 21g; Saturated Fat: 6g; Carbohydrates: <1g; Fiber: 0g; Sodium: 709mg; Protein: 81g

Spanish Chicken With Creamy Herbed Rice

Servings:4

Cooking Time:x

Ingredients:

- 2 tablespoons plus 2 teaspoons garlic-infused olive oil
- 1 heaping tablespoon smoked paprika
- 1 heaping tablespoon ground cumin
- ½ teaspoon ground turmeric
- Salt and freshly ground black pepper
- Four 6-ounce (170 g) boneless, skinless chicken breasts
- 2 cups (300 g) cooked basmati rice, at room temperature (made from ⅔ cup/130 g uncooked rice)
- 2 teaspoons garlic-infused olive oil
- 3 tablespoons olive oil
- ¼ cup (60 ml) red wine vinegar
- ¾ cup (200 g) gluten-free low-fat plain yogurt
- ⅓ cup (90 g) Basil Pesto
- ¼ cup (15 g) flat-leaf parsley leaves
- 2 heaping tablespoons finely chopped mint
- Mint or flat-leaf parsley leaves, for garnish

Directions:

1. Preheat the oven to 350°F (180°C).
2. Combine the garlic-infused oil, paprika, cumin, turmeric, salt, and pepper in a small bowl. Place the chicken in a large baking dish and rub with about three quarters of the spice mixture.
3. Bake the chicken for 20 minutes or until cooked through. Remove from the oven, reserve any cooking juices separately, and set aside for 1 to 2 hours.
4. To make the creamy herbed rice, combine all the ingredients in a large bowl and mix together well.
5. Combine the remaining spice mix and the cooking juices with a little water in a small frying pan over medium heat. Simmer until warmed through.
6. Cut the chicken into thick slices and serve at room temperature with the rice, a drizzle of the spicy sauce, and a scattering of mint or parsley leaves. Serve cold or at room temperature.

Nutrition Info:

- 593 calories; 47 g protein; 35 g total fat; 6 g saturated fat; 37 g carbohydrates; 2 g fiber; 385 mg sodium

Breaded Thin-cut Pork Chops

Servings:4

Cooking Time: 20 Minutes

Ingredients:

- 2 cups gluten-free bread crumbs
- 1 teaspoon dried thyme
- 1 teaspoon sea salt
- ¼ teaspoon freshly ground black pepper
- 4 (4- to 6-ounce) thin-cut pork chops
- ¼ cup Dijon mustard

Directions:

1. Preheat the oven to 425°F.

2. In a small bowl, stir together the bread crumbs, thyme, salt, and pepper.

3. Spread the pork chops on both sides with mustard. Dip them into the seasoned bread crumbs to coat. Put the pork chops on a nonstick rimmed baking sheet.

4. Bake for about 20 minutes to an internal temperature of 165°F measured with a meat thermometer.

Nutrition Info:

- Calories:589; Total Fat: 32g; Saturated Fat: 11; Carbohydrates: 40g; Fiber: 3g; Sodium: 1,120mg; Protein: 33g

Chicken Enchiladas

Servings:8

Cooking Time: 45 Minutes

Ingredients:

- FOR THE SAUCE
- 2 tablespoons grapeseed oil
- 2 tablespoons gluten-free all-purpose flour
- 1 tablespoon Garlic Oil (here)
- ¼ cup gluten-, onion-, and garlic-free chili powder
- ½ teaspoon salt
- ¼ teaspoon ground cumin
- 1 tablespoon minced fresh oregano
- 2 cups homemade (onion- and garlic-free) chicken broth
- FOR THE ENCHILADAS
- Oil for preparing the baking sheet
- 1½ pounds cooked, shredded chicken breast (boneless, skinless)
- 1 cup fresh or frozen (thawed) corn kernels
- 1 (4-ounce) can diced green chiles
- 1 teaspoon ground chipotle
- 1 (14-ounce) can onion- and garlic-free diced tomatoes, drained
- ½ teaspoon salt
- 16 corn tortillas
- 1 cup shredded cheddar or Monterey Jack cheese
- ¼ cup chopped fresh cilantro

Directions:

1. To make the sauce, heat the grapeseed oil in a small saucepan over medium-high heat. Whisk in the flour and cook, stirring, for 1 minute. Stir in the Garlic Oil, chili powder, salt, cumin, and oregano. While stirring constantly, gradually add the broth. Bring to a boil, then reduce the heat to low and simmer, stirring occasionally, for 10 to 15 minutes, until the sauce has thickened. Transfer the sauce to a large, shallow bowl.

2. To make the enchiladas, begin by preheating the oven to 350°F.

3. Oil a 9-by-13-inch baking dish.

4. In a large bowl, combine the chicken, corn, green chiles, ground chipotle, tomatoes, and salt, and stir to mix well. Wrap the tortillas in a clean dish towel, and microwave them on high for about 30 seconds.

5. Coat the bottom of the prepared baking dish with several spoonfuls of the sauce. Dip each tortilla in the sauce to coat it lightly. Spoon about ¼ cup of the chicken mixture into the tortilla in a line down the center. Roll the tortilla up around the filling and place it in the prepared baking dish, seam-side down. Repeat with the remaining tortillas and filling. When all of the tortillas are filled and in the baking dish, spoon the remaining sauce over the top, covering all of the tortillas. Sprinkle with the cheese.

6. Bake the enchiladas in the preheated oven until the sauce is bubbly and the cheese is melted, for 15 to 20 minutes. Serve hot, garnished with cilantro.

Nutrition Info:

- Calories: 415; Protein: 37g; Total Fat: 13g; Saturated Fat: 3g; Carbohydrates: 41g; Fiber: 9g; Sodium: 759mg;

Lemon-pepper Shrimp

Servings:4

Cooking Time: 8 Minutes

Ingredients:

- 2 tablespoons Garlic Oil
- 1 pound medium shrimp, shelled and deveined
- Juice of 2 lemons
- ½ teaspoon sea salt
- ½ teaspoon freshly ground black pepper

Directions:

1. In a large nonstick skillet over medium-high heat, heat the garlic oil until it shimmers.

2. Add the shrimp. Cook for about 5 minutes, stirring occasionally, until it is pink.

3. Squeeze in the lemon juice, then add the salt and pepper. Simmer for 3 minutes more.

Nutrition Info:

- Calories:119; Total Fat: 2g; Saturated Fat: 0g; Carbohydrates: 2g; Fiber: 0g; Sodium: 494mg; Protein: 25g

Mild Lamb Curry

Servings:6

Cooking Time:x

Ingredients:

- ½ cup (75 g) cornstarch
- 2 pounds 10 ounces (1.2 kg) lean lamb steaks, cut into ¾-inch (2 cm) pieces
- 2 teaspoons garlic-infused olive oil
- 2 tablespoons rice bran oil or sunflower oil

- 2 teaspoons ground cinnamon
- 2 heaping tablespoons ground cumin
- 2 teaspoons ground ginger
- 1 heaping tablespoon ground turmeric
- 2 teaspoons paprika
- 1 teaspoon cayenne pepper
- 1 teaspoon salt
- 1 teaspoon freshly ground black pepper
- 4 cups (1 liter) gluten-free, onion-free beef stock*
- 2 heaping tablespoons light brown sugar
- One 14.5-ounce (425 g) can crushed tomatoes
- Steamed rice and cilantro leaves, for serving

Directions:

1. Place the cornstarch in a shallow bowl. Add the lamb pieces and toss to coat well. Shake off any excess.
2. Heat the garlic-infused oil and rice bran oil in a large heavy-bottomed saucepan or Dutch oven over medium heat. Add the cinnamon, cumin, ginger, turmeric, paprika, cayenne, salt, and pepper and cook for 1 to 2 minutes, until fragrant. Add the lamb and cook, stirring occasionally, for 5 to 7 minutes, until nicely browned. Add the stock and brown sugar and bring to a boil, then reduce the heat and simmer gently for 1½ hours, stirring occasionally.
3. Stir in the crushed tomatoes and cook for another hour or until the meat is very tender. Make sure the heat is kept very low so the lamb does not boil dry. (Add a little water if necessary.)
4. Season to taste with salt and pepper and serve with steamed rice, garnished with cilantro.

Nutrition Info:

- 538 calories; 27 g protein; 39 g total fat; 15 g saturated fat; 16 g carbohydrates; 2 g fiber; 647 mg sodium

Sautéed Shrimp With Cilantro-lime Rice

Servings:4

Cooking Time: 10 Minutes

Ingredients:

- 3 tablespoons Garlic Oil
- 1 pound medium shrimp, peeled and deveined
- 2 cups cooked brown rice
- ¼ cup Cilantro-Lime Vinaigrette
- ½ teaspoon sea salt

Directions:

1. In a large nonstick skillet over medium-high heat, heat the garlic oil until it shimmers.
2. Add the shrimp. Cook for about 5 minutes, stirring occasionally, until the shrimp is pink.
3. Stir in the rice, vinaigrette, and salt. Cook for 2 minutes more, stirring.

Nutrition Info:

- Calories:360; Total Fat: 11g; Saturated Fat: 2g; Carbohydrates: 38g; Fiber: 2g; Sodium: 494mg; Protein: 28g

Breaded Fish Fillets With Spicy Pepper Relish

Servings:4

Cooking Time: 15 Minutes

Ingredients:

- 2 cups gluten-free bread crumbs (see Tip)
- 1¼ teaspoons sea salt, divided
- 1 teaspoon dried thyme
- ⅛ teaspoon freshly ground black pepper
- 2 eggs, beaten
- 1 tablespoon Dijon mustard
- 1 pound cod, cut into 8 pieces
- 1 red bell pepper, chopped
- 2 tablespoons capers, drained and rinsed
- 1 jalapeño pepper, minced
- Juice of 1 lime
- ¼ teaspoon red pepper flakes

Directions:

1. Preheat the oven to 425°F.
2. In a small bowl, whisk the bread crumbs, 1 teaspoon salt, thyme, and pepper.
3. In another small bowl, whisk the eggs and mustard.
4. Dip the fish into the egg mixture and into the breading mixture to coat. Place the fish on a nonstick rimmed baking sheet. Bake for about 15 minutes, until the crust is golden and the fish is opaque.
5. While the fish cooks, in a small bowl, stir together the bell pepper, capers, jalapeño, lime juice, red pepper flakes, and the remaining ¼ teaspoon salt.
6. Serve the fish topped with the relish.

Nutrition Info:

- Calories:209; Total Fat: 3g; Saturated Fat: <1g; Carbohydrates: 13g; Fiber: 2g; Sodium: 699mg; Protein: 30g

Roasted Garlic Shrimp And Red Peppers

Servings:4

Cooking Time: 17 Minutes

Ingredients:

- 2 pounds peeled and deveined shrimp (tails left intact)
- 2 red bell peppers, cut into 1½-inch triangles
- 4 tablespoons Garlic Oil (here)
- 1½ tablespoons smoked paprika
- ¾ teaspoon cayenne
- 1 teaspoon salt
- ½ teaspoon freshly ground black pepper

- 1 tablespoon chopped fresh oregano

Directions:

1. Preheat the oven to 400°F.

2. In a large baking dish, combine the shrimp, peppers, Garlic Oil, paprika, cayenne, salt, and pepper, and toss to coat. Spread the shrimp and peppers out in a single layer.

3. Roast the shrimp and peppers in the preheated oven for 10 minutes. Using tongs, flip the shrimp and peppers over, sprinkle the oregano over the top, and continue to roast for another 5 to 7 minutes, until the shrimp are cooked through. Serve hot.

Nutrition Info:

- Calories: 260; Protein: 50g; Total Fat: 4g; Saturated Fat: 0g; Carbohydrates: 9g; Fiber: 3g; Sodium: 1099mg;

Easy Salmon Cakes

Servings:4
Cooking Time: 10 Minutes

Ingredients:

- 1 pound canned salmon, flaked
- ½ cup gluten-free bread crumbs
- 1 egg, beaten
- 1 tablespoon Dijon mustard
- 1 tablespoon chopped fresh dill
- ½ teaspoon sea salt
- ⅛ teaspoon freshly ground black pepper

Directions:

1. Preheat the oven to 375°F.

2. Line a baking sheet with parchment paper and set it aside.

3. In a large bowl, mix the salmon and the bread crumbs.

4. In a small bowl, whisk together the egg, mustard, dill, salt, and pepper. Fold this into the salmon and bread crumbs. Form the salmon mixture into 4 patties and place them on the prepared sheet.

5. Bake for 5 minutes, flip, and bake for 5 minutes more, until the patties are golden.

Nutrition Info:

- Calories:184; Total Fat: 8g; Saturated Fat: 1g; Carbohydrates: 4g; Fiber: 0g; Sodium: 362mg; Protein: 24g

Beef Satay Stir-fry With Peanut Sauce

Servings:6
Cooking Time:x

Ingredients:

- 1 heaping tablespoon cornstarch
- ¾ cup (210 g) creamy peanut butter
- 2 cups (500 ml) gluten-free, onion-free beef stock*
- 2 teaspoons garlic-infused olive oil

- 2 tablespoons rice bran oil or peanut oil
- ¼ cup (60 ml) gluten-free soy sauce
- ¼ cup (55 g) packed light brown sugar
- Salt and freshly ground black pepper
- 2 tablespoons peanut oil, plus more if needed
- 1½ pounds (700 g) lean beef, sliced ⅛-inch (3 mm) thick
- 5 ounces (150 g) green beans, trimmed (1-⅓ cups)
- 1 red bell pepper, seeded and cut into strips
- 1½ cups (150 g) broccoli florets
- 2 carrots, diced
- Steamed rice, for serving

Directions:

1. To make the peanut sauce, blend the cornstarch with the peanut butter and 2 tablespoons of the stock to make a smooth paste. Stir in the garlic-infused oil, rice bran oil, soy sauce, brown sugar, and remaining stock, and season to taste with salt and pepper.

2. Heat the peanut oil in a wok over medium heat. Add one third of the beef and stir-fry until just cooked (it should still be pink on the inside). Remove from the wok and set aside. Cook the remaining beef in two batches and set aside.

3. Add the vegetables to the wok and stir-fry over high heat for 2 to 5 minutes, until just tender, adding a little extra oil if needed. Return the beef and any juices to the wok. Add the sauce and stir-fry until thickened and heated through. Serve with rice.

Nutrition Info:

- 450 calories; 23 g protein; 32 g total fat; 8 g saturated fat; 19 g carbohydrates; 4 g fiber; 718 mg sodium

Pecan-crusted Maple-mustard Salmon

Servings:4
Cooking Time: 12 Minutes

Ingredients:

- Cooking spray
- 2 tablespoons Dijon mustard
- 2 tablespoons maple syrup
- 4 (6-ounce) salmon fillets
- ½ cup finely chopped pecans

Directions:

1. Preheat the oven to 425°F.

2. Coat a baking dish with cooking spray. In a small bowl, stir together the mustard and maple syrup. Arrange the salmon fillets in a single layer in the baking dish. Spread the mustard–maple syrup mixture over the tops of the fillets. Sprinkle the pecans on top, pressing them into the mustard mixture.

3. Bake in the preheated oven for about 12 minutes, until the salmon is cooked through and flakes easily with a fork. Serve immediately.

Nutrition Info:

- Calories: 305; Protein: 34g; Total Fat: 16g; Saturated Fat: 2g; Carbohydrates: 8g; Fiber: 1g; Sodium: 165mg;

Indian-spiced Prawns With Coconut Milk

Servings:4

Cooking Time: 10 Minutes

Ingredients:

- 2 red jalapeño or serrano chiles, seeded and chopped
- 1-inch piece peeled fresh ginger, sliced
- 1 tablespoon grapeseed oil
- 1 teaspoon black mustard seeds
- ½ teaspoon fenugreek seeds
- ½ teaspoon ground turmeric
- ½ teaspoon cracked black peppercorns
- 1½ pounds peeled and deveined prawns
- ¾ cup canned coconut milk
- ½ cup chopped fresh basil
- Juice of 1 lime
- 2 tablespoons chopped fresh cilantro

Directions:

1. In a food processor, pulse the chiles and ginger with 3 tablespoons of water until finely chopped.

2. Heat the oil in a heavy skillet over medium-high heat and add the mustard and fenugreek seeds. Cook, shaking the pan, for about 10 seconds. Add the chile-ginger purée and reduce the heat to low. Cook, stirring, for about 3 minutes.

3. Stir in the turmeric, peppercorns, prawns, and coconut milk, and bring to a simmer. Cook for 2 to 3 minutes, until the prawns are cooked through and fully opaque. Stir in the basil and lime juice, and serve immediately, garnished with cilantro.

Nutrition Info:

- Calories: 305; Protein: 38g; Total Fat: 17g; Saturated Fat: 10g; Carbohydrates: 4g; Fiber: 2g; Sodium: 392mg;

Grilled Halibut Tacos With Cabbage Slaw

Servings:4

Cooking Time: 10 Minutes

Ingredients:

- FOR THE FISH TACOS
- 4 teaspoons gluten-, onion-, and garlic-free chili powder
- 2 tablespoons lime juice
- 2 tablespoons olive oil
- 1 teaspoon ground cumin
- 1 teaspoon salt

- ½ teaspoon freshly ground black pepper
- 4 (6-ounce) halibut fillets
- Cooking spray
- 12 corn tortillas, warmed
- ½ avocado, thinly sliced
- FOR THE SLAW
- ½ cup mayonnaise
- 2 tablespoons chopped fresh cilantro
- Zest and juice of 1 lime
- 1 teaspoon sugar
- ⅛ teaspoon salt
- ⅛ teaspoon pepper
- 3 cups finely shredded green cabbage

Directions:

1. In a small bowl, combine the chili powder, lime juice, oil, cumin, salt, and pepper. Rub the spice mixture all over the fish fillets and refrigerate for about 20 minutes.

2. While the fish is marinating, make the coleslaw. In a large bowl, combine the mayonnaise, cilantro, lime zest and juice, sugar, salt, and pepper, and stir to mix. Add the cabbage and toss well. Cover and refrigerate until ready to serve.

3. To cook the fish, spray a grill or grill pan with cooking spray and heat it to medium-high.

4. Cook the fish for 3 to 5 minutes per side, until it flakes easily with a fork. Transfer to a cutting board and break into chunks.

5. To serve, place 2 tortillas on each serving plate. Top with some of the fish and a handful of coleslaw.

Nutrition Info:

- Calories: 547; Protein: 36g; Total Fat: 25g; Saturated Fat: 4g; Carbohydrates: 47g; Fiber: 9g; Sodium: 983mg;

Rib-eye Steak With Creamy Shrimp Sauce

Servings:6

Cooking Time:x

Ingredients:

- 2 teaspoons garlic-infused olive oil
- 2 teaspoons olive oil
- 1 tablespoon plus 1 teaspoon fresh lemon juice
- Salt and freshly ground black pepper
- Six 6- to 7-ounce (190 g) rib-eye steaks (2½ pounds/1.125 kg total), trimmed of excess fat
- ½ cup (125 ml) light cream
- 1 teaspoon cornstarch
- 1 teaspoon garlic-infused olive oil
- 1 pound (450 g) raw jumbo shrimp, peeled and deveined, tails intact

- 2 teaspoons roughly chopped flat-leaf parsley
- Salt and freshly ground black pepper
- Green salad or vegetables, for serving

Directions:

1. Combine the garlic-infused oil, olive oil, lemon juice, salt, and pepper in a baking dish. Add the steaks and turn to coat. Cover and refrigerate for at least 3 hours.

2. To make the sauce, blend the cream and cornstarch in a small bowl, stirring well to remove any lumps. Heat the garlic-infused oil in a medium frying pan. Add the cream mixture, shrimp, and parsley and cook until the shrimp have turned just pink and the sauce has thickened. Season to taste with salt and pepper.

3. Heat a ridged grill pan, cast-iron skillet, or grill to medium-high. Cook the steaks to your preferred doneness. Remove from the pan, cover, and let rest for a few minutes.

4. Serve the steaks with the shrimp sauce and your choice of salad or vegetables.

Nutrition Info:

- 459 calories; 60 g protein; 25 g total fat; 9 g saturated fat; 2 g carbohydrates; 0 g fiber; 433 mg sodium

Fish And Potato Pie

Servings:6

Cooking Time: 50 Minutes

Ingredients:

- 2 large potatoes
- 4 tablespoons butter, divided
- 1½ teaspoons salt, divided
- 1 teaspoon freshly ground black pepper, divided
- ¾ pound smoked whitefish (such as haddock), cut into bite-size pieces
- ¾ pound skinless salmon fillet, cut into ½-inch pieces
- 1 medium carrot, coarsely grated
- 2 (8-inch) stalks celery, coarsely grated
- 4 cups chopped fresh spinach
- 4 ounces grated sharp white cheddar cheese

Directions:

1. Preheat the oven to 400°F.

2. Bring a pot of salted water to a boil. Add the potatoes and cook for 10 to 12 minutes, until the potatoes are tender. Drain and then mash the potatoes along with 2 tablespoons of the butter, ¾ teaspoon of the salt, and ½ teaspoon of the pepper.

3. In a large baking dish, toss together the smoked fish, salmon, carrot, celery, and spinach. Season with the remaining ¾ teaspoon salt and ½ teaspoon pepper. Spread the mixture out in an even layer. Spread the mashed potatoes over the top in an even layer. Melt the remaining 2 tablespoons of butter and drizzle it over the top. Sprinkle the cheese over the top.

4. Bake in the preheated oven for 30 to 40 minutes, until the top is golden brown and the dish is hot all the way through. Serve immediately.

Nutrition Info:

- Calories: 366; Protein: 34g; Total Fat: 16g; Saturated Fat: 10g; Carbohydrates: 22g; Fiber: 4g; Sodium: 1312mg;

Chicken Carbonara

Servings:4

Cooking Time: 5 Minutes

Ingredients:

- 2 tablespoons Garlic Oil
- 8 ounces boneless skinless chicken breast, chopped
- 3 bacon slices, chopped
- 8 ounces gluten-free pasta, cooked according to the package directions and drained
- 3 eggs, beaten
- 2 tablespoons unsweetened almond milk
- ½ teaspoon sea salt
- ⅛ teaspoon freshly ground black pepper
- ½ cup grated Parmesan cheese

Directions:

1. In a large nonstick skillet over medium-high heat, heat the garlic oil until it shimmers.

2. Add the chicken and bacon. Cook for about 5 minutes, until the bacon is crisp and chicken is cooked through.

3. Add the cooked pasta to the pan, stir to combine, and turn off the heat.

4. In a small bowl, whisk the eggs, almond milk, salt, and pepper. Stir the egg mixture into the hot pasta. The hot ingredients and residual heat from the stove will cook the eggs and turn it into a sauce.

5. Toss with the cheese.

Nutrition Info:

- Calories:727; Total Fat: 32g; Saturated Fat: 12g; Carbohydrates: 33g; Fiber: 0g; Sodium: 1,105mg; Protein: 73g

Chapter 4 Soups, Salads And Sandwiches Recipes

Caramelized Squash Salad With Sun-dried Tomatoes And Basil

Servings:4
Cooking Time:x
Ingredients:
- 2 pounds 10 ounces (1.2 kg) kabocha or other suitable winter squash, peeled, seeded, and cut into ¾-inch (2 cm) cubes
- 1 eggplant, cut into ¼-inch (5 mm) slices
- ¼ cup (60 ml) olive oil
- 12 or 13 pieces (50 g) sun-dried tomatoes in oil, drained and sliced
- ½ cup (100 g) thawed frozen corn kernels
- Small handful of basil leaves, roughly chopped

Directions:
1. Preheat the oven to 350°F (180°C).
2. Spread the squash and eggplant on two separate baking sheets and brush with 2 tablespoons of the olive oil. Bake for 25 minutes or until tender and golden brown. Let cool to room temperature, then roughly chop the eggplant.
3. Combine the squash, eggplant, sun-dried tomatoes, corn, basil, and the remaining 2 tablespoons of olive oil in a large bowl. Refrigerate for 2 to 3 hours to allow the flavors to develop. Bring to room temperature before serving.

Nutrition Info:
- 288 calories; 5 g protein; 15 g total fat; 2 g saturated fat; 41 g carbohydrates; 8 g fiber; 148 mg sodium

Curried Potato And Parsnip Soup

Servings:4
Cooking Time:x
Ingredients:
- 1 tablespoon canola oil
- 2 parsnips (14 ounces/400 g), peeled and cut into ¾-inch (2 cm) pieces
- 4 potatoes (1¾ pounds/800 g), peeled and cut into ¾-inch (2 cm) pieces
- 6½ cups (1.5 liters) gluten-free, onion-free chicken or vegetable stock*
- 1 teaspoon gluten-free curry powder, or to taste
- 1 cup (250 ml) low-fat milk, lactose-free milk, or suitable plant-based milk
- Salt and freshly ground black pepper
- Chopped flat-leaf parsley, to garnish

Directions:
1. Heat the canola oil in a large heavy-bottomed saucepan over medium heat. Add the parsnips and potatoes and cook, stirring regularly, for 3 to 5 minutes, until lightly golden. Add the stock and bring to a boil. Reduce the heat and simmer for 15 to 20 minutes, stirring occasionally, until the vegetables are tender. Remove from the heat and let cool for about 10 minutes.
2. Puree with an immersion blender (or in batches in a regular blender) until smooth. Add the curry powder and milk and blend again until well combined. Season to taste with salt and pepper. Reheat gently without boiling. Garnish with a sprinkling of parsley and serve.

Nutrition Info:
- 215 calories; 10 g protein; 4 g total fat; 1 g saturated fat; 36 g carbohydrates; 12 g fiber; 766 mg sodium

Open-faced Bacon, Tomato, And Cheese Sandwich

Servings:2
Cooking Time: 6 Minutes
Ingredients:
- 6 bacon slices
- 2 slices gluten-free sandwich bread, toasted
- 1 tablespoon Garlic Oil
- 1 tomato, sliced
- ½ cup grated Cheddar cheese, divided

Directions:
1. In a large nonstick skillet over medium-high heat, cook the bacon for about 6 minutes, until crisp on both sides. Transfer to paper towels to drain.
2. Preheat the broiler to high and adjust a rack to the top position.
3. Brush one side of the toasted bread slices with garlic oil. Place the bread on a baking sheet, oiled-side up, and top with the tomato slices.
4. Top each sandwich with 3 bacon slices and sprinkle each with ¼ cup cheese.
5. Broil for about 3 minutes, until the cheese melts.

Nutrition Info:
- Calories:634; Total Fat: 48g; Saturated Fat: 19g; Carbohydrates: 22g; Fiber: 4g; Sodium: 1,516mg; Protein: 31g

Mussels In Chili, Bacon, And Tomato Broth

Servings:4
Cooking Time:x
Ingredients:
- 4 ounces (113 g) lean bacon slices, cut crosswise into thin strips
- 2 tablespoons olive oil
- 3 cups (750 ml) tomato puree
- ½ teaspoon cayenne pepper (or to taste)
- 6½ cups (1.5 liters) reduced sodium gluten-free, onion-free chicken stock*
- 5½ pounds (2.5 kg) mussels, scrubbed and debearded
- Salt and freshly ground black pepper
- Gluten-free bread, for serving

Directions:
1. In a large heavy-bottomed saucepan over medium heat, cook the bacon until just golden. Spoon out and discard any excess fat, then add the olive oil, tomato puree, cayenne, and 2 cups (500 ml) of the stock. Bring to a boil, reduce the heat to low, and simmer for 30 to 40 minutes to develop the smoky bacon flavor.
2. Add the remaining stock. Increase the heat to medium-high and bring to a boil. Add the mussels and cook, covered, for 5 to 8 minutes, until all the mussels have opened. Shake the pan to redistribute the mussels and cook for an extra minute. Shake again. Discard any unopened mussels. Season to taste with salt and pepper and serve immediately with plenty of gluten-free bread to mop up the delicious broth.

Nutrition Info:
- 612 calories; 59 g protein; 26 g total fat; 7 g saturated fat; 33 g carbohydrates; 4 g fiber; 2082 mg sodium

Smoked Gouda And Tomato Sandwich

Servings:2
Cooking Time: 6 Minutes
Ingredients:
- 2 tablespoons garlic oil
- 4 slices gluten-free sandwich bread
- ⅔ cup grated smoked Gouda cheese, divided
- 1 tomato, cut into 6 slices

Directions:
1. Heat a nonstick skillet over medium-high heat.
2. Brush the outside of each bread slice with the garlic oil.
3. Place 2 pieces of bread, oil-side down, in the skillet. Top each with ⅓ cup cheese and 3 tomato slices. Top with the remaining 2 bread slices, oil side up.
4. Cook for about 3 minutes per side until the cheese melts and the bread browns on each side.

Nutrition Info:
- Calories:536; Total Fat: 37g; Saturated Fat: 18g; Carbohydrates: 41g; Fiber: 9g; Sodium: 761mg; Protein: 15g

Potato Leek Soup

Servings:4
Cooking Time: 13 Minutes
Ingredients:
- 6 cups Low-FODMAP Vegetable Broth
- 5 russet potatoes, peeled and chopped
- 2 leeks, green parts only, thoroughly washed (see Tip) and chopped
- ½ teaspoon sea salt
- ⅛ teaspoon freshly ground black pepper

Directions:
1. In a large pot over medium-high heat, stir together the broth, potatoes, leeks, salt, and pepper. Bring the soup to a boil. Reduce the heat to medium and simmer the soup for about 10 minutes, until the potatoes and leeks are soft.
2. In a blender or food processor, purée the soup, in batches if needed, until smooth. For safe puréeing of hot soup, see the Tip for Carrot and Ginger Soup.

Nutrition Info:
- Calories:234; Total Fat: <1g; Saturated Fat: 0g; Carbohydrates: 55g; Fiber: 7g; Sodium: 304mg; Protein: 5g

Potato And Corn Chowder

Servings:6
Cooking Time:x
Ingredients:
- 8 ounces (225 g) lean bacon slices, diced (optional)
- Nonstick cooking spray
- 3 large potatoes, peeled (if desired) and diced
- 8 cups (2 liters) reduced sodium gluten-free, onion-free chicken or vegetable stock*
- One 14.7-ounce (417 g) can no-salt-added, gluten-free cream-style corn
- 1 teaspoon ground mustard
- 1 teaspoon fresh thyme leaves
- 1 heaping tablespoon roughly chopped flat-leaf parsley
- Salt and freshly ground black pepper

Directions:
1. If using the bacon, add to a large heavy-bottomed saucepan over medium heat and cook, stirring, until crisp. Remove to paper towels to drain. Spray the same saucepan with cooking spray, add the potatoes, and cook, still over medium heat, stirring regularly.

2. Pour in the stock and bring to a boil. Reduce the heat to a simmer and cook for 15 minutes, stirring occasionally, until the potatoes are tender.

3. Puree with an immersion blender (or in batches in a regular blender) until smooth. Stir in the corn, mustard, thyme, parsley, and reserved bacon, and season to taste with salt and pepper. Reheat gently without boiling and serve.

Nutrition Info:

- 283 calories; 18 g protein; 15 g total fat; 6 g saturated fat; 18 g carbohydrates; 3 g fiber; 1148 mg sodium

Creamy Seafood Soup

Servings:6
Cooking Time:x
Ingredients:

- 3 tablespoons (45 g) salted butter
- 2 large carrots, diced
- ½ cup (100 g) long-grain white rice
- 5 cups (1.25 liters) gluten-free, onion-free chicken stock*
- 2 tablespoons plus 2 teaspoons fish sauce, or 4 teaspoons soy sauce plus 2 teaspoons fresh lime juice
- ½ cup (125 ml) tomato puree
- ½ fennel bulb, finely chopped
- ½ cup (125 ml) white wine (optional)
- 1 pound (450 g) raw medium shrimp, peeled and deveined
- 2 large or 5 small squid bodies, cleaned and sliced (5 ounces/150 g)
- 5 ounces (150 g) boneless, skinless firm fish fillets, cut into cubes
- 6 cooked jumbo shrimp
- 1 cup (250 ml) low-fat milk, lactose-free milk, or suitable plant-based milk
- Salt and freshly ground black pepper
- Extra virgin olive oil, to garnish (optional)

Directions:

1. Melt the butter in a large heavy-bottomed saucepan over medium heat. Add the carrots and rice and cook, stirring regularly, for 5 minutes.

2. Add the stock, fish sauce, tomato puree, fennel, and wine (if using) and stir to combine. Bring to a boil, reduce the heat to low, and simmer for 20 minutes, until the rice is tender.

3. Let cool for 10 minutes. Puree with an immersion blender (or in batches in a regular blender) until smooth.

4. Return the pan to the stove over medium heat and bring the soup to a simmer. Add the uncooked shrimp, squid, and fish and simmer for 4 to 5 minutes, until the seafood is just

cooked. Add the jumbo shrimp and milk and stir until heated through and combined. Season to taste with salt and pepper, finish with a drizzle of olive oil (if desired), and serve immediately.

Nutrition Info:

- 296 calories; 32 g protein; 9 g total fat; 4 g saturated fat; 17 g carbohydrates; 2 g fiber; 1300 mg sodium

Vegetable Soup

Servings:4
Cooking Time:x
Ingredients:

- 2 tablespoons garlic-infused olive oil
- 2 celery stalks, tough strings removed, halved lengthwise and cut into ¼-inch (5 mm) slices
- 1 head broccoli, cut into chunks (including stalks)
- 3 rutabagas, peeled and cut into chunks
- 2 large carrots, cut into chunks
- 14 ounces (400 g) kabocha or other suitable winter squash, peeled, seeded, and cut into chunks
- 3 potatoes, cut into chunks
- 4 cups (1 liter) gluten-free, onion-free vegetable stock*
- 1½ cups (375 ml) low-fat milk, lactose-free milk, or suitable plant-based milk
- Salt and freshly ground black pepper

Directions:

1. Heat the oil in a large heavy-bottomed stockpot over medium heat. Add the celery and cook, stirring, until golden brown. Add the broccoli, rutabagas, carrots, squash, and potatoes. Pour in the stock. Bring to a boil, reduce the heat, and simmer, covered, for 1 hour or until the vegetables are tender.

2. Remove from the heat and leave to cool to room temperature. Use an immersion blender to puree the vegetables to a smooth consistency. (Alternatively, carefully transfer the vegetables to a food processor and process until smooth.)

3. Stir in the milk, season to taste with salt and pepper, and reheat gently.

Nutrition Info:

- 231 calories; 10 g protein; 6 g total fat; 1 g saturated fat; 39 g carbohydrates; 12 g fiber; 579 mg sodium

Pesto Ham Sandwich

Servings:2

Cooking Time: 0 Minutes

Ingredients:

- 4 slices gluten-free sandwich bread, toasted
- 4 tablespoons Macadamia Spinach Pesto, divided
- 4 ounces thinly sliced prosciutto, divided
- 4 pieces jarred roasted red pepper

Directions:

1. Spread 2 bread slices with 2 tablespoons pesto each.
2. Top each with half the prosciutto and half the roasted red pepper.
3. Top with the remaining bread slices.

Nutrition Info:

- Calories:238; Total Fat: 12g; Saturated Fat: 2g; Carbohydrates: 25g; Fiber: 5g; Sodium: 790mg; Protein: 9g

Philly Steak Sandwich

Servings:2

Cooking Time: 15 Minutes

Ingredients:

- 2 tablespoons Garlic Oil
- 1 green bell pepper, sliced
- 1 red bell pepper, sliced
- 6 scallions, green parts only, sliced
- 6 ounces thinly sliced deli roast beef, chopped
- 2 slices gluten-free sandwich bread, toasted
- ½ cup grated Monterey Jack cheese

Directions:

1. In a large nonstick skillet over medium-high heat, heat the garlic oil until it shimmers.
2. Add the green and red bell peppers and the scallions. Cook for about 7 minutes, stirring occasionally, until soft.
3. Add the roast beef, and cook for about 3 minutes more, until the beef is warmed through.
4. Preheat the broiler to high and adjust a rack to the top position.
5. Place the toasted bread on a baking sheet and top each with half the bell peppers and beef.
6. Sprinkle each with ¼ cup grated cheese.
7. Broil for about 3 minutes, until the cheese melts.

Nutrition Info:

- Calories:501; Total Fat: 31g; Saturated Fat: 9g; Carbohydrates: 30g; Fiber: 7g; Sodium: 641mg; Protein: 28g

Roasted Sweet Potato Salad With Spiced Lamb And Spinach

Servings:4

Cooking Time:x

Ingredients:

- 4 small sweet potatoes, peeled (if desired) and cut into ¾-inch (2 cm) cubes (about 4½ cups/600 g)
- 1 red bell pepper, seeded and cut into quarters
- Olive oil
- 1 heaping tablespoon ground cumin
- 2 teaspoons ground coriander
- ½ teaspoon ground cardamom
- 2 teaspoons ground turmeric
- ½ teaspoon ground sumac, or ½ teaspoon paprika plus ½ teaspoon lemon zest
- 1 pound (450 g) lean lamb steak, cut into thin strips
- 8 ounces (225 g) baby spinach leaves (8 cups), rinsed and dried

Directions:

1. Preheat the oven to 350°F (180°C).
2. Place the sweet potato and bell pepper on a large baking sheet and brush with olive oil. Roast for 30 minutes or until tender and browned. Set aside to cool. When cool enough to handle, remove the skin from the bell pepper.
3. Heat a little olive oil in a medium frying pan over medium-low heat. Add the cumin, coriander, cardamom, turmeric, and sumac and heat for 1 minute or until fragrant. Add the lamb and stir to coat with the spice mix. Cook for 3 to 5 minutes, until just browned. Remove from the heat.
4. Combine the spinach, sweet potato, and bell pepper in a large bowl. Top with the lamb and any pan juices and finish with a drizzle of olive oil.

Nutrition Info:

- 392 calories; 27 g protein; 14 g total fat; 3 g saturated fat; 40 g carbohydrates; 8 g fiber; 171 mg sodium

Vietnamese Beef Noodle Salad

Servings:4

Cooking Time:x

Ingredients:

- 2 teaspoons garlic-infused olive oil
- 2 teaspoons olive oil
- 1 heaping tablespoon Chinese five-spice powder
- ¼ cup (60 ml) fish sauce, or 3 tablespoons soy sauce and 1 tablespoon fresh lime juice
- ¼ cup (60 ml) seasoned rice vinegar
- 2 teaspoons grated ginger
- 1 heaping tablespoon light brown sugar
- 1 pound (450 g) beef sirloin or top round steak, cut into thin strips
- 8 ounces (225 g) gluten-free rice vermicelli
- 2 tablespoons sesame oil
- 1 cup (50 g) snow pea shoots or bean sprouts

- ¼ cup (15 g) roughly chopped Vietnamese mint, or a combination of mint and cilantro

Directions:

1. To make the marinade, combine the garlic-infused oil, olive oil, five-spice powder, fish sauce, vinegar, ginger, and brown sugar in a medium glass or ceramic bowl. Add the beef strips and toss so the meat is well coated in the marinade. Cover and refrigerate for 3 hours.
2. Fill a large bowl with very hot water. Add the vermicelli and soak for 4 to 5 minutes, until softened. Drain and rinse under cold water, then drain again.
3. Heat the sesame oil in a nonstick frying pan or wok over medium heat. Add the beef strips and any remaining marinade and toss until just cooked through, 2 to 4 minutes. Don't overcook the meat—you want it to be nice and tender.
4. Combine the beef and any juices, vermicelli, snow pea shoots, and mint in a bowl and serve immediately.

Nutrition Info:

- 598 calories; 28 g protein; 28 g total fat; 8 g saturated fat; 50 g carbohydrates; 3 g fiber; 1457 mg sodium

Roasted Squash And Chestnut Soup

Servings:4
Cooking Time:x
Ingredients:

- 4½ pounds (2 kg) peeled, seeded, and cubed kabocha or other suitable winter squash
- 2 tablespoons olive oil
- 2 cups (500 g) unsweetened chestnut puree
- 8 cups (2 liters) gluten-free, onion-free chicken or vegetable stock*
- 2 teaspoons ground ginger
- 1 cup (250 ml) low-fat milk, lactose-free milk, or suitable plant-based milk, warmed, plus more for serving (optional)
- Salt and freshly ground black pepper

Directions:

1. Preheat the oven to 350°F (180°C).
2. Spread the squash on a baking sheet and drizzle with the olive oil. Bake, turning occasionally, for 30 to 40 minutes, until golden and cooked through.
3. Transfer the squash to a large saucepan or stockpot. Add the chestnut puree, stock, and ginger and bring to a boil. Reduce the heat and simmer over medium-low heat for 15 to 20 minutes, stirring occasionally, until the squash is tender. Let cool for about 10 minutes.
4. Add the warmed milk to the soup and puree with an immersion blender (or in batches in a regular blender) until smooth. Season to taste with salt and pepper. Finish with a swirl of extra milk (if desired) and serve.

Nutrition Info:

- 466 calories; 9 g protein; 10 g total fat; 2 g saturated fat; 92 g carbohydrates; 8 g fiber; 928 mg sodium

Spinach And Bell Pepper Salad With Fried Tofu Puffs

Servings:4
Cooking Time:x
Ingredients:

- ¼ cup (60 ml) gluten-free soy sauce
- ¼ cup (60 ml) fresh lemon juice
- 1 tablespoon plus 1 teaspoon seasoned rice vinegar
- ¼ cup (55 g) packed light brown sugar
- ¼ cup (60 ml) sesame oil
- 10½ ounces (300 g) baby spinach leaves (10 cups), rinsed and dried
- 1½ cups (75 g) snow pea shoots or bean sprouts
- 1 green bell pepper, seeded and sliced
- 14 ounces (400 g) fried tofu puffs, cut into cubes
- ⅓ cup (50 g) pine nuts
- Salt and freshly ground black pepper

Directions:

1. Combine the soy sauce, lemon juice, vinegar, brown sugar, and sesame oil in a small bowl and whisk well.
2. Toss the spinach, snow pea shoots, bell pepper, tofu, and pine nuts in a large bowl until well combined. Drizzle with the dressing and toss briefly. Season to taste with salt and pepper and serve.

Nutrition Info:

- 571 calories; 24 g protein; 40 g total fat; 6 g saturated fat; 40 g carbohydrates; 9 g fiber; 1054 mg sodium

Spicy Clear Soup

Servings:4
Cooking Time:x
Ingredients:

- 1 tablespoon sesame oil
- 2 teaspoons garlic-infused olive oil
- 2 teaspoons rice bran oil or sunflower oil
- 2 heaping tablespoons finely chopped lemongrass (white portion only)
- ½ to 1 red chile pepper, seeded and finely chopped
- 6 pieces dried galangal root (optional)
- 6½ cups (1.5 liters) gluten-free, onion-free chicken or vegetable stock*
- 2 tablespoons plus 2 teaspoons fish sauce, or 4 teaspoons soy sauce and 2 teaspoons fresh lime juice
- 1 tablespoon plus 1 teaspoon fresh lime juice
- 3 bunches baby bok choy, quartered, rinsed, and drained

- 2 heaping tablespoons chopped cilantro
- One 8-ounce (225 g) can bamboo shoots, drained
- One 14- to 15-ounce (400 g) can baby corn, drained, or 7½ ounces (215 g) fresh baby corn, cut on the diagonal (about 1½ cups/360 ml)
- 3½ ounces (100 g) gluten-free rice vermicelli (about 2 cups)

Directions:

1. Heat the sesame oil, garlic-infused oil, and rice bran oil in a large saucepan over medium heat. Add the lemongrass and chile and cook for 2 minutes or until fragrant.
2. Add the galangal (if using), stock, fish sauce, and lime juice and bring to a boil. Add the bok choy, cilantro, bamboo shoots, baby corn, and vermicelli. Reduce the heat and simmer for 3 minutes or until the vegetables and noodles are tender. (Remove the galangal.) Serve immediately.

Nutrition Info:

- 227 calories; 7 g protein; 8 g total fat; 1 g saturated fat; 28 g carbohydrates; 4 g fiber; 1671 mg sodium

Chicken Noodle Soup

Servings:4
Cooking Time: 15 Minutes

Ingredients:

- 2 tablespoons Garlic Oil
- 6 scallions, green parts only, chopped
- 3 carrots, chopped
- 1 red bell pepper, chopped
- 6 cups Low-FODMAP Poultry Broth
- ½ teaspoon sea salt
- ⅛ teaspoon freshly ground black pepper
- 4 ounces gluten-free spaghetti, cooked according to instructions on package
- 4 cups chopped cooked chicken

Directions:

1. In a large pot over medium-high heat, heat the garlic oil until it shimmers.
2. Add the scallions, carrots, and bell pepper. Cook for 3 minutes, stirring occasionally.
3. Stir in the broth, salt, and pepper. Bring to a boil.
4. Add the spaghetti. Cook for 8 to 10 minutes, stirring occasionally, until the pasta is cooked. Drain.
5. Stir in the chicken. Cook for 2 minutes more.

Nutrition Info:

- Calories:441; Total Fat: 35g; Saturated Fat: 3g; Carbohydrates: 24g; Fiber: 2g; Sodium: 560mg; Protein: 52g

Turkey-ginger Soup

Servings:4
Cooking Time: 17 Minutes

Ingredients:

- 2 tablespoons Garlic Oil
- 1 pound ground turkey
- 6 scallions, green parts only, chopped
- 2 carrots, chopped
- 2 tablespoons peeled, minced fresh ginger
- 7 cups Low-FODMAP Poultry Broth
- ½ teaspoon sea salt
- ⅛ teaspoon freshly ground black pepper
- 2 cups cooked brown rice

Directions:

1. In a large pot over medium-high heat, heat the garlic oil until it shimmers.
2. Add the turkey. Cook for about 5 minutes, crumbling it with the back of a spoon, until browned.
3. Add the scallions, carrots, and ginger. Cook for 3 minutes, stirring.
4. Stir in the broth, salt, and pepper. Bring to a simmer. Cook for about 7 minutes, until the carrots soften.
5. Stir in the brown rice and cook for 2 minutes more to heat through.

Nutrition Info:

- Calories:482; Total Fat: 16g; Saturated Fat: 3g; Carbohydrates: 44g; Fiber: 3g; Sodium: 610mg; Protein: 44g

Greens And Lemon Soup

Servings:4
Cooking Time: 15 Minutes

Ingredients:

- 2 tablespoons Garlic Oil
- 5 scallions, green parts only, chopped
- 5 cups stemmed, chopped Swiss chard
- 6 cups Low-FODMAP Vegetable Broth
- ½ teaspoon sea salt
- ¼ teaspoon freshly ground black pepper
- Juice of 2 lemons

Directions:

1. In a large pot over medium-high heat, heat the garlic oil until it shimmers.
2. Add the scallions and chard. Cook for 3 minutes, stirring.
3. Stir in the broth, salt, and pepper. Simmer for 10 minutes, stirring occasionally.
4. Squeeze in the lemon juice.

Nutrition Info:

- Calories:106; Total Fat: 7g; Saturated Fat: 1g; Carbohydrates: 11g; Fiber: 1g; Sodium: 387mg; Protein: 2g

Chicken Noodle Soup With Bok Choy

Servings:4
Cooking Time:x
Ingredients:
- 8 cups (2 liters) gluten-free, onion-free chicken or vegetable stock*
- 1 heaping tablespoon grated ginger
- 4 kaffir lime leaves
- 1 pound (450 g) boneless, skinless chicken breasts, very thinly sliced
- 8 ounces (225 g) gluten-free rice vermicelli, broken into 2-inch (5 cm) pieces
- 3 bunches baby bok choy, leaves separated, rinsed and drained
- ½ cup (40 g) bean sprouts
- 2 teaspoons gluten-free soy sauce

Directions:
1. Place the stock, ginger, and lime leaves in a large heavy-bottomed saucepan and bring to a boil. Add the chicken, reduce the heat, and simmer for 5 minutes.
2. Add the rice noodles, bok choy, and bean sprouts and simmer for another 5 minutes or until the noodles are tender. Remove the lime leaves, stir in the soy sauce, and serve immediately.

Nutrition Info:
- 362 calories; 31 g protein; 2 g total fat; 0 g saturated fat; 46 g carbohydrates; 2 g fiber; 1023 mg sodium

Peppered Beef And Citrus Salad

Servings:4
Cooking Time:x
Ingredients:
- 2 teaspoons olive oil
- 1 pound (450 g) beef sirloin or top round steak
- 2 teaspoons garlic-infused olive oil
- 1 heaping tablespoon freshly ground black pepper, plus more for serving
- ¼ cup (60 ml) fresh lemon juice
- 1 heaping tablespoon light brown sugar
- Salt
- 1 orange, peeled and cut into segments
- 1 head butter lettuce (Boston or Bibb), leaves separated
- One 8-ounce (225 g) can water chestnuts, drained and roughly chopped

Directions:

1. Heat the olive oil in a frying pan over medium heat. Add the beef and cook for 4 minutes on each side for medium-rare, or to your preferred doneness. Let the beef rest for 10 minutes, then slice it thinly.
2. Make the marinade by whisking together the garlic-infused oil, pepper, lemon juice, brown sugar, and salt to taste in a medium bowl. Add the beef and toss until well coated in the marinade. Cover and refrigerate for 3 hours.
3. Combine the orange segments, lettuce, water chestnuts, beef, and any remaining marinade in a large bowl. Finish with several grinds of black pepper and serve immediately.

Nutrition Info:
- 369 calories; 23 g protein; 23 g total fat; 8 g saturated fat; 18 g carbohydrates; 4 g fiber; 361 mg sodium

Shrimp Chowder

Servings:4
Cooking Time: 20 Minutes
Ingredients:
- 2 tablespoons Garlic Oil
- 6 scallions, green parts only, chopped
- 1 fennel bulb, chopped
- 2 carrots, chopped
- 7 cups Low-FODMAP Poultry Broth
- 8 baby red potatoes, quartered
- ½ teaspoon sea salt
- ¼ teaspoon freshly ground black pepper
- 12 ounces medium shrimp, peeled, deveined, and tails removed
- 1 cup unsweetened almond milk
- 2 tablespoons cornstarch
- 2 tablespoons chopped fennel fronds

Directions:
1. In a large pot over medium-high, heat the garlic oil until it shimmers.
2. Add the scallions, fennel bulb, and carrots. Cook for about 3 minutes, stirring occasionally, until soft.
3. Stir in the broth, potatoes, salt, and pepper. Simmer for 10 minutes, until the potatoes are tender.
4. Add the shrimp. Cook for 5 minutes more.
5. In a small bowl, whisk the almond milk and cornstarch into a slurry. Stir this mixture into the soup in a thin stream. Simmer the soup for about 2 minutes more until it thickens.
6. Stir in the fennel fronds.

Nutrition Info:
- Calories:325; Total Fat: 10g; Saturated Fat: 2g; Carbohydrates: 33g; Fiber: 5g; Sodium: 671mg; Protein: 27g

Egg Salad Sandwich

Servings:2

Cooking Time: 0 Minutes

Ingredients:

- 6 hardboiled eggs, peeled and chopped
- 3 scallions, green parts only, finely chopped
- 1 teaspoon Dijon mustard
- ¼ cup Low-FODMAP Mayonnaise
- ¼ teaspoon sea salt
- 4 slices gluten-free sandwich bread

Directions:

1. In a small bowl, mix the eggs, scallions, mustard, mayonnaise, and salt.

2. Divide the egg salad between 2 bread slices and spread it out. Top with the remaining bread slices to make 2 sandwiches.

Nutrition Info:

- Calories:532; Total Fat: 31g; Saturated Fat: 6g; Carbohydrates: 47g; Fiber: 9g; Sodium: 654mg; Protein: 19g

Hearty Lamb Shank And Vegetable Soup

Servings:4

Cooking Time:x

Ingredients:

- 3 tablespoons olive oil
- 1 tablespoon garlic-infused olive oil
- 2 lamb shanks (about 2 pounds/900 g)
- 1½ pounds (700 g) kabocha or other suitable winter squash, peeled, seeded, and cut into ¾-inch (2 cm) pieces
- 3 large carrots, cut into ⅓-inch (1 cm) pieces
- 3 celery stalks, cut into ⅓-inch (1 cm) slices
- 6½ cups (1.5 liters) gluten-free, onion-free beef stock*
- ⅔ cup (130 g) long-grain white rice
- Salt and freshly ground black pepper

Directions:

1. Heat the olive oil and garlic-infused oil in a large heavy-bottomed saucepan over medium heat. Add the lamb shanks and cook on all sides until lightly browned, 5 to 10 minutes total, searing for 2 to 3 minutes on each side before turning. Remove the shanks and set aside on a plate. Add the squash, carrots, and celery to the pan and cook in the remaining oil and meat juices for 2 to 3 minutes, until lightly golden.

2. Increase the heat to medium-high and return the shanks to the pan. Add the stock and rice and bring to a boil, then reduce the heat and simmer, stirring occasionally, for 50 to 60 minutes, until the meat is very tender.

3. Remove the lamb shanks, then remove the meat from the bones and shred or cut into large pieces. Discard the bones and fat. Return the lamb to the pan and stir until well combined, breaking up the squash pieces. Season well with salt and pepper and serve.

Nutrition Info:

- 623 calories; 40 g protein; 30 g total fat; 8 g saturated fat; 49 g carbohydrates; 5 g fiber; 804 mg sodium

Carrot And Ginger Soup

Servings:4

Cooking Time: 18 Minutes

Ingredients:

- 2 tablespoons extra-virgin olive oil
- 2 tablespoons peeled, minced fresh ginger
- 7 cups Low-FODMAP Vegetable Broth
- 10 carrots, chopped
- ½ teaspoon sea salt
- 2 tablespoons fresh cilantro leaves

Directions:

1. In a large pot over medium-high heat, heat the olive oil until it shimmers.

2. Add the ginger. Cook for about 1 minute, stirring until fragrant.

3. Stir in the broth, carrots, and salt. Bring to a boil. Reduce the heat to medium-low. Simmer for about 15 minutes, until the carrots are soft.

4. Carefully transfer the soup to a blender or food processor (or use an immersion blender). Blend until smooth. See the Tip for safe handling of hot soup when puréeing.

5. Garnish with the cilantro leaves.

Nutrition Info:

- Calories:136; Total Fat: 7g; Saturated Fat: 1g; Carbohydrates: 18g; Fiber: 4g; Sodium: 347mg; Protein: 2g

Blue Cheese And Arugula Salad With Red Wine Dressing

Servings:4

Cooking Time:x

Ingredients:

- 4 handfuls of arugula
- 1 cup (50 g) snow pea shoots or bean sprouts
- 7 ounces (200 g) blue cheese, cut into small chunks
- ½ English cucumber, sliced
- 1 avocado, pitted, peeled, and sliced (optional)
- ½ green bell pepper, seeded and thinly sliced
- ¼ cup (60 ml) olive oil
- 2 tablespoons plus 2 teaspoons fresh lemon juice
- 1 tablespoon red wine vinegar
- 1 teaspoon gluten-free whole grain mustard
- 1 teaspoon sugar

- 2 heaping tablespoons chopped tarragon or flat-leaf parsley

Directions:

1. Combine the arugula, snow pea shoots, blue cheese, cucumber, avocado (if using), and bell pepper in a large bowl.

2. To make the dressing, combine all the ingredients in a small screw-top jar and shake until well mixed.

3. Just before serving, pour the dressing over the salad and gently toss to combine.

Nutrition Info:

- 403 calories; 13 g protein; 36 g total fat; 3 g saturated fat; 12 g carbohydrates; 4 g fiber; 728 mg sodium

Vermicelli Salad With Chicken, Cilantro, And Mint

Servings:4
Cooking Time:x

Ingredients:

- 10½ ounces (300 g) gluten-free rice vermicelli
- 2 tablespoons fresh lime juice
- 1 tablespoon fish sauce, or 2 teaspoons soy sauce and 1 extra teaspoon fresh lime juice
- 2 tablespoons light brown sugar
- ½ red chile pepper, seeded and finely chopped
- 1 tablespoon sesame oil
- 4-⅓ cups (350 g) shredded cooked chicken breasts
- Small handful of cilantro leaves, roughly chopped
- Small handful of mint leaves, roughly chopped
- Salt and freshly ground black pepper

Directions:

1. Fill a large bowl with very hot water. Add the vermicelli and soak for 4 to 5 minutes, until softened. Drain and rinse under cold water, then drain again.

2. To make the dressing, combine all the ingredients in a small screw-top jar and shake until well mixed.

3. Combine the noodles, chicken, cilantro, and mint in a large bowl. Add the dressing, season to taste with salt and pepper, and toss well to combine. Refrigerate for 2 to 3 hours before serving to allow the flavors to meld.

Nutrition Info:

- 395 calories; 35 g protein; 6 g total fat; 1 g saturated fat; 42 g carbohydrates; 2 g fiber; 406 mg sodium

Smoked Chicken And Walnut Salad

Servings:4
Cooking Time:x

Ingredients:

- ½ cup (150 g) gluten-free mayonnaise

- ½ teaspoon gluten-free soy sauce
- 3 tablespoons fresh lemon juice
- 2 heads baby romaine lettuce, leaves separated
- ½ cup (20 g) alfalfa sprouts
- 4 large hard-boiled eggs, halved
- 1 avocado, pitted, peeled, and sliced (optional)
- 14 ounces (400 g) smoked chicken or plain roast chicken, thinly sliced
- ¼ cup (25 g) toasted walnuts
- Salt and freshly ground black pepper

Directions:

1. To make the dressing, whisk together the mayonnaise, soy sauce, and lemon juice in a small bowl.

2. Combine the lettuce, sprouts, eggs, and avocado (if using) in a large salad bowl. Drizzle the dressing over the top and toss gently to coat. Just before serving, add the chicken and walnuts, season to taste, and serve.

Nutrition Info:

- 442 calories; 22 g protein; 36 g total fat; 5 g saturated fat; 8 g carbohydrates; 4 g fiber; 1009 mg sodium

Vegetable Beef Soup

Servings:4
Cooking Time: 15 Minutes

Ingredients:

- 1 pound ground beef
- 7 cups Low-FODMAP Poultry Broth
- 6 scallions, green parts only, chopped
- 2 carrots, chopped
- 1 zucchini, chopped
- 1 red bell pepper, chopped
- 1 teaspoon dried thyme
- ½ teaspoon sea salt
- ⅛ teaspoon freshly ground black pepper
- 1 cup shredded cabbage

Directions:

1. In a large pot over medium-high heat, cook the ground beef for about 5 minutes, breaking it up with the back of a spoon, until browned.

2. Add the broth, scallions, carrots, zucchini, bell pepper, thyme, salt, and pepper. Bring the soup to a simmer and reduce the heat to medium. Cook for about 7 minutes, stirring occasionally, until the veggies are crisp-tender.

3. Stir in the cabbage. Cook for 3 minutes more.

Nutrition Info:

- Calories:279; Total Fat: 7g; Saturated Fat: 3g; Carbohydrates: 11g; Fiber: 3g; Sodium: 465mg; Protein: 40g

Turkey-tapenade Sandwich

Servings:2

Cooking Time: 0 Minutes

Ingredients:

- 2 teaspoons Dijon mustard, divided
- 4 slices gluten-free sandwich bread, toasted
- 4 pieces jarred roasted red pepper
- 4 tablespoons Olive Tapenade, divided
- 6 ounces sliced deli turkey
- 2 slices Havarti cheese

Directions:

1. Spread 1 teaspoon mustard on each of 2 bread slices.

2. Top each with 2 pieces roasted red pepper, 2 tablespoons tapenade, 3 ounces turkey, 1 slice cheese, and the second bread slice.

Nutrition Info:

- Calories:487; Total Fat: 22g; Saturated Fat: 6g; Carbohydrates: 55g; Fiber: 10g; Sodium: 2,043mg; Protein: 22g

Lentil And Potato Soup

Servings:4

Cooking Time: 13 Minutes

Ingredients:

- 6 cups Low-FODMAP Vegetable Broth
- 4 Yukon Gold potatoes, chopped
- 2 cups canned lentils, drained
- 1 carrot, chopped
- 1 teaspoon dried thyme
- ½ teaspoon sea salt
- ⅛ teaspoon freshly ground black pepper

Directions:

1. In a large pot over medium-high heat, combine the broth, potatoes, lentils, carrot, thyme, salt, and pepper. Bring to a boil.

2. Reduce the heat to medium and simmer for about 10 minutes, until the potatoes are soft.

Nutrition Info:

- Calories:497; Total Fat: 1g; Saturated Fat: 0g; Carbohydrates: 97g; Fiber: 32g; Sodium: 313mg; Protein: 5g

Chapter 5 Vegetarian And Vegan Recipes

Smoky Corn Chowder With Red Peppers

Servings:4

Cooking Time: 45 Minutes

Ingredients:

- 1 tablespoon olive oil
- 1 tablespoon Garlic Oil (here)
- 1 (10-inch) stalk celery, diced
- 2 carrots, diced
- 1 leek (green part only), halved lengthwise and thinly sliced
- 2 red bell peppers, seeded and diced
- 4 Yukon Gold potatoes, diced (about 1 pound)
- 2 cups canned corn kernels, divided
- 4 cups homemade (onion- and garlic-free) vegetable broth
- 1 teaspoon ground cumin
- ½ teaspoon smoked paprika
- ⅛ teaspoon cayenne
- 1 teaspoon salt
- 1 cup rice milk
- 3 scallions, green parts only, thinly sliced

Directions:

1. Heat the olive oil and Garlic Oil in a stockpot over medium heat. Add the celery and carrots and cook, stirring occasionally, for about 5 minutes, until the vegetables begin to soften. Add the leek, red bell peppers, potatoes, 1 cup of the corn, broth, cumin, smoked paprika, cayenne, and salt, and bring to a boil. Reduce the heat to low and simmer for about 30 minutes, until the potatoes are very tender.

2. Using an immersion blender or in batches in a countertop blender, purée the soup.

3. Stir in the remaining cup of corn and the rice milk, and cook over low heat for about 10 minutes more, until the soup is heated through and the corn kernels are tender. Serve immediately, garnished with sliced scallions.

Nutrition Info:

- Calories: 355; Protein: 13g; Total Fat: 7g; Saturated Fat: 1g; Carbohydrates: 69g; Fiber: 8g; Sodium: 1416mg;

Coconut-curry Tofu With Vegetables

Servings:4
Cooking Time: 25 Minutes
Ingredients:
- FOR THE SAUCE
- 1 cup canned coconut milk
- 2 tablespoons chopped fresh cilantro
- 1 tablespoon gluten-free, onion- and garlic-free curry powder
- 1 teaspoon brown sugar
- 1 teaspoon salt
- FOR THE TOFU AND VEGETABLES
- 1 tablespoon grapeseed oil
- 14 ounces extra-firm tofu, drained and cut into cubes
- 1 red bell pepper, sliced
- 1 zucchini, halved lengthwise and sliced
- 2 cups broccoli florets
- 1 bunch baby bok choy, cut into 2-inch pieces

Directions:
1. To make the sauce, in a small bowl, stir together the coconut milk, cilantro, curry powder, brown sugar, and salt.
2. To prepare the tofu and vegetables, heat the oil in a large skillet over high heat. Arrange the tofu in the pan in a single layer and cook, without stirring, for about 5 minutes, until it begins to brown on the bottom. Scrape the tofu from the pan with a spatula and continue to cook, stirring occasionally, until it is golden brown all over, for about 7 more minutes.
3. Add the bell pepper, zucchini, broccoli, and bok choy to the pan, along with the sauce mixture, and continue to cook, stirring, for about 8 to 10 minutes, until the vegetables are tender. Serve immediately.

Nutrition Info:
- Calories: 321; Protein: 16g; Total Fat: 25g; Saturated Fat: 14g; Carbohydrates: 17g; Fiber: 6g; Sodium: 756mg;

Zucchini Pasta Alla Puttanesca

Servings:4
Cooking Time: 15 Minutes
Ingredients:
- 2 tablespoons olive oil
- 1½ cups diced tomatoes
- 1 tablespoon Garlic Oil (here)
- 2 tablespoons chopped Kalamata olives
- 1 tablespoon capers, drained
- 1 teaspoon salt
- ½ teaspoon freshly ground black pepper
- ½ teaspoon red pepper flakes
- ¼ cup chopped fresh basil
- 3 large zucchini, cut into ribbons with a spiral slicer
- ½ cup freshly grated Parmesan cheese

Directions:
1. Heat the olive oil in a large skillet over medium-high heat. Add the tomatoes and Garlic Oil, and cook for about 10 minutes, until the tomatoes begin to break down and become saucy. Add the olives, capers, salt, pepper, and red pepper flakes, and cook for 5 minutes more. Stir in the basil.
2. Remove the pan from the heat and add the zucchini. Toss until the zucchini noodles soften and are well coated with the sauce. Serve immediately, garnished with Parmesan cheese.

Nutrition Info:
- Calories: 226; Protein: 14g; Total Fat: 15g; Saturated Fat: 5g; Carbohydrates: 16g; Fiber: 5g; Sodium: 974mg;

Roasted-veggie Gyros With Tzatziki Sauce

Servings:4
Cooking Time: 35 Minutes
Ingredients:
- FOR THE ROASTED VEGETABLES
- 1 large zucchini, chopped into half moons
- 1 large yellow squash, chopped into half moons
- 1 large eggplant, cut into 1-inch cubes
- 1 cup cherry tomatoes, halved
- ¼ cup olive oil
- 1 tablespoon chopped fresh oregano
- 1½ teaspoons salt
- ¾ teaspoon freshly ground black pepper
- FOR THE SAUCE
- 1 medium cucumber, peeled, seeded, coarsely grated and squeezed in a clean dish towel to remove excess moisture
- 8 ounces plain lactose-free yogurt
- 1 tablespoon Garlic Oil (here)
- 1 tablespoon white-wine vinegar
- 1 tablespoon chopped fresh dill
- 1 tablespoon lemon juice
- TO SERVE
- 4 gluten-free pita pockets or gluten-free naan
- 4 large lettuce leaves

Directions:
1. Preheat the oven to 425°F.
2. On a large, rimmed baking sheet, toss the zucchini, yellow squash, eggplant, and cherry tomatoes together with the olive oil, oregano, salt, and pepper. Spread the vegetables out in an even layer and roast in the preheated oven for about 35 minutes, until they are soft and browned.

3. While the vegetables are roasting, make the sauce. In a medium bowl, combine the cucumber, yogurt, Garlic Oil, vinegar, dill, and lemon juice, and stir to combine. Refrigerate, covered, until ready to serve.

4. Wrap the pitas in foil and heat in the oven (you can place them in the oven along with the vegetables while they're roasting) for about 10 minutes.

5. To serve, fill each pita with the roasted vegetables, top with a dollop of the tzatziki sauce, and garnish each with a lettuce leaf. Serve immediately.

Nutrition Info:

- Calories: 342; Protein: 14g; Total Fat: 15g; Saturated Fat: 2g; Carbohydrates: 46g; Fiber: 12g; Sodium: 1023mg;

Vegetable Stir-fry

Servings:4
Cooking Time: 10 Minutes

Ingredients:

- 2 tablespoons Garlic Oil
- 2⅔ cups chopped firm tofu
- 8 scallions, green parts only, chopped
- 2 cups broccoli florets
- ½ cup Stir-Fry Sauce

Directions:

1. In a large skillet over medium-high heat, heat the garlic oil until it shimmers.

2. Add the tofu, scallions, and broccoli. Cook for about 7 minutes, stirring frequently, until the broccoli is crisp-tender.

3. Stir in the stir-fry sauce. Cook for about 3 minutes, stirring, until it thickens.

Nutrition Info:

- Calories:231; Total Fat: 14g; Saturated Fat: 3g; Carbohydrates: 14g; Fiber: 4g; Sodium: 426mg; Protein: 16g

Chipotle Tofu And Sweet Potato Tacos With Avocado Salsa

Servings:4
Cooking Time: 20 Minutes

Ingredients:

- FOR THE FILLING
- 2 tablespoons olive oil
- 2 sweet potatoes, peeled and cut into ½-inch cubes
- 1 pound firm tofu, diced
- ½ to 1 teaspoon ground chipotle chiles
- 2 tablespoons sugar
- Juice of 1 lime
- FOR THE AVOCADO SALSA
- 2 tomatoes
- ½ avocado, diced

- ¼ serrano chile, diced
- Juice of ½ lime
- ¼ teaspoon salt
- 2 tablespoons chopped fresh cilantro
- TO SERVE
- 8 soft corn tortillas

Directions:

1. Heat the olive oil in a large skillet over medium heat. Add the sweet potatoes and cook for about 5 minutes, until the potatoes begin to soften. Add the tofu, chipotle, sugar, and lime juice. Reduce the heat to low and cook, stirring occasionally, until the sweet potatoes are tender, about 15 minutes.

2. Meanwhile, wrap the tortillas in aluminum foil and heat them in a 350°F oven for 10 minutes.

3. To make the avocado salsa, combine the tomatoes, avocado, chile, lime juice, and salt in a medium bowl. Stir in the cilantro.

4. To serve, fill the tortillas with the filliing, dividing equally, and spoon a dollop of avocado salsa on top of each. Serve immediately.

Nutrition Info:

- Calories: 421; Protein: 15g; Total Fat: 18g; Saturated Fat: 3g; Carbohydrates: 55g; Fiber: 10g; Sodium: 229mg;

Pineapple Fried Rice

Servings:4
Cooking Time: 10 Minutes

Ingredients:

- 2 tablespoons Garlic Oil
- 6 scallions, green parts only, finely chopped
- ½ cup canned water chestnuts, drained
- 1 tablespoon peeled and grated fresh ginger
- 3 cups cooked brown rice
- 2 cups canned pineapple (in juice), drained, ¼ cup juice reserved
- 2 tablespoons gluten-free soy sauce
- ¼ cup chopped fresh cilantro leaves

Directions:

1. In a large skillet over medium-high heat, heat the garlic oil until it shimmers.

2. Add the scallions, water chestnuts, and ginger. Cook for 5 minutes, stirring.

3. Add the brown rice, pineapple, reserved pineapple juice, and soy sauce. Cook for 5 minutes, stirring, until the rice is warmed through.

4. Stir in the cilantro.

Nutrition Info:

- Calories:413; Total Fat: 9g; Saturated Fat: 1g; Carbohydrates: 77g; Fiber: 4g; Sodium: 396mg; Protein: 7g

Watercress Zucchini Soup

Servings:4
Cooking Time: 15 Minutes
Ingredients:
- 2 tablespoons extra-virgin olive oil
- 1 leek, white part removed and the greens finely chopped
- 3 cups homemade (onion- and garlic-free) vegetable broth
- 1 pound zucchini, chopped
- 8 ounces chopped watercress
- 2 tablespoons dried tarragon
- 1 teaspoon salt
- ¼ teaspoon freshly ground black pepper
- 2 tablespoons heavy cream

Directions:
1. In a large pot, heat the olive oil over medium-high heat until it shimmers.
2. Add the leek greens and cook, stirring occasionally, until the vegetables are soft, about seven minutes.
3. Add the vegetable broth and zucchini and simmer, stirring occasionally, for eight minutes.
4. Add the watercress, tarragon, salt, and pepper. Cook, stirring occasionally, an additional five minutes.
5. Carefully transfer the soup mixture to a blender or food processor. You may need to work in batches.
6. Fold a towel and place it over the top of the blender with your hand on top of it. Purée the soup for 30 seconds, and then remove the lid to vent steam. Close the blender and purée for another 30 seconds, until the mixture is smooth.
7. Transfer the mixture back to the cooking pot and stir in the heavy cream. Serve immediately.

Nutrition Info:
- Calories: 161; Total Fat: 11g; Saturated Fat: 3g; Cholesterol: 10mg; Carbohydrates: 9g; Fiber: 2g; Protein: 7g;

Tempeh Enchiladas With Red Chili Sauce

Servings:4
Cooking Time: 60 Minutes
Ingredients:
- FOR THE SAUCE
- 2 tablespoons grapeseed oil
- 2 tablespoons gluten-free all-purpose flour
- 1 tablespoon Garlic Oil (here)
- ¼ cup gluten-free, onion- and garlic-free chili powder
- ½ teaspoon salt
- ¼ teaspoon ground cumin
- 1 tablespoon minced fresh oregano
- 2 cups homemade (onion- and garlic-free) vegetable broth
- FOR THE ENCHILADAS
- 12 ounces crumbled tempeh
- 2 cups canned corn kernels
- 1 (4-ounce) can diced green chiles
- 10 small corn tortillas
- 1½ cups shredded sharp white cheddar cheese (optional)

Directions:
1. To make the sauce, heat the grapeseed oil in a small saucepan over medium-high heat. Whisk in the flour and cook, stirring, for 1 minute. Stir in the Garlic Oil, chili powder, salt, cumin, and oregano. While stirring constantly, gradually add the broth. Bring to a boil, then reduce the heat to low and simmer, stirring occasionally, for 10 to 15 minutes, until the sauce has thickened. Transfer the sauce to a wide, shallow bowl.
2. In a bowl, stir together the crumbled tempeh, corn, and green chiles.
3. To make the enchiladas, spoon about ⅓ cup of the sauce into a 9-by-13-inch baking dish and spread it out over the bottom of the dish. Wrap the tortillas in a clean dish towel and heat them in the microwave on high for about 30 seconds. Dip each tortilla in the sauce to coat it lightly, then spoon about ¼ cup of the tempeh mixture in a line down the center. Roll the tortilla up around the filling. Set the filled tortilla in the prepared baking dish, seam-side down. Repeat with the remaining tortillas and filling.
4. Spoon the remaining sauce over the top, covering all of the tortillas. Sprinkle the cheese over the top, if using, and bake in the preheated oven for about 40 minutes, until heated through and bubbling. Serve immediately.

Nutrition Info:
- Calories: 724; Protein: 38g; Total Fat: 35g; Saturated Fat: 12g; Carbohydrates: 76g; Fiber: 15g; Sodium: 998mg;

Baked Tofu Báhn Mì Lettuce Wrap

Servings:4
Cooking Time: 20 Minutes
Ingredients:
- FOR THE TOFU
- 1 (16-ounce) package firm tofu, drained and cut into ½-inch-thick slabs
- 2 tablespoons gluten-free soy sauce
- 2 teaspoons grated fresh ginger
- Vegetable oil or coconut oil to prepare the baking sheet
- FOR THE VEGETABLES

- ½ cup rice vinegar
- ¼ cup water
- ¼ cup sugar
- 1 teaspoon salt
- 1½ cups shredded carrot
- 1½ cups shredded daikon radish
- FOR THE WRAPS
- 8 large lettuce leaves
- 2 tablespoons mayonnaise
- ½ medium cucumber, peeled, seeded, and cut into matchsticks
- 2 large jalapeño chiles, thinly sliced
- 1 cup cilantro leaves

Directions:

1. Line a rimmed baking sheet with paper towels and place the cut tofu on the sheet in a single layer. Top with another layer of paper towels and then another baking sheet. Weight the top baking sheet down with something heavy (cans of tomatoes or beans work well). Let sit for 30 minutes.

2. While the tofu is draining, prepare the vegetables. In a small saucepan, combine the vinegar, water, sugar, and salt and cook, stirring, over medium heat, until the sugar has dissolved, for about 3 minutes. Remove the pan from the heat and add the carrot and daikon, stirring to coat well. Let sit for 20 minutes.

3. In a large bowl, combine the soy sauce and ginger. Add the pressed tofu and toss to coat well.

4. Let the tofu sit for about 15 minutes, and preheat the oven to 350°F.

5. Oil a large baking sheet with vegetable or coconut oil.

6. Arrange the tofu slabs in a single layer on the prepared baking sheet and bake in the preheated oven for about 10 minutes. Turn the pieces over and bake for another 10 minutes, until the tofu is browned. Remove from the oven and cut into 1-inch-wide sticks.

7. To make the wraps, arrange the lettuce leaves on your work surface and spread a bit of mayonnaise on each, dividing equally. Fill with the baked tofu, cucumber, chiles, and cilantro. Drain the pickled carrots and daikon, and place a handful onto each wrap. Serve immediately.

Nutrition Info:

- Calories: 180; Protein: 6g; Total Fat: 3g; Saturated Fat: 0g; Carbohydrates: 28g; Fiber: 2g; Sodium: 4138mg;

Tofu Burger Patties

Servings:4
Cooking Time: 10 Minutes
Ingredients:
- 8 ounces firm tofu, mashed with a fork

- 4 scallions, green parts only, minced
- 1 cup rolled oats
- 1 egg, beaten
- 2 teaspoons ground cumin
- 2 teaspoons chili powder
- ½ teaspoon sea salt
- ¼ teaspoon freshly ground black pepper
- Nonstick cooking spray

Directions:

1. In a medium bowl, stir together the tofu, scallions, oats, egg, cumin, chili powder, salt, and pepper. Form the mixture into 4 patties.

2. Spray a large nonstick skillet with cooking spray and place it over medium-high heat.

3. Add the patties and cook for about 5 minutes per side, until browned on both sides.

Nutrition Info:

- Calories:146; Total Fat: 5g; Saturated Fat: 1g; Carbohydrates: 17g; Fiber: 4g; Sodium: 275mg; Protein: 10g

Cheese Strata

Servings:4
Cooking Time: 30 Minutes
Ingredients:
- Nonstick cooking spray
- 3 eggs, beaten
- 1 cup unsweetened almond milk
- ½ teaspoon sea salt
- ⅛ teaspoon freshly ground black pepper
- 5 slices gluten-free sandwich bread, crusts removed, cut into cubes
- ¾ cup grated Monterey Jack cheese

Directions:

1. Preheat the oven to 350°F.

2. Spray a 9-by-5-inch loaf pan with nonstick cooking spray.

3. In a medium bowl, whisk together the eggs, almond milk, salt, and pepper.

4. Fold in the bread until it is coated with the egg mixture.

5. Fold in the cheese.

6. Pour the mixture into the prepared dish and bake for 30 to 35 minutes, until set.

Nutrition Info:

- Calories:402; Total Fat: 29g; Saturated Fat: 18g; Carbohydrates: 28g; Fiber: 6g; Sodium: 628mg; Protein: 12g

Stuffed Zucchini Boats

Servings:4

Cooking Time: 40 Minutes

Ingredients:

- 4 medium zucchini, halved lengthwise with the middles scooped out, chopped, and reserved
- 2 cups cooked brown rice
- ½ cup canned crushed tomatoes, drained
- ½ cup grated Parmesan cheese
- ¼ cup chopped fresh basil leaves
- ½ teaspoon sea salt
- ⅛ teaspoon freshly ground black pepper

Directions:

1. Preheat the oven to 400°F.
2. Place the zucchini halves on a rimmed baking sheet, cut-side up.
3. In a medium bowl, stir together the brown rice, reserved chopped zucchini, tomatoes, Parmesan cheese, basil, salt, and pepper. Spoon the mixture into the zucchini boats.
4. Bake for 40 to 45 minutes, until the zucchini are soft.

Nutrition Info:

- Calories:262; Total Fat: 5g; Saturated Fat: 2g; Carbohydrates: 46g; Fiber: 5g; Sodium: 447mg; Protein: 11g

Zucchini Pizza Bites

Servings:4

Cooking Time: 15 Minutes

Ingredients:

- 2 medium zucchini, cut into ¼-inch-thick slices
- 1 cup tomato sauce
- 2 tablespoons Garlic Oil
- 2 teaspoons dried Italian seasoning
- ½ teaspoon sea salt
- 1 cup grated mozzarella cheese

Directions:

1. Preheat the oven to 350°F.
2. Line two rimmed baking sheets with parchment paper. Arrange the zucchini slices in a single layer on the prepared sheets.
3. In a small bowl, whisk the tomato sauce, garlic oil, Italian seasoning, and salt. Spread the sauce on the zucchini slices.
4. Top with the cheese.
5. Bake for about 15 minutes, until the zucchini is soft and the cheese melts.

Nutrition Info:

- Calories:124; Total Fat: 6g; Saturated Fat: 3g; Carbohydrates: 9g; Fiber: 2g; Sodium: 736mg; Protein: 10g

Potato Frittata

Servings:2

Cooking Time: 35 Minutes

Ingredients:

- 6 eggs, beaten
- 2 tablespoons unsweetened almond milk
- ½ teaspoon sea salt
- ⅛ teaspoon freshly ground black pepper
- 2 tablespoons Garlic Oil
- 2 russet potatoes, sliced
- ½ cup grated Parmesan cheese
- 4 cherry tomatoes, quartered
- Arugula, for garnishing (optional)

Directions:

1. Preheat the broiler to high.
2. In a medium bowl, whisk together the eggs, almond milk, salt, and pepper. Set it aside.
3. In a large (12-inch) ovenproof skillet heat over medium-high heat, heat the garlic oil until it shimmers.
4. Add the potatoes. Cook for about 20 minutes, stirring occasionally, until soft.
5. Carefully pour the egg mixture over the potatoes. Cook for about 5 minutes, until the eggs start to set around the edges. With a heat-proof spatula, pull the edges away from the pan and tilt the pan to allow the egg mixture to flow into any spaces you've made. Cook for about 5 minutes more, until the edges set again. Sprinkle with the cheese and top with the tomatoes.
6. Place the skillet under the broiler for 3 to 5 minutes, until the frittata sets and puffs and the cheese melts.
7. Garnish with arugula (if using).

Nutrition Info:

- Calories:445; Total Fat: 37g; Saturated Fat: 13g; Carbohydrates: 5g; Fiber: 1g; Sodium: 954mg; Protein: 27g

Peanut Butter Soba Noodles

Servings:4

Cooking Time: 0 Minutes

Ingredients:

- 6 tablespoons sugar-free natural peanut butter
- ¼ cup low-sodium gluten-free soy sauce
- 2 tablespoons freshly squeezed lime juice
- 1 tablespoon Garlic Oil
- 1 teaspoon peeled and grated fresh ginger
- 1 packet stevia
- 8 ounces soba noodles, cooked according to the package directions, drained, and hot

Directions:

1. In a small bowl (or a blender), whisk together the peanut butter, soy sauce, lime juice, garlic oil, ginger, and stevia until smooth.

2. In a large serving bowl, combine the hot noodles and sauce and toss to coat.

Nutrition Info:

- Calories:357; Total Fat: 13g; Saturated Fat: 3g; Carbohydrates: 49g; Fiber: 2g; Sodium: 1,501mg; Protein: 17g

Polenta With Roasted Vegetables And Spicy Tomato Sauce

Servings:4

Cooking Time: 60 Minutes

Ingredients:

- FOR THE POLENTA
- Oil for preparing the baking sheet
- 4 cups water
- 1 teaspoon salt
- 1 cup uncooked polenta
- 2 tablespoons butter or nondairy butter substitute (optional)
- FOR THE VEGETABLES
- 2 medium red bell peppers, seeded and cut into ¼-inch-thick rings
- 2 cups assorted grape tomatoes
- 8 pieces oil-packed sun-dried tomatoes, julienned
- 2 tablespoons olive oil
- 1 teaspoon salt
- 1 teaspoon gluten-free, onion- and garlic-free chili powder
- 4 ounces crumbled queso fresco or feta cheese (optional)
- FOR THE SAUCE
- 2 jalapeño chiles, seeded and diced
- 1 tablespoon Garlic Oil (here)
- 1 teaspoon salt
- 1 (14½-ounce) can onion- and garlic-free diced tomatoes, preferably fire-roasted
- 2 tablespoons chopped fresh flat-leafed parsley

Directions:

1. Preheat the oven to 475°F.

2. Oil a large, rimmed baking sheet.

3. To make the polenta, combine the water and salt in a large saucepan, and bring to a boil over medium-high heat. While whisking continuously, slowly add the polenta. Reduce the heat to low and cook, whisking continuously, until the polenta becomes thick. Cover the saucepan and cook for about 30 minutes, stirring every once in a while,

until the polenta is creamy and no grittiness remains. Just before serving, stir in the butter, if using.

4. In a large bowl, toss the bell peppers, grape tomatoes, and sun-dried tomatoes with the olive oil. Spread the vegetables on the baking sheet in a single layer. Sprinkle with the salt and chili powder. Roast in the preheated oven, stirring once or twice, until the vegetables are tender and starting to brown, for about 25 minutes.

5. Meanwhile, make the sauce. In a blender, combine the chiles, Garlic Oil, and salt, and blend until smooth. Add the tomatoes and pulse to a chunky, smooth texture. Transfer the mixture to a small saucepan and heat over medium heat. Simmer until the sauce is thickened, for about 6 minutes.

6. To serve, spoon some of the polenta into each of 4 serving bowls. Top with some of the roasted vegetables and spoon some of the warm sauce over the top. Sprinkle the cheese on top, if using. Garnish with parsley and serve immediately.

Nutrition Info:

- Calories: 457; Protein: 12g; Total Fat: 24g; Saturated Fat: 10g; Carbohydrates: 53g; Fiber: 8g; Sodium: 2135mg;

Quinoa-stuffed Eggplant Roulades With Feta And Mint

Servings:4

Cooking Time: 45 Minutes

Ingredients:

- 3 tablespoons olive oil, divided
- ½ cup uncooked quinoa, rinsed
- 1 cup water
- ¼ cup toasted pine nuts
- 2 medium eggplants, sliced lengthwise into ¼-inch-thick slices
- ½ teaspoon salt
- ½ teaspoon freshly ground black pepper
- 1½ cups onion- and garlic-free tomato sauce or marinara sauce (such as Rao's Sensitive Formula Marinara Sauce)
- 2 tablespoons chopped fresh mint
- ½ cup crumbled feta cheese

Directions:

1. Preheat the oven to 375°F.

2. Grease a large baking dish with 1 tablespoon of the olive oil.

3. In a small saucepan, combine the quinoa and water, and bring to a boil over high heat. Reduce the heat to low, cover, and simmer for about 15 minutes, until the water has evaporated and the quinoa is tender. Stir in the pine nuts.

4. While the quinoa is cooking, prepare the eggplant slices. Heat the remaining 2 tablespoons of olive oil in a large

skillet over medium-high heat. Sprinkle the eggplant slices on both sides with salt and pepper, and add them to the pan, cooking in a single layer (you'll need to cook them in batches). Cook for about 3 minutes per side, until golden brown. Transfer the eggplant slices to a plate as they are cooked.

5. To make the roulades, lay an eggplant slice on your work surface and spoon some of the quinoa onto the bottom. Roll the eggplant up into a tube around the filling. Place the rolls as you complete them into a baking dish, and spoon the marinara sauce over the top. Sprinkle the mint and cheese over the roulades, and bake in the preheated oven until they are heated through and the sauce is bubbly, for about 15 minutes.

Nutrition Info:

- Calories: 422; Protein: 11g; Total Fat: 25g; Saturated Fat: 6g; Carbohydrates: 44g; Fiber: 14g; Sodium: 894mg;

Eggplant And Chickpea Curry

Servings:4
Cooking Time: 15 Minutes
Ingredients:

- 2 tablespoons Garlic Oil
- 6 scallions, green parts only, minced
- 2 cups chopped eggplant
- 1 cup canned chickpeas, drained
- 1 cup unsweetened almond milk
- 1 tablespoon curry powder
- ¼ teaspoon freshly ground black pepper

Directions:

1. In a large skillet over medium-high heat, heat the garlic oil until it shimmers.
2. Add the scallions and eggplant. Cook for about 5 minutes, stirring, until the eggplant is soft.
3. Add the chickpeas, almond milk, curry powder, and pepper. Bring to a boil. Reduce the heat to medium-low and simmer for 10 minutes.

Nutrition Info:

- Calories:275; Total Fat: 11g; Saturated Fat: 1g; Carbohydrates: 36g; Fiber: 12g; Sodium: 62mg; Protein: 11g

Spanish Rice

Servings:4
Cooking Time: 10 Minutes
Ingredients:

- 2 tablespoons Garlic Oil
- 6 scallions, green parts only, chopped
- 2 cups hot cooked brown rice
- 1 cup canned crushed tomatoes, drained
- ½ cup Low-FODMAP Vegetable Broth

- ½ cup chopped black olives
- ½ cup pine nuts
- 1 teaspoon dried oregano
- ½ teaspoon sea salt
- ¼ teaspoon freshly ground black pepper

Directions:

1. In a large skillet over medium-high heat, heat the garlic oil until it shimmers.
2. Add the scallions. Cook for 3 minutes, stirring occasionally.
3. Stir in the brown rice, tomatoes, broth, olives, pine nuts, oregano, salt, and pepper. Cook for about 5 minutes more, stirring, until warmed through.

Nutrition Info:

- Calories:399; Total Fat: 22g; Saturated Fat: 2g; Carbohydrates: 46g; Fiber: 6g; Sodium: 506mg; Protein: 8g

Crustless Spinach Quiche

Servings:4
Cooking Time: 20 Minutes
Ingredients:

- Nonstick cooking spray
- 6 eggs, beaten
- ¼ cup unsweetened almond milk
- ½ teaspoon sea salt
- ⅛ teaspoon freshly ground black pepper
- 1 teaspoon dried thyme
- 2 cups (2 [8-ounce] boxes) frozen spinach, thawed and squeezed of excess moisture
- ½ cup grated Swiss cheese

Directions:

1. Preheat the oven to 350°F.
2. Spray a 9-inch pie pan with nonstick cooking spray.
3. In a medium bowl, whisk together the eggs, almond milk, salt, pepper, and thyme.
4. Fold in the spinach and cheese. Pour the mixture into the prepared pie pan.
5. Bake for 20 to 25 minutes, until the quiche sets.

Nutrition Info:

- Calories:187; Total Fat: 14g; Saturated Fat: 8g; Carbohydrates: 3g; Fiber: <1g; Sodium: 368mg; Protein: 13g

Tofu And Red Bell Pepper Quinoa

Servings:4
Cooking Time: 21 Minutes
Ingredients:
- Rest: 5 minutes
- 2 tablespoons Garlic Oil
- 1 red bell pepper, chopped
- 6 ounces firm tofu, chopped
- 1 cup quinoa, rinsed well
- 2 cups Low-FODMAP Vegetable Broth
- 1 teaspoon dried thyme
- ½ teaspoon sea salt
- ¼ teaspoon freshly ground black pepper

Directions:
1. In a large saucepan over medium-high heat, heat the garlic oil until it shimmers.
2. Add the bell pepper and the tofu. Cook for about 5 minutes, stirring, until the pepper is soft.
3. Add the quinoa. Cook for 1 minute, stirring.
4. Add the broth, thyme, salt, and pepper. Bring to a boil. Reduce the heat to medium and simmer for 15 minutes.
5. Turn off the heat. Cover the pot and let it sit for 5 minutes more.
6. Fluff with a fork.

Nutrition Info:
- Calories:276; Total Fat: 12g; Saturated Fat: 2g; Carbohydrates: 31g; Fiber: 4g; Sodium: 624mg; Protein: 12g

Kale-pesto Soba Noodles

Servings:4
Cooking Time: 10 Minutes
Ingredients:
- 1 (10-ounce) package gluten-free soba noodles
- 4 cups kale, removed from stems and roughly chopped
- Zest and juice of 1 lemon
- 1 cup pine nuts
- ¾ cup grated Parmesan cheese, plus more for serving
- ¾ cup olive oil
- 2 tablespoons Garlic Oil (here)
- ¾ teaspoon salt
- ½ teaspoon freshly ground black pepper

Directions:
1. Cook the soba noodles according to the instructions on the package.
2. While the noodles are cooking, prepare the pesto. In a food processor, combine the kale, lemon zest and juice, pine nuts, and cheese, and pulse until the kale is finely chopped. With the processor running, slowly add the olive oil in a thin stream, and continue to process to a smooth purée. Add the Garlic Oil, salt, and pepper, and pulse to combine.
3. When the noodles are finished cooking, drain them and immediately toss them with the pesto. Serve immediately, garnished with additional cheese, if desired.

Nutrition Info:
- Calories: 922; Protein: 26g; Total Fat: 68g; Saturated Fat: 11g; Carbohydrates: 67g; Fiber: 4g; Sodium: 1293mg;

Lentil-walnut Burgers

Servings:6
Cooking Time: 10 Minutes
Ingredients:
- 1½ cups canned lentils, rinsed and drained
- 1 tablespoon homemade (onion- and garlic-free) vegetable broth or water
- 2 teaspoons olive oil
- 8 ounces fresh baby spinach
- Juice of ½ lemon
- 1 teaspoon salt, divided
- ½ teaspoon freshly ground black pepper
- ½ teaspoon ground cumin
- 1 cup gluten-free bread crumbs
- ½ cup walnuts, toasted and finely chopped
- Cooking spray
- TO SERVE
- 6 gluten-free hamburger buns
- 2 cups baby arugula
- 1 large tomato, sliced
- 2 tablespoons spicy mustard

Directions:
1. In a medium bowl, mash the lentils with a potato masher, adding the tablespoon of broth or water.
2. Heat the oil in a large skillet set over medium heat. Add the spinach, lemon juice, ¼ teaspoon of the salt, pepper, and cumin and cook, stirring, until the spinach is cooked, about 3 minutes.
3. Add the spinach mixture, bread crumbs, walnuts, and the remaining ¾ teaspoon of salt to the mashed lentils, and stir to mix well. Refrigerate, covered, for at least 1 hour.
4. Coat a grill or grill pan with cooking spray and heat it to medium-high heat. Shape the lentil mixture into six patties, each about 4 inches across. Cook the patties for about 3 minutes on each side, until grill marks appear. Serve the patties hot on gluten-free buns, garnished with arugula, tomato, and spicy mustard.

Nutrition Info:
- Calories: 292; Protein: 13g; Total Fat: 6g; Saturated Fat: 1g; Carbohydrates: 48g; Fiber: 7g; Sodium: 764mg;

Tempeh Lettuce Wraps

Servings:4
Cooking Time: 8 Minutes
Ingredients:

- 2 tablespoons Garlic Oil
- 4 cups chopped tempeh
- 1 tablespoon Chinese five-spice powder
- ¼ cup creamy sugar-free natural peanut butter
- ¼ cup Low-FODMAP Vegetable Broth
- 1 tablespoon gluten-free soy sauce
- 1 teaspoon ground ginger
- 8 large lettuce leaves
- Minced scallions, green parts only, for garnishing (optional)
- Chopped fresh cilantro leaves, for garnishing (optional)
- Bean sprouts, for garnishing (optional)
- Chopped peanuts, for garnishing (optional)

Directions:

1. In a large skillet over medium-high heat, heat the garlic oil until it shimmers.
2. Add the tempeh and five-spice powder. Cook for 3 to 4 minutes, stirring, until the tempeh is warmed through.
3. In a small bowl, whisk the peanut butter, broth, soy sauce, and ginger. Stir the sauce into the tempeh. Cook for 3 minutes more, stirring.
4. Serve with the lettuce leaves to wrap and the garnishes (if using) on the side.

Nutrition Info:

- Calories:433; Total Fat: 27g; Saturated Fat: 6g; Carbohydrates: 21g; Fiber: 2g; Sodium: 367mg; Protein: 36g

Vegan Noodles With Gingered Coconut Sauce

Servings:4
Cooking Time: 10 Minutes
Ingredients:

- 1 tablespoon Garlic Oil (here)
- 2½ tablespoons minced fresh ginger
- 1 (15-ounce) can light coconut milk
- 2 teaspoons sugar
- 2 teaspoons lemon juice
- 1 teaspoon salt
- ½ teaspoon freshly ground black pepper
- Red pepper flakes, to taste
- 1 bunch of Swiss chard leaves, thick center stems removed, leaves julienned
- 2 cups baby spinach
- 1 (16-ounce) package gluten-free spaghetti, cooked al dente according to package directions and drained
- 2 tablespoons chopped fresh basil

Directions:

1. Heat the Garlic Oil in a large sauté pan over medium heat. Add the ginger and cook, stirring, for about 3 minutes. Stir in the coconut milk, sugar, lemon juice, salt, pepper, and red pepper flakes and bring just to a boil. Reduce the heat to medium low and add the chard and spinach to the simmering sauce. Cook, stirring occasionally, until the greens are completely wilted, about 5 minutes.
2. Transfer the sauce mixture to a blender and purée, or transfer it to a bowl and purée it using an immersion blender.
3. Return the puréed sauce to the pan and bring it back to a simmer over medium heat. Add the prepared noodles and cook, stirring, until heated through, about 2 to 3 minutes. Serve immediately, garnished with basil.

Nutrition Info:

- Calories: 569; Protein: 11g; Total Fat: 15g; Saturated Fat: 1g; Carbohydrates: 99g; Fiber: 8g; Sodium: 908mg;

Curried Squash Soup With Coconut Milk

Servings:4
Cooking Time: 15 Minutes
Ingredients:

- 1 tablespoon coconut oil
- 1 tablespoon Garlic Oil (here)
- 1 tablespoon minced fresh ginger
- 8 pattypan squash, diced
- 2 medium zucchini, diced
- 1 teaspoon gluten-free, onion- and garlic-free curry powder
- 1 teaspoon salt
- ¾ teaspoon ground coriander
- ½ teaspoon ground cumin
- ¼ teaspoon ground cloves
- ¼ teaspoon cayenne
- 4 cups homemade (onion- and garlic-free) vegetable broth
- ½ cup light coconut milk
- 1 cup pure pumpkin purée
- 2 tablespoons chopped fresh cilantro, for garnish

Directions:

1. Heat the coconut oil and Garlic Oil in a stockpot over medium-high heat. Add the ginger and cook for 1 minute. Add the pattypan squash and zucchini, and cook, stirring frequently, until the squash softens, about 3 minutes. Stir in the curry powder, salt, coriander, cumin, cloves, and cayenne, and cook, stirring, for 1 minute more. Add the

broth, coconut milk, and pumpkin purée, and bring to a boil. Reduce the heat to low and simmer for about 10 minutes.

2. Purée the soup either in a blender in batches or in the pot using an immersion blender. Return to the heat if needed and heat through.

3. Serve hot, garnished with cilantro.

Nutrition Info:

- Calories: 155; Protein: 3g; Total Fat: 10g; Saturated Fat: 4g; Carbohydrates: 17g; Fiber: 4g; Sodium: 638mg;

Moroccan-spiced Lentil And Quinoa Stew

Servings:4

Cooking Time: 30 Minutes

Ingredients:

- 1 tablespoon olive oil
- 4 carrots, diced
- 1 leek (green part only), halved lengthwise and thinly sliced
- 1 tablespoon Garlic Oil (here)
- 1 teaspoon ground cumin
- 1 teaspoon ground coriander
- 1 teaspoon ground turmeric
- ¼ teaspoon ground cinnamon
- 1½ teaspoons salt
- ¼ teaspoon freshly ground black pepper
- 8 cups homemade (onion- and garlic-free) vegetable broth
- ¾ cup uncooked quinoa, rinsed
- 1¾ cups canned lentils
- 1 (28-ounce) can onion- and garlic-free diced tomatoes, drained
- 2 tablespoons tomato paste
- 4 cups chopped fresh spinach or 1 (10-ounce) package frozen chopped spinach, thawed
- ½ cup chopped fresh cilantro
- 2 tablespoons lemon juice

Directions:

1. Heat the olive oil in a medium stockpot set over medium heat. Add the carrots and leek, and cook, stirring frequently, for about 10 minutes, until the carrots soften. Add the Garlic Oil, cumin, coriander, turmeric, cinnamon, salt, and pepper. Cook, stirring, for about 1 minute more.

2. Stir in the broth, quinoa, lentils, tomatoes, and tomato paste, and bring the mixture to a boil. Reduce the heat to low and simmer, stirring occasionally, for about 20 minutes, until the quinoa is tender.

3. Stir in the spinach and cook for 5 minutes more.

4. Stir in the cilantro and lemon juice, and serve immediately.

Nutrition Info:

- Calories: 638; Protein: 43g; Total Fat: 11g; Saturated Fat: 2g; Carbohydrates: 97g; Fiber: 36g; Sodium: 2541mg;

Pasta With Tomato And Lentil Sauce

Servings:4

Cooking Time: 10 Minutes

Ingredients:

- 2 tablespoons Garlic Oil
- 6 scallions, green parts only, chopped
- 2 cups canned lentils, drained
- 1½ cups canned crushed tomatoes, undrained
- 1 tablespoon dried Italian seasoning
- ½ teaspoon sea salt
- Pinch red pepper flakes
- ¼ cup chopped fresh basil leaves
- 8 ounces gluten-free pasta (any shape), cooked according to the package directions, drained

Directions:

1. In a large skillet over medium-high heat, heat the garlic oil until it shimmers.

2. Add the scallions and cook for 3 minutes.

3. Stir in the lentils, tomatoes, Italian seasoning, salt, and red pepper flakes. Simmer for 5 minutes, stirring.

4. Stir in the basil.

5. Add the hot pasta and toss to coat.

Nutrition Info:

- Calories:426; Total Fat: 3g; Saturated Fat: 0g; Carbohydrates: 73g; Fiber: 34g; Sodium: 461mg; Protein: 28g

Pasta With Pesto Sauce

Servings:4

Cooking Time: 0 Minutes

Ingredients:

- 8 ounces gluten-free angel hair pasta, cooked according to the package instructions. Drained
- 1 recipe Macadamia Spinach Pesto
- ¼ cup grated Parmesan cheese

Directions:

1. In the warm pot that you used to cook the pasta, toss the noodles with the pesto.

2. Sprinkle with the cheese.

Nutrition Info:

- Calories:449; Total Fat: 25g; Saturated Fat: 6g; Carbohydrates: 46g; Fiber: 3g; Sodium: 444mg; Protein: 13g

Chapter 6 Sauces, Dressings, And Condiments Recipes

Low-fodmap Worcestershire Sauce

Servings:1
Cooking Time: 20 Minutes
Ingredients:

- 2 cups rice vinegar
- 1 teaspoon balsamic vinegar
- ½ cup gluten-free soy sauce or tamari
- ¼ cup light-brown sugar
- 1 teaspoon ground ginger
- 1 teaspoon dry mustard
- 1 teaspoon cumin seeds
- ½ teaspoon fennel seeds
- ½ teaspoon ground cinnamon
- ½ teaspoon freshly ground black pepper

Directions:

1. In a medium saucepan, combine all of the ingredients and bring to a boil over medium-high heat. Reduce the heat to low and simmer, stirring occasionally, for 20 minutes or until the liquid has been reduced by about half.
2. Strain the mixture through a fine-meshed sieve, discarding the solids, and let cool to room temperature. Store in a covered container in the refrigerator for up to 3 months.

Nutrition Info:

- Calories: 21; Protein: 0g; Total Fat: 0g; Saturated Fat: 0g; Carbohydrates: 2g; Fiber: 0g; Sodium: 17mg;

Low-fodmap Vegetable Broth

Servings:8
Cooking Time: 3 To 8 Hours
Ingredients:

- 3 carrots, roughly chopped
- 2 leeks, green parts only, roughly chopped
- 1 fennel bulb, roughly chopped
- 8 peppercorns
- 1 fresh rosemary sprig

Directions:

1. In a large stockpot or slow cooker, combine the carrots, leeks, fennel, peppercorns, and rosemary.
2. Fill the pot about ¾ full, with enough water to cover the ingredients.
3. If using a stockpot: Place the pot over medium-low heat and bring the liquid to a simmer.
4. Simmer for 3 hours.
5. If using a slow cooker: Cover the cooker, set the temperature to low, and cook for 8 hours.
6. Strain and discard the solids. Refrigerate or freeze the stock in 1-cup servings. The broth will keep in the refrigerator for about 5 days or in the freezer for up to 12 months.

Nutrition Info:

- Calories:15; Total Fat: 0g; Saturated Fat: 0g; Carbohydrates: 5g; Fiber: 0g; Sodium: 30mg; Protein: <1g

Thai Red Curry Paste

Servings:1
Cooking Time: 1 Minute
Ingredients:

- 6 dry red chiles
- 1 teaspoon ground cumin
- 1 teaspoon ground coriander
- 1 teaspoon paprika
- 3-inch piece fresh ginger
- 2 (6-inch) pieces fresh lemongrass
- 2 tablespoons chopped fresh cilantro
- 2 teaspoons shrimp paste
- 2 Kaffir lime leaves
- ¼ teaspoon salt

Directions:

1. Place the chiles in a heatproof bowl and cover them with boiling water. Let soak for 15 minutes, then drain.
2. Heat a medium skillet over medium-high heat, add the cumin, coriander, and paprika, and cook, stirring, for about 1 minute, until fragrant. Transfer the spices to a food processor.
3. Add the ginger, lemongrass, cilantro, shrimp paste, lime leaves, and salt to the food processor, along with the drained chiles. Process to a smooth paste.
4. Refrigerate in a sealed container for up to a week, or freeze for up to 3 months.

Nutrition Info:

- Calories: 23; Protein: 1g; Total Fat: 0g; Saturated Fat: 0g; Carbohydrates: 5g; Fiber: 1g; Sodium: 193mg;

Teriyaki Sauce

Servings:1
Cooking Time: 5 Minutes
Ingredients:

- ½ cup water
- ½ cup gluten-free soy sauce
- ¼ cup packed brown sugar
- 2 tablespoons mirin
- 1 tablespoon Garlic Oil
- 1 tablespoon peeled and grated fresh ginger

Directions:

1. In a small saucepan over medium-high heat, whisk together all the ingredients.

2. Simmer for about 5 minutes, whisking, until the sauce thickens.

Nutrition Info:

- Calories:52; Total Fat: 2g; Saturated Fat: 0g; Carbohydrates: 8g; Fiber: 0g; Sodium: 1,040mg; Protein: 2g

Easy Lemon Vinaigrette

Servings:1

Cooking Time: None

Ingredients:

- 1 teaspoon finely grated lemon zest
- 3 tablespoons lemon juice
- 1 teaspoon sugar
- ¾ teaspoon Dijon mustard
- ¾ teaspoon salt
- ¼ teaspoon freshly ground black pepper
- 6 tablespoons olive oil

Directions:

1. Whisk the lemon zest, lemon juice, sugar, mustard, salt, and pepper together in a small bowl. While whisking, add the oil in a thin stream, whisking until the mixture thickens.

2. Use immediately or store in a covered container in the refrigerator for up to a week.

Nutrition Info:

- Calories: 125; Protein: 0g; Total Fat: 14g; Saturated Fat: 2g; Carbohydrates: 1g; Fiber: 0g; Sodium: 299mg;

Homemade Barbecue Sauce

Servings:1

Cooking Time: 10 Minutes

Ingredients:

- 6 scallions, green parts only, minced
- ½ cup apple cider vinegar
- 2 tablespoons Garlic Oil
- 2 tablespoons tomato paste
- 1 teaspoon liquid smoke
- 1 packet stevia
- 1 teaspoon chili powder
- ½ teaspoon sea salt
- ⅛ teaspoon freshly ground black pepper

Directions:

1. In a small saucepan over medium heat, combine all the ingredients.

2. Simmer for 5 minutes, stirring. Refrigerate any leftovers for up to 5 days.

Nutrition Info:

- Calories:41; Total Fat: 4g; Saturated Fat: 0g; Carbohydrates: 2g; Fiber: <1g; Sodium: 127mg; Protein: <1g

Cilantro-lime Vinaigrette

Servings:1

Cooking Time: 0 Minutes

Ingredients:

- 2 tablespoons freshly squeezed lime juice
- 2 tablespoons Garlic Oil
- ¼ cup extra-virgin olive oil
- ¼ teaspoon sea salt
- 2 tablespoons chopped fresh cilantro leaves

Directions:

1. In a small bowl, whisk together the lime juice, garlic oil, olive oil, salt, and cilantro.

2. Whisk again just before serving.

Nutrition Info:

- Calories:170; Total Fat: 20g; Saturated Fat: 3g; Carbohydrates: <1g; Fiber: 0g; Sodium: 119mg; Protein: <1g

Sweet-and-sour Sauce

Servings:1

Cooking Time: 5 Minutes

Ingredients:

- ½ cup pineapple juice
- ⅓ cup rice vinegar
- ¼ cup packed brown sugar
- ¼ cup tomato sauce
- 1 tablespoon gluten-free soy sauce
- 1 tablespoon cornstarch

Directions:

1. In a small saucepan over medium-high heat, whisk together all the ingredients.

2. Simmer for about 5 minutes, whisking, until the sauce thickens.

Nutrition Info:

- Calories:39; Total Fat: 0g; Saturated Fat: 0g; Carbohydrates: 8g; Fiber: 0g; Sodium: 155mg; Protein: <1g

Cilantro-coconut Pesto

Servings:1
Cooking Time: None
Ingredients:
- 1 bunch cilantro
- 6 tablespoons unsweetened shredded coconut
- 6 tablespoons toasted peanuts
- ½ jalapeño, serrano, or Thai chile (optional)
- Juice of ½ lemon
- 1 tablespoon Garlic Oil (here)
- 1 tablespoon olive oil
- Salt to taste

Directions:
1. In a food processor, roughly chop the cilantro. Add the coconut, peanuts, chile (if using), and lemon juice, and process to a paste.
2. With the processor running, add the Garlic Oil and olive oil, and process until the desired texture has been achieved. If the mixture is too thick, add more oil or lemon juice or a bit of water. Taste and add salt as needed.

Nutrition Info:
- Calories: 90; Protein: 2g; Total Fat: 8g; Saturated Fat: 3g; Carbohydrates: 3g; Fiber: 1g; Sodium: 23mg;

Chimichurri Sauce

Servings:1
Cooking Time: None
Ingredients:
- 1 cup fresh flat-leaf parsley
- ¼ cup lemon juice
- ¼ cup olive oil
- ¼ cup Garlic Oil (here)
- ¼ cup fresh cilantro
- ¾ teaspoon red-pepper flakes
- ½ teaspoon ground cumin
- ½ teaspoon salt

Directions:
1. Combine all the ingredients in a blender or food processor and process until smooth.
2. Use immediately or cover and refrigerate for up to a week.

Nutrition Info:
- Calories: 88; Protein: 1g; Total Fat: 9g; Saturated Fat: 1g; Carbohydrates: 3g; Fiber: 1g; Sodium: 203mg;

Garlic Oil

Servings:1
Cooking Time: 5 Minutes
Ingredients:
- 1 cup olive oil
- 6 cloves garlic, sliced

Directions:
1. Heat the olive oil in a small saucepan over medium-low heat.
2. Add the garlic and cook at a low simmer, stirring often, for 5 minutes.
3. Strain the oil through a fine-meshed sieve and discard the solids.
4. Refrigerate the oil in a covered container for up to a week.

Nutrition Info:
- Calories: 108; Protein: 0g; Total Fat: 13g; Saturated Fat: 2g; Carbohydrates: 0g; Fiber: 0g; Sodium: 0mg;

Raspberry Sauce

Servings:4
Cooking Time: 10 Minutes
Ingredients:
- 1 cup fresh raspberries
- ¼ cup sugar
- 2 tablespoons water

Directions:
1. In a large saucepan over medium-high heat, cook the raspberries, sugar, and water, stirring frequently and mashing the raspberries with a spoon. Bring to a boil. Reduce the heat to low and simmer for 5 minutes.
2. Strain the sauce through a fine-mesh sieve to remove the seeds. Chill before serving.

Nutrition Info:
- Calories:63; Total Fat: 0g; Saturated Fat: 0g; Carbohydrates: 16g; Fiber: 2g; Sodium: 1mg; Protein: <1g

Stir-fry Sauce

Servings:5
Cooking Time: 0 Minutes
Ingredients:
- ¼ cup freshly squeezed orange juice
- 3 tablespoons gluten-free soy sauce
- 2 tablespoons cornstarch
- 1 tablespoon peeled and grated fresh ginger
- Pinch red pepper flakes

Directions:
1. In a small bowl, whisk together the orange juice, soy sauce, cornstarch, ginger, and red pepper flakes.

Nutrition Info:
- Calories:33; Total Fat: <1g; Saturated Fat: 0g; Carbohydrates: 7g; Fiber: 0g; Sodium: 677mg; Protein: 1g

Low-fodmap Poultry Broth Or Meat Broth

Servings:8

Cooking Time: 3 To 8 Hours

Ingredients:

- 3 pounds meaty bones
- 3 carrots, roughly chopped
- 2 leeks, green parts only, roughly chopped
- 8 peppercorns
- 1 fresh thyme sprig

Directions:

1. In a large stockpot or slow cooker, combine the bones, carrots, leeks, peppercorns, and thyme.
2. Fill the pot about ¾ full, with enough water to cover the ingredients.
3. If using a stockpot: Place the pot over medium-low heat and bring the liquid to a simmer.
4. Simmer for 3 hours.
5. If using a slow cooker: Cover the cooker, set the temperature to low, and cook for 8 hours.
6. Strain and discard the solids.
7. Refrigerate the broth overnight. Skim the fat from the surface and discard.
8. Refrigerate or freeze the stock in 1-cup servings. The broth will keep in the refrigerator for about 5 days or in the freezer for up to 12 months.

Nutrition Info:

- Calories:Calories: 15; Total Fat: 0g; Saturated Fat: 0g; Carbohydrates: 1.5g; Fiber: 0g; Sodium: 60mg; Protein: 1.5g

Tangy Lemon Curd

Servings:2

Cooking Time: 10 Minutes

Ingredients:

- 1 cup granulated sugar
- 1 tablespoon finely grated lemon zest
- 1 cup lemon juice (from about 5 large lemons)
- 3 tablespoons chilled butter
- 3 eggs, lightly beaten

Directions:

1. In a medium saucepan over medium heat, whisk together the sugar, lemon zest, and lemon juice. Whisk in the butter and eggs, and cook the mixture, stirring constantly (be careful not to let it come to a boil), until it becomes thick, for 8 to 10 minutes.
2. Transfer the mixture to a ramekin or custard bowl, and cover with plastic wrap, pressing the plastic directly onto the surface of the curd to prevent a skin from forming, and chill for 4 hours.

Nutrition Info:

- Calories: 240; Protein: 3g; Total Fat: 12.4g; Saturated Fat: 7.2g; Carbohydrates: 32g; Fiber: 2g; Sodium: 42mg;

Olive Tapenade

Servings:1

Cooking Time: 0 Minutes

Ingredients:

- 1 cup chopped black olives
- 2 tablespoons Garlic Oil
- 2 tablespoons chopped fresh basil leaves
- 1 anchovy fillet, minced
- 1 tablespoon capers, chopped
- Juice of ½ lemon
- ½ teaspoon sea salt
- ⅛ teaspoon freshly ground black pepper

Directions:

1. In a small bowl, stir together all the ingredients until well mixed.

Nutrition Info:

- Calories:61; Total Fat: 6g; Saturated Fat: <1g; Carbohydrates: 2g; Fiber: <1g; Sodium: 388mg; Protein: <1g

Luscious Hot Fudge Sauce

Servings:2

Cooking Time: 5 Minutes

Ingredients:

- ⅔ cup full-fat coconut milk
- ½ cup granulated sugar
- ⅓ cup brown sugar
- ¼ cup unsweetened cocoa powder
- ¼ teaspoon salt
- 6 ounces bittersweet chocolate (dairy-free and gluten-free), chopped, divided
- 2 tablespoons coconut oil
- 1 teaspoon vanilla extract

Directions:

1. In a medium saucepan combine the coconut milk, sugars, cocoa powder, salt, and half of the chocolate, and bring to a boil. Reduce the heat to low and simmer, stirring occasionally, for 5 minutes.
2. Remove the pan from the heat and whisk in the remaining chocolate along with the coconut oil and vanilla. Stir until smooth.
3. Let cool for 15 to 20 minutes before serving. Serve warm or store in a covered container in the refrigerator for up to 2 weeks.

Nutrition Info:

- Calories: 135; Protein: 2g; Total Fat: 8g; Saturated Fat: 6g; Carbohydrates: 17g; Fiber: 1g; Sodium: 48mg;

Homemade Mayonnaise

Servings:1
Cooking Time: None
Ingredients:
- 1 large pasteurized egg yolk
- 1½ teaspoons fresh lemon juice
- 1 teaspoon white wine vinegar
- ¼ teaspoon Dijon mustard
- ½ teaspoon salt
- ¾ cup light olive oil

Directions:
1. In a blender or food processor, combine the egg yolk, lemon juice, vinegar, mustard, and salt, and process to combine. With the processor running, slowly add the oil. Continue processing until all of the oil has been added and the mixture is thick.
2. Transfer to a storage container and store, covered, in the refrigerator for up to 3 days.

Nutrition Info:
- Calories: 113; Protein: 0g; Total Fat: 13g; Saturated Fat: 2g; Carbohydrates: 0g; Fiber: 0g; Sodium: 99mg;

Low-fodmap Mayonnaise

Servings:1
Cooking Time: 0 Minutes
Ingredients:
- 1 egg yolk
- 1 tablespoon red wine vinegar
- ½ teaspoon Dijon mustard
- ¼ teaspoon sea salt
- ¾ cup extra-virgin olive oil

Directions:
1. In a blender or food processor, combine the egg yolk, vinegar, mustard, and salt. Process for about 30 seconds until well combined. With a rubber spatula, scrape down the sides of the blender jar or food processor bowl.
2. Turn the blender or processor to medium speed. Very slowly, drip in the olive oil, 1 drop at a time as the processor or blender runs. After about 10 drops, leave the blender or processor running, then add the rest of the olive oil in a thin stream until it is incorporated and emulsified.
3. The mayo will keep refrigerated for up to 5 days.

Nutrition Info:
- Calories:169; Total Fat: 20g; Saturated Fat: 3g; Carbohydrates: <1g; Fiber: 0g; Sodium: 63mg; Protein: <1g

Thai Sweet Chili Sauce

Servings:1
Cooking Time: 7 Minutes
Ingredients:
- 1 cup plus 2 tablespoons water, divided
- 2 tablespoons cornstarch
- 2 tablespoons finely chopped chiles (use red jalapeños, red Thai, Fresno, or other red chiles)
- ⅔ cup sugar
- ⅓ cup rice vinegar
- 2 teaspoons salt

Directions:
1. In a small bowl, stir together 2 tablespoons of the water and the cornstarch until smooth.
2. In a medium saucepan over medium heat, combine the remaining 1 cup water, chiles, sugar, vinegar, and salt, and bring to a boil. Reduce the heat to low and simmer, uncovered, until the sauce starts to become syrupy, about 5 minutes.
3. Give the cornstarch mixture a stir and whisk it into the simmering sauce. Cook, stirring, for 1 minute more, until the sauce is thickened. Remove from the heat and let cool slightly before using.
4. Store in a covered container in the refrigerator for up to a week.

Nutrition Info:
- Calories: 85; Protein: 0g; Total Fat: 0g; Saturated Fat: 0g; Carbohydrates: 20g; Fiber: 0g; Sodium: 582mg;

Egg-free Caesar Dressing

Servings:1
Cooking Time: None
Ingredients:
- 4 whole anchovy fillets
- 2 tablespoons Dijon mustard
- 1 tablespoon red-wine vinegar
- 1 teaspoon gluten-free soy sauce or coconut aminos
- Juice of ½ lemon
- ¼ teaspoon salt
- ¼ teaspoon freshly ground black pepper
- ¼ cup olive oil
- ¼ cup Garlic Oil (here)
- ¼ cup freshly grated Parmesan cheese

Directions:
1. In a blender or food processor, combine the anchovies, mustard, vinegar, soy sauce or coconut aminos, lemon juice, salt, and pepper. Pulse to chop the anchovies and combine well.

2. With the processor running, slowly add the olive oil and Garlic Oil in a thin stream. Process until the mixture is thickened. Add the cheese and pulse just to incorporate.

3. Serve immediately or store in a covered container in the refrigerator for up to a week.

Nutrition Info:

*   Calories: 229; Protein: 18g; Total Fat: 17g; Saturated Fat: 4g; Carbohydrates: 2g; Fiber: 0g; Sodium: 3632mg;

Pico De Gallo Salsa

Servings:2

Cooking Time: None

Ingredients:

*   5 medium tomatoes, chopped
*   1 jalapeño chile, minced
*   ½ cup minced fresh cilantro
*   Juice of 1 lime
*   2 tablespoons Garlic Oil (here)
*   2 tablespoons olive oil
*   ½ teaspoon salt

Directions:

1. In a medium bowl, combine all of the ingredients and toss to combine well.

2. Let sit at room temperature for 15 minutes. Serve immediately or store, covered, in the refrigerator for up to 3 days.

Nutrition Info:

*   Calories: 95; Protein: 2g; Total Fat: 7g; Saturated Fat: 1g; Carbohydrates: 8g; Fiber: 2g; Sodium: 300mg;

Maple-mustard Vinaigrette

Servings:1

Cooking Time: None

Ingredients:

*   2 tablespoons balsamic vinegar
*   2 tablespoons maple syrup
*   2 tablespoons Dijon mustard
*   ¼ teaspoon salt
*   ¼ teaspoon freshly ground black pepper
*   6 tablespoons olive oil

Directions:

1. Whisk the vinegar, maple syrup, mustard, salt, and pepper together in a small bowl. While whisking, add the oil in a thin stream, whisking until the mixture thickens.

2. Use immediately or store in a covered container in the refrigerator for up to a week.

Nutrition Info:

*   Calories: 142; Protein: 0g; Total Fat: 14g; Saturated Fat: 2g; Carbohydrates: 5g; Fiber: 0g; Sodium: 157mg;

Sun-dried Tomato Spread

Servings:x

Cooking Time:x

Ingredients:

*   1 cup (150 g) sun-dried tomatoes in oil, drained and roughly chopped (oil reserved)
*   ¼ cup (15 g) roughly chopped flat-leaf parsley
*   2 heaping tablespoons reduced-fat cream cheese, at room temperature
*   1 tablespoon garlic-infused olive oil
*   3 tablespoons olive oil
*   Salt and freshly ground black pepper

Directions:

1. Place the sun-dried tomatoes and reserved oil, parsley, and cream cheese in a food processor or blender and process until well combined.

2. Gradually add the garlic-infused oil and olive oil until the mixture is almost smooth.

3. Season to taste with salt and pepper.

4. Spoon into a bowl or jar, cover, and store in the fridge for up to 3 days.

Nutrition Info:

*   134 calories; 1 g protein; 13 g total fat; 3 g saturated fat; 3 g carbohydrates; 1 g fiber; 122 mg sodium

Balsamic Vinaigrette

Servings:5

Cooking Time: 0 Minutes

Ingredients:

*   2 tablespoons balsamic vinegar
*   1 tablespoon freshly squeezed orange juice
*   ½ teaspoon grated orange zest
*   ½ teaspoon Dijon mustard
*   ⅓ cup extra-virgin olive oil
*   ¼ teaspoon sea salt
*   ⅛ teaspoon freshly ground black pepper

Directions:

1. In a small bowl, whisk together all the ingredients.

2. Whisk again just before serving.

Nutrition Info:

*   Calories:146; Total Fat: 17g; Saturated Fat: 2g; Carbohydrates: <1g; Fiber: 0g; Sodium: 117mg; Protein: <1g

Low-fodmap Spicy Ketchup

Servings:1
Cooking Time: 20 Minutes
Ingredients:

- 2 tablespoons Garlic Oil (here)
- ¼ cup tomato paste
- ¼ cup light-brown sugar
- ½ teaspoon ground ginger
- ¼ teaspoon cayenne
- ¼ teaspoon ground allspice
- ⅛ teaspoon ground cinnamon
- ⅛ teaspoon ground cloves
- ¼ cup red-wine vinegar
- 1 (15-ounce) can tomato sauce
- ½ teaspoon salt
- ¼ teaspoon freshly ground black pepper

Directions:

1. Heat the Garlic Oil in a small saucepan over medium heat. Add the tomato paste and cook, stirring, for 1 minute.
2. Add the sugar, ginger, cayenne, allspice, cinnamon, and cloves, and cook, stirring frequently, until the sugar is fully dissolved. Stir in the vinegar, tomato sauce, salt, and pepper. Cook, stirring occasionally, for 15 to 20 minutes, until the sauce is very thick.
3. Let cool to room temperature. Serve immediately or store in a covered container in the refrigerator for up to a week.

Nutrition Info:

- Calories: 28; Protein: 1g; Total Fat: 0g; Saturated Fat: 0g; Carbohydrates: 7g; Fiber: 1g; Sodium: 289mg;

Salsa Verde

Servings:x
Cooking Time:x
Ingredients:

- 2 handfuls of flat-leaf parsley, rinsed and dried
- 3 anchovy fillets in oil, drained (optional)
- 2 teaspoons capers, rinsed and drained
- 1 tablespoon garlic-infused olive oil
- 2 tablespoons olive oil
- 2 tablespoons fresh lemon juice, or to taste
- Salt and freshly ground black pepper

Directions:

1. Combine the parsley, anchovy fillets (if using), and capers in a food processor or blender and process until well combined.
2. Gradually add the garlic-infused oil and olive oil until well blended.

3. Add the lemon juice and salt and pepper to taste.
4. Spoon into a bowl or jar, cover, and store in the fridge for up to 5 days.

Nutrition Info:

- 53 calories; 1 g protein; 5 g total fat; 1 g saturated fat; 1 g carbohydrates; 0 g fiber; 158 mg sodium

Basil "hollandaise" Sauce

Servings:1
Cooking Time: None
Ingredients:

- ½ cup cold rice milk
- ½ cup fresh basil leaves
- 4 teaspoons lemon juice
- 1 tablespoon nutritional yeast
- ½ teaspoon salt
- ⅛ teaspoon cayenne pepper
- ⅛ teaspoon turmeric
- ¼ teaspoon xanthan gum
- ½ cup light olive oil

Directions:

1. In a blender, combine the rice milk, basil, lemon juice, nutritional yeast, salt, cayenne, and turmeric, and process until smooth.
2. Add the xanthan gum and blend on high until the mixture becomes foamy.
3. With the blender running, slowly add the oil, blending until the sauce is thick.

Nutrition Info:

- Calories: 161; Protein: 1g; Total Fat: 17g; Saturated Fat: 2g; Carbohydrates: 3g; Fiber: 0g; Sodium: 203mg;

Lemon-dill Vinaigrette

Servings:5
Cooking Time: 0 Minutes
Ingredients:

- ¼ cup Garlic Oil
- 3 tablespoons freshly squeezed lemon juice
- ½ teaspoon grated lemon zest
- 2 tablespoons chopped fresh dill
- ½ teaspoon Dijon mustard
- ¼ teaspoon sea salt
- ⅛ teaspoon freshly ground black pepper

Directions:

1. In a small bowl, whisk together all the ingredients.
2. Whisk again just before serving.

Nutrition Info:

- Calories:128; Total Fat: 14g; Saturated Fat: 2g; Carbohydrates: 1g; Fiber: 0g; Sodium: 130mg; Protein: <1g

Basil Pesto

Servings:x
Cooking Time:x
Ingredients:

- 2 handfuls of basil leaves, rinsed and dried
- 2 tablespoons garlic-infused olive oil
- 2 tablespoons olive oil, plus more as needed
- ⅓ cup (50 g) pine nuts
- ⅓ cup (25 g) grated Parmesan
- Salt and freshly ground black pepper

Directions:

1. Combine the basil, garlic-infused oil, olive oil, pine nuts, and Parmesan in a food processor or blender and process until well combined.
2. Season to taste with salt and pepper.
3. Add more oil if you prefer a more liquid pesto for drizzling.
4. Spoon into a bowl or jar and cover with a thin layer of olive oil.
5. Cover and store in the fridge for up to 5 days or in the freezer for up to 2 months.

Nutrition Info:

- 107 calories; 3 g protein; 10 g total fat; 2 g saturated fat; 1 g carbohydrates; 0 g fiber; 102 mg sodium

Whipped Coconut Cream

Servings:2
Cooking Time: None
Ingredients:

- 1 can full-fat coconut milk, refrigerated overnight
- 2 tablespoons maple syrup
- ½ teaspoon vanilla extract

Directions:

1. Carefully turn over the can of coconut milk and open the bottom of the can. Pour off the liquid coconut milk, leaving the thick cream (you should end up with about 1 cup of cream). Add some of the coconut milk, if needed, so that it equals 1 cup, saving the rest of the coconut milk for another purpose). Place the coconut cream in a large bowl and, using an electric mixer set on high speed, whip the cream until it becomes very fluffy and forms soft peaks.
2. Add the maple syrup and vanilla, and gently whip until just incorporated.

3. Refrigerate until ready to serve, or up to 3 days.
Nutrition Info:

- Calories: 83; Protein: 1g; Total Fat: 7g; Saturated Fat: 6g; Carbohydrates: 5g; Fiber: 1g; Sodium: 5mg;

Italian Basil Vinaigrette

Servings:5
Cooking Time: 0 Minutes
Ingredients:

- 2 tablespoons apple cider vinegar
- 2 tablespoons extra-virgin olive oil
- 2 tablespoons Garlic Oil
- 2 tablespoons chopped fresh basil leaves
- ½ teaspoon Dijon mustard
- ¼ teaspoon sea salt
- ⅛ teaspoon freshly ground black pepper

Directions:

1. In a small bowl, whisk together all the ingredients.
2. Whisk again just before serving.

Nutrition Info:

- Calories:124; Total Fat: 14g; Saturated Fat: 2g; Carbohydrates: <1g; Fiber: 0g; Sodium: 118mg; Protein: <1g

Macadamia Spinach Pesto

Servings:1
Cooking Time: 0 Minutes
Ingredients:

- 2 cups fresh baby spinach
- ½ cup fresh basil leaves
- ½ cup grated Parmesan cheese
- ¼ cup Garlic Oil
- ¼ cup macadamia nuts
- Zest of 1 lemon
- ½ teaspoon sea salt

Directions:

1. In a blender or food processor, combine all the ingredients.
2. Process until everything is well chopped and combined.

Nutrition Info:

- Calories:115; Total Fat: 12g; Saturated Fat: 2g; Carbohydrates: 1g; Fiber: <1g; Sodium: 189mg; Protein: 3g

Chapter 7 Salads And Sides Recipes

Green Beans And New Potatoes With Tomato

Servings: 8
Cooking Time: 10 Minutes
Ingredients:

- 1 tablespoon olive oil
- 1 tablespoon Garlic Oil (here)
- 1¼ pounds green beans, trimmed
- 1½ cups diced red new potatoes
- 1 teaspoon salt
- ¼ cup water
- ⅓ cup chopped cilantro
- ¾ pound plum tomatoes, peeled and coarsely chopped
- ¼ teaspoon freshly ground black pepper
- ¼ teaspoon cayenne

Directions:

1. Heat the olive oil and Garlic Oil in a large skillet over medium-high heat. Add the green beans, potatoes, and salt, and cook, stirring, for 1 minute.
2. Stir in the water, cover the pan, and cook until the beans are barely tender, about 5 minutes.
3. Stir in the cilantro and tomatoes, cover the pan again, reduce the heat to low, and cook for about 4 minutes more, until the tomatoes begin to break down.
4. Just before serving, stir in the pepper and cayenne. Serve hot.

Nutrition Info:

- Calories: 244; Protein: 7g; Total Fat: 4g; Saturated Fat: 1g; Carbohydrates: 49g; Fiber: 11g; Sodium: 615mg;

Chicken Cheese Fritters

Servings: 4
Cooking Time: 20 Minutes
Ingredients:

- Fritters
- 1 lb ground chicken
- 2 eggs, large
- ¼ cup mayonnaise
- ¼ cup gluten-free, all-purpose flour
- ¾ cup mozzarella cheese, grated
- 2 tbsp basil, fresh and finely chopped
- 2 tbsp chives, dried
- Pinch of salt
- Pinch black pepper
- 1 tsp sunflower oil

- Aioli
- ¼ cup mayonnaise
- ¼ tsp garlic-infused oil
- ½ tbsp lemon juice
- 1 tsp lemon zest
- Pinch of salt
- Pinch of black pepper

Directions:

1. In a bowl, mix the chicken with the fritter ingredients. Mix until combined thoroughly.
2. Over medium heat, place a pan greased with oil. When the oil is hot, measure a ¼ cup of the fritter mixture and pour it into the pan and flatten with a spatula.
3. Fry for 3-4 minutes until the fritters are golden brown. Add oil if needed. Place the cooked fritters onto a paper towel to absorb the oil.
4. The aioli is made by mixing the ingredients in a small bowl until smooth.
5. Serve the fritters with aioli on the side.

Nutrition Info:

- 415g Calories, 26.8g Total fat, 8g Saturated fat, 11.4g Carbohydrates, 0.4 g Fiber, 31.5g Protein, 1.7g Sodium.

Veggie Dip

Servings: 16
Cooking Time: 5 Minutes
Ingredients:

- 1 cup mayonnaise
- 2 cups Greek yogurt
- 2 cups kale, chopped finely
- 1 ½ cups bell peppers, variety of colors, chopped finely
- 2 cups water chestnuts, chopped finely
- 3 spring onions, green parts only, chopped finely
- 1 tsp garlic-infused oil
- Pinch of salt
- Fresh sliced vegetables and corn chips for serving

Directions:

1. In a bowl, mix all the ingredients well, except for the fresh sliced vegetables. Place in the fridge until serving.
2. Serve with the fresh vegetables.

Nutrition Info:

- 123g Calories, 10g Total fat, 1g Saturated fat, 3g Carbohydrates, 3 g Fiber, 3g Protein, 1g Sodium.

Parmesan Mayo Corn On The Cob

Servings:6

Cooking Time: 10 Minutes

Ingredients:

- 6 ears of corn, leaves still attached
- ½ cup mayonnaise
- ⅔ cup grated Parmesan
- 1 tbsp coriander, chopped

Directions:

1. In a pot of salted, boiling water, cook the corn for 7 minutes before draining. Leave to cool. Once cooled, pull back the leaves and place the corn onto a hot, greased skillet and grill for 5 minutes making sure to roll them until there are char marks.

2. In a bowl, mix the mayonnaise, Parmesan, and coriander. When the corn is ready, spread a tablespoon of the mayonnaise mixture onto each cob.

3. Serve warm.

Nutrition Info:

- 254g Calories, 15g Total fat, 5.8g Saturated fat, 20g Carbohydrates, 1.8 g Fiber, 12.8g Protein, 3.8g Sodium.

Bacon Mashed Potatoes

Servings:4

Cooking Time: 15 Minutes

Ingredients:

- 1 pound new or baby potatoes, cut into 1-inch cubes
- 2 slices bacon
- ⅓ cup lactose-free milk
- ½ teaspoon salt
- ¼ teaspoon freshly ground black pepper
- ¼ cup unsalted butter
- 4 scallions, green parts only, sliced

Directions:

1. Put the potatoes in a large saucepan, cover with 2 inches of water, and bring to a boil over medium-high heat. Lower the heat to medium and cook for 10 to 12 minutes, until the potatoes are tender. Drain the potatoes and place them in a large bowl.

2. While the potatoes are cooking, cook the bacon in a large skillet over medium heat for about 4 minutes per side, until browned and crisp. Drain on paper towels, and then crumble.

3. In the large bowl, mash the potatoes with a potato masher. Add the milk, salt, pepper, and butter. Continue mashing until the potatoes are smooth, the butter is melted, and everything is well mixed. Stir in the bacon and scallions. Serve immediately.

Nutrition Info:

- Calories: 203; Protein: 5g; Total Fat: 14g; Saturated Fat: 8g; Carbohydrates: 16g; Fiber: 3g; Sodium: 479mg;

Mashed Potatoes

Servings:4

Cooking Time: 10 Minutes

Ingredients:

- 4 russet potatoes, peeled and cut into 1-inch cubes
- 2 tablespoons unsalted butter
- ¼ cup unsweetened almond milk
- ½ teaspoon sea salt
- ¼ teaspoon freshly ground black pepper

Directions:

1. In a large pot over medium-high heat, combine the potatoes with enough water to cover. Bring to a boil and cook for 10 to 15 minutes, until soft. Drain and return the potatoes to the pot.

2. Add the butter, almond milk, salt, and pepper. With a potato masher, mash until smooth.

Nutrition Info:

- Calories:233; Total Fat: 10g; Saturated Fat: 7g; Carbohydrates: 34g; Fiber: 6g; Sodium: 290mg; Protein: 4g

Easy Fruit Salad

Servings:4

Cooking Time: 0 Minutes

Ingredients:

- 6 clementines, sectioned
- 2 cups sliced fresh strawberries
- 1 pint fresh blueberries
- 2 bananas, sliced

Directions:

1. In a large bowl, gently stir together the clementines, strawberries, blueberries, and bananas.

Nutrition Info:

- Calories:133; Total Fat: <1g; Saturated Fat: 0g; Carbohydrates: 34g; Fiber: 5g; Sodium: 2mg; Protein: 2g

Quinoa With Cherry Tomatoes, Olives, And Radishes

Servings:4

Cooking Time: 20 Minutes

Ingredients:

- 1 cup uncooked quinoa
- 1 teaspoon salt
- ¼ cup white wine vinegar or white balsamic vinegar
- ¼ cup olive oil
- 1 cup cherry tomatoes, halved or quartered

- 1 cup pitted cured black olives, halved, quartered, or left whole if small
- 4 to 6 radishes, thinly sliced

Directions:

1. In a medium saucepan, combine the quinoa and salt with 2 cups water and bring to a boil. Reduce the heat to low, cover, and let simmer for 15 to 20 minutes, until tender.

2. Meanwhile, in a small bowl, whisk together the vinegar and olive oil. When the quinoa is cooked, immediately toss it together with the dressing in a large bowl. Add the tomatoes, olives, and radishes and toss together. Serve immediately or refrigerate, covered, for up to 3 days.

Nutrition Info:

- Calories: 309; Protein: 7g; Total Fat: 19g; Saturated Fat: 3g; Carbohydrates: 31g; Fiber: 5g; Sodium: 886mg;

Caramelized Fennel

Servings:4

Cooking Time: 60 Minutes

Ingredients:

- ¼ cup olive oil
- 4 large fennel bulbs, cut into ¼-inch-thick slices
- 1 teaspoon salt
- ¼ cup freshly grated Parmesan
- 2 tablespoons chopped fresh parsley
- 1 teaspoon lemon zest
- 2 teaspoons lemon juice

Directions:

1. In a large, heavy skillet, heat the olive oil over medium-high heat. Stir in the fennel and salt, reduce the heat to medium, and cook, stirring occasionally, for 45 to 60 minutes, lowering the heat if needed, until the fennel is golden brown and very tender.

2. Just before serving, stir in the cheese, parsley, lemon zest, and lemon juice.

Nutrition Info:

- Calories: 228; Protein: 8g; Total Fat: 16g; Saturated Fat: 4g; Carbohydrates: 18g; Fiber: 7g; Sodium: 836mg;

Festive Stuffing

Servings:12

Cooking Time: 20 Minutes

Ingredients:

- 10 slices gluten-free bread, can use other approved bread
- 4 tbsp butter or margarine
- 1 tsp garlic-infused oil
- 1 ½ cups leeks, only the green tips
- ½ cup parsley, fresh

- 1 tsp sage, dried
- 1 tsp oregano, dried
- ½ tsp thyme, dried
- Pinch of salt
- Pinch of pepper
- ½ cup vegetable stock, low-FODMAP-approved, without onion or garlic

Directions:

1. Preheat the oven to 350°F.

2. In a large bowl, tear the bread into small pieces.

3. In a smaller bowl, melt the butter and mix the garlic-infused oil into it before drizzling and tossing it onto the bread. Spread the bread over an oven tray, then place it in the oven for 5 minutes. Toss the bread and bake for another 5 minutes.

4. Depending on the desired texture, place the bread and other ingredients into a bowl for a chunky texture or a blender for a smooth texture. Mix well.

5. Grease a muffin tin with oil. Mix the stock into the bread, being careful not to make the bread soggy. Spoon the mixture into the muffin tin, fill each space to the top, and press down gently.

6. Bake for 10-15 minutes. When finished, the top should be crunchy.

Nutrition Info:

- 120g Calories, 5.6g Total fat, 0.9g Saturated fat, 14.8g Carbohydrates, 0.9 g Fiber, 3g Protein, 1.6g Sodium.

Beetroot Dip

Servings:6

Cooking Time: -

Ingredients:

- 1 ¼ cups baby beetroot, canned, drained
- 1 tbsp lemon juice
- 1 cup mint leaves, unchopped
- 1 tsp cumin seeds, whole
- ½ tsp fennel seeds
- ½ tsp coriander, ground
- ½ cup coconut yogurt, or other approved yogurts

Directions:

1. In a blender or food processor, place the beetroot, lemon juice, coriander, cumin, and fennel. Add the yogurt to the mixture and mix until the dip is smooth and at the desired consistency. The dip will thicken when it is cooled in the fridge.

2. Serve with plain chips, fresh vegetables, or rice crackers.

Nutrition Info:

- 63g Calories, 4.6g Total fat, 4g Saturated fat, 5g Carbohydrates, 1.6 g Fiber, 1.1g Protein, 3g Sodium.

Classic Coleslaw

Servings:6

Cooking Time: None

Ingredients:

- 1 cup mayonnaise
- 3 tablespoons Dijon mustard
- 1 tablespoon white-wine vinegar
- Juice of 1 lemon
- Pinch sugar
- ½ teaspoon celery seed
- Several dashes onion- and garlic-free hot-pepper sauce
- ¾ teaspoon salt
- ½ teaspoon freshly ground black pepper
- 1 head green cabbage, shredded
- 2 carrots, grated
- 1 fresh red chile, sliced

Directions:

1. In a large bowl, combine the mayonnaise, mustard, vinegar, lemon juice, sugar, celery seed, hot sauce, salt, and pepper, and stir together.
2. Add the cabbage and carrots to the dressing, and toss together until evenly coated.
3. Cover and chill the coleslaw for at least 2 hours before serving.

Nutrition Info:

- Calories: 198; Protein: 5g; Total Fat: 14g; Saturated Fat: 2g; Carbohydrates: 19g; Fiber: 4g; Sodium: 694mg;

Sesame Rice Noodles

Servings:4

Cooking Time: About 10 Minutes

Ingredients:

- 1 package rice noodles, such as pad Thai noodles
- FOR THE SAUCE
- ¼ cup gluten-free soy sauce
- 3 tablespoons dark sesame oil
- 2 tablespoons rice vinegar
- 2 tablespoons sugar
- 1 tablespoon Garlic Oil (here)
- ½ teaspoon chili oil or onion- and garlic-free chili paste
- 2 tablespoons chopped cilantro (optional)

Directions:

1. Cook the noodles according to the package instructions.
2. While the noodles are cooking, make the sauce. In a small bowl, whisk together the soy sauce, sesame oil, vinegar, sugar, Garlic Oil, and chili oil or paste until well combined.

3. In a large bowl, toss the warm, cooked noodles with the sauce until well coated. Serve immediately, garnished with cilantro if desired.

Nutrition Info:

- Calories: 270; Protein: 1g; Total Fat: 11g; Saturated Fat: 2g; Carbohydrates: 40g; Fiber: 1g; Sodium: 74mg;

Roasted Lemon-parmesan Broccoli

Servings:6

Cooking Time: 25 Minutes

Ingredients:

- 1½ pounds broccoli, cut into florets
- 2 tablespoons olive oil
- 1 teaspoon salt
- ½ teaspoon freshly ground black pepper
- 2 teaspoons grated lemon zest
- 2 tablespoons lemon juice
- ¼ cup freshly grated Parmesan cheese
- 2 tablespoons toasted pine nuts

Directions:

1. Preheat the oven to 425°F.
2. On a large, rimmed sheet pan, toss the broccoli with the olive oil, sprinkle with salt and pepper, and spread into a single layer. Roast in the preheated oven for about 25 minutes, until the broccoli begins to brown on the edges.
3. Transfer the broccoli to a large serving platter and toss with the lemon zest, lemon juice, and cheese. Garnish with the pine nuts and serve immediately.

Nutrition Info:

- Calories: 117; Protein: 5g; Total Fat: 8g; Saturated Fat: 2g; Carbohydrates: 9g; Fiber: 3g; Sodium: 500mg;

Zucchini Fritters

Servings:3

Cooking Time: 15 Minutes

Ingredients:

- Fritters
- 2 cups broccoli, cut into florets
- ¼ cup zucchini, grated
- ½ cup cheddar cheese, grated (other approved cheeses can be substituted)
- Pinch of salt
- Pinch of pepper
- 1 egg
- ½ cup gluten-free flour
- 3 tbsp lactose-free milk, can be substituted with other approved milk
- 1 tbsp garlic-infused oil
- Lime aioli

- ¼ cup mayonnaise
- 2 tsp lime juice, fresh
- ½ tsp lime zest

Directions:

1. Cut the broccoli, steam it, then mash it. Grate the zucchini.

2. In a bowl, mix the wet ingredients. Add the dry ingredients, excluding the black pepper, into the bowl, then fold in the broccoli, zucchini, and cheese. Do not over mix.

3. Over medium heat, place a large pan that has been greased lightly with oil. With a ¼-cup measuring spoon, scoop some mixture and pour it into the pan then flatten gently with a spatula. Cook 2-3 fritters per batch.

4. Whisk the lime juice, zest, and mayonnaise and season with black pepper.

5. Serve the fritters topped with the aioli.

Nutrition Info:

- 310g Calories, 17.2g Total fat, 5.8g Saturated fat, 28.2g Carbohydrates, 2.1 g Fiber, 10.7g Protein, 4.3g Sodium.

Parmesan Baked Zucchini

Servings:4

Cooking Time: 17 Minutes

Ingredients:

- 4 zucchini, quartered lengthwise
- 2 tablespoons Garlic Oil
- ¼ cup freshly grated Parmesan cheese
- ½ teaspoon chopped fresh thyme leaves
- ½ teaspoon sea salt
- ¼ teaspoon freshly ground black pepper

Directions:

1. Preheat the oven to 350°F.

2. In a large bowl, toss together the zucchini, garlic oil, cheese, thyme, salt, and pepper. Place the zucchini, skin-side down, in a single layer on a rimmed baking sheet.

3. Bake for about 15 minutes, until soft.

4. Set the oven to broil.

5. Broil the zucchini for 2 to 3 minutes, until browned and crisp.

Nutrition Info:

- Calories:183; Total Fat: 13g; Saturated Fat: 5g; Carbohydrates: 8g; Fiber: 2g; Sodium: 517mg; Protein: 12g

Chive Dip

Servings:10

Cooking Time: 30 Minutes

Ingredients:

- 2 tbsp parsley, fresh, chopped finely
- 1 cup mayonnaise

- 2 tbsp chives, dried
- 2 tbsp oil (best with onion-infused but can be substituted with other approved oils)
- Pinch of salt
- 1 tsp lemon juice

Directions:

1. Mix the mayonnaise, oil, chives, salt, and parsley together in a bowl. Add lemon juice or herbs of choice to taste.

2. Chill in the fridge for 30 minutes and serve with approved fresh vegetables or chips.

Nutrition Info:

- 82g Calories, 7.8g Total fat, 1.2g Saturated fat, 2.9g Carbohydrates, 0.3 g Fiber, 0.4g Protein, 0.8g Sodium.

Cucumber And Sesame Salad

Servings:4

Cooking Time: 0 Minutes

Ingredients:

- 4 medium cucumbers, peeled and chopped
- 6 scallions, green parts only, chopped
- 1 tablespoon sesame seeds
- 1 teaspoon sesame oil
- ¼ cup Cilantro-Lime Vinaigrette

Directions:

1. In a large bowl, combine the cucumbers, scallions, and sesame seeds.

2. In a small bowl, whisk together the sesame oil and vinaigrette. Add the dressing to the cucumber mix and toss to coat.

Nutrition Info:

- Calories:145; Total Fat: 10g; Saturated Fat: 2g; Carbohydrates: 14g; Fiber: 2g; Sodium: 10mg; Protein: 3g

Warm Spinach Salad

Servings:4

Cooking Time: 8 Minutes

Ingredients:

- 6 cups fresh baby spinach
- 4 bacon slices, chopped
- 4 scallions, green parts only, finely chopped
- ¼ cup red wine vinegar
- ½ teaspoon sea salt
- ¼ teaspoon freshly ground black pepper

Directions:

1. Place the spinach in a large bowl and refrigerate until ready to serve.

2. In a large skillet over medium-high heat, cook the bacon for about 5 minutes, stirring occasionally, until browned.

With a slotted spoon, transfer the bacon to a plate and set it aside. Leave the fat in the pan. Return the skillet to medium-high heat.

3. Stir the scallions, vinegar, salt, and pepper into the bacon fat. Bring to a simmer. Reduce the heat to low and cook the dressing for 3 to 5 minutes, stirring occasionally, until it thickens.

4. Pour the warm dressing over the spinach and gently toss to coat and lightly wilt the leaves.

Nutrition Info:

- Calories:172; Total Fat: 12g; Saturated Fat: 4g; Carbohydrates: 3g; Fiber: 1g; Sodium: 928mg; Protein: 12g

Chopped Italian Salad

Servings:4

Cooking Time: 0 Minutes

Ingredients:

- 4 cups chopped romaine lettuce
- 8 cherry tomatoes, halved
- 1 medium zucchini, chopped
- 1 cup black olives, halved
- ¼ cup Italian Balsamic Vinaigrette

Directions:

1. In a medium bowl, combine the lettuce, tomatoes, zucchini, and olives.

2. Add the vinaigrette and toss to coat.

Nutrition Info:

- Calories:158; Total Fat: 10g; Saturated Fat: 2g; Carbohydrates: 16g; Fiber: 5g; Sodium: 433mg; Protein: 3g

Tomato, Basil, And Olive Risotto

Servings:4

Cooking Time: 40 Minutes

Ingredients:

- 3 cups homemade (onion- and garlic-free) chicken or vegetable broth
- 3 tablespoons unsalted butter, divided
- 2 tablespoons olive oil
- 1 cup Arborio rice
- 1 (14-ounce) can onion- and garlic-free diced tomatoes, drained
- 6 Kalamata olives, finely chopped
- ½ cup chopped fresh basil
- ¾ cup freshly grated Parmesan cheese

Directions:

1. In a small saucepan, bring the broth to a boil over medium heat. Reduce the heat to low to maintain a gentle simmer.

2. In a large saucepan, heat 1 tablespoon of the butter and the olive oil over medium heat. Add the rice and stir to coat. Add the tomatoes, olives, and about 1 cup of the broth and cook, stirring constantly, until most of the liquid has been absorbed.

3. Continue adding the broth, one ladleful at time, and cook, stirring frequently, until each addition is fully absorbed, about 30 minutes. When all the liquid has been used up and the rice is tender, remove the pan from the heat and stir in the basil, the remaining butter, and the cheese.

4. Cover the risotto and let rest for about 5 minutes. Serve hot, garnished with additional cheese, if desired.

Nutrition Info:

- Calories: 583; Protein: 44g; Total Fat: 26g; Saturated Fat: 12g; Carbohydrates: 43g; Fiber: 3g; Sodium: 456mg;

Rice Paper "spring Rolls" With Satay Sauce

Servings:3

Cooking Time: 30 Minutes

Ingredients:

- Satay sauce
- 4 tbsp peanut butter
- 2 tbsp lemon juice
- 2 tbsp water
- 2 tsp brown sugar
- 1 tsp white sugar
- Rice spring rolls
- 12 rice paper wrappers
- 1 cucumber, small
- 1 carrot, large, cut into matchstick pieces
- 1 cup red cabbage, sliced finely
- ½ cup mint, fresh, chopped roughly
- ½ cup cilantro, fresh, roughly cut

Directions:

1. Prepare the satay sauce first. Soften the peanut butter in a microwaveable bowl for about 30 seconds. Place the rest of the sauce ingredients into the bowl and use a fork to mix until smooth. Add a tbsp of water if the mixture is too thick.

2. Put warm water into a large bowl. One at a time, dip a rice wrapper into the water until it softens slightly then place it on a clean, damp cloth.

3. Place a small amount of the fresh vegetables and herbs onto the bottom third of the wrapper. Do not overfill as it will affect the rolling process.

4. To roll, first, fold the small sides up like a burrito. Next, pull the bottom of the wrapper up gently over the filling. It is best to hold the end with the filling in it in your hands.

5. The rolls are best when dipped in the satay sauce.

Nutrition Info:

- 472g Calories, 23.5g Total fat, 4.7g Saturated fat, 48.2g Carbohydrates, 3.7 g Fiber, 24.4g Protein, 17g Sodium.

Roasted Potato Wedges

Servings:4
Cooking Time: 30 Minutes
Ingredients:

- 1 pound Yukon Gold potatoes, quartered lengthwise
- 2 tablespoons Garlic Oil
- 1 tablespoon chopped fresh rosemary leaves
- ½ teaspoon sea salt
- ¼ teaspoon freshly ground black pepper

Directions:

1. Preheat the oven to 425°F.
2. In a large bowl, toss the potatoes with the garlic oil, rosemary, salt, and pepper. Divide them between two baking sheets and spread into a single layer.
3. Bake for about 30 minutes until the potatoes are browned. Stir them once or twice and rotate the pans (switching racks) halfway through cooking.

Nutrition Info:

- Calories:143; Total Fat: 7g; Saturated Fat: 1g; Carbohydrates: 19g; Fiber: 2g; Sodium: 241mg; Protein: 2g

Easy Rice Pilaf

Servings:4
Cooking Time: 10 Minutes
Ingredients:

- 2 tablespoons extra-virgin olive oil
- 6 scallions, green parts only, chopped
- 2 carrots, chopped
- 2 cups cooked brown rice
- ¼ cup pine nuts
- ½ teaspoon sea salt
- ⅛ teaspoon freshly ground black pepper
- ¼ cup chopped fresh parsley leaves

Directions:

1. In a large skillet over medium-high heat, heat the olive oil until it shimmers.
2. Add the scallions and carrots. Cook for about 4 minutes, stirring occasionally.
3. Stir in the brown rice, pine nuts, salt, and pepper. Cook for about 5 minutes more, stirring occasionally, until the rice is warm.
4. Stir in the parsley just before serving.

Nutrition Info:

- Calories:307; Total Fat: 13g; Saturated Fat: 2g; Carbohydrates: 43g; Fiber: 2g; Sodium: 263mg; Protein: 5g

Crispy Rosemary-roasted Potatoes

Servings:6
Cooking Time: 60 Minutes
Ingredients:

- 2 pounds small red- or white-skinned new potatoes, halved
- 2 tablespoons olive oil
- 2 tablespoons chopped fresh rosemary
- 1 teaspoon salt

Directions:

1. Preheat the oven to 400°F.
2. Toss the potatoes, oil, rosemary, and salt together in a large baking dish. Spread the potatoes out in an even layer and roast in the preheated oven for about 60 minutes, until the potatoes are nicely browned and crisp. Serve hot.

Nutrition Info:

- Calories: 106; Protein: 1g; Total Fat: 5g; Saturated Fat: 1g; Carbohydrates: 13g; Fiber: 2g; Sodium: 401mg;

Quinoa With Swiss Chard

Servings:4
Cooking Time: 25 Minutes
Ingredients:

- 1 tablespoon Garlic Oil (here)
- 1 bunch Swiss chard, stems removed and leaves julienned
- 1 teaspoon ground cumin
- 1 teaspoon ground coriander
- 2 teaspoons paprika
- ½ teaspoon salt
- 1 cup quinoa
- 2 cups homemade (onion- and garlic-free) vegetable broth

Directions:

1. Heat the oil in a large skillet set over medium heat. Add the Swiss chard, cumin, coriander, paprika, salt, quinoa, and broth and bring to a boil.
2. Cover, reduce the heat to low, and cook for 20 minutes, until the liquid has evaporated and the quinoa is tender. Serve hot.

Nutrition Info:

- Calories: 207; Protein: 9g; Total Fat: 7g; Saturated Fat: 1g; Carbohydrates: 29g; Fiber: 4g; Sodium: 753mg;

Rice Pilaf With Vegetables

Servings:4

Cooking Time: 25 Minutes

Ingredients:

- 1 tablespoon Garlic Oil (here)
- ½ medium red bell pepper, finely chopped
- 2 teaspoons salt, divided
- 2 cups long-grain white rice
- Pinch saffron threads steeped in ¼ cup hot (not boiling) water
- 2½ cups homemade (onion- and garlic-free) vegetable or chicken broth
- 2 bay leaves
- 1 cup fresh or frozen green beans, cut into 2-inch pieces
- ¼ cup golden raisins

Directions:

1. Preheat the oven to 350°F.
2. Heat the Garlic Oil in a medium, oven-safe saucepan over medium heat. Add the bell pepper and ½ teaspoon of the salt and cook, stirring, for 3 to 4 minutes, until the pepper begins to soften.
3. Add the rice and cook, stirring frequently, until the rice just begins to brown, for about 3 minutes.
4. Add the saffron threads and their soaking water, broth, bay leaves, and the remaining 1½ teaspoons salt. Increase the heat and bring to a boil.
5. Scatter the green beans over the top of the rice, cover the pan, and bake in the preheated oven for 15 minutes. Remove the pan from the oven and let rest, without removing the lid, for 15 minutes. Just before serving, fluff with a fork and stir in the raisins. Serve hot.

Nutrition Info:

- Calories: 405; Protein: 11g; Total Fat: 2g; Saturated Fat: 0g; Carbohydrates: 85g; Fiber: 3g; Sodium: 1648mg;

Coconut Rice

Servings:4

Cooking Time: 30 Minutes

Ingredients:

- 2 cups jasmine rice
- 1 cup water
- 1 (14-ounce) can light coconut milk
- 1 teaspoon salt

Directions:

1. In a medium saucepan, combine the rice, water, coconut milk, and salt, and bring to a boil over high heat. Reduce the heat to low, cover, and cook for 30 to 40 minutes, until the rice is tender and the liquid has evaporated.

2. Remove the pot from the heat and let the rice rest, without taking the lid off, for about 10 minutes. Just before serving, fluff with a fork. Serve hot.

Nutrition Info:

- Calories: 416; Protein: 7g; Total Fat: 8g; Saturated Fat: 0g; Carbohydrates: 76g; Fiber: 1g; Sodium: 610mg;

Sesame-broccoli Stir-fry

Servings:4

Cooking Time: 10 Minutes

Ingredients:

- 2 tablespoons extra-virgin olive oil
- 2 cups broccoli florets
- 2 tablespoons gluten-free soy sauce
- ½ teaspoon sesame oil
- 2 tablespoons sesame seeds

Directions:

1. In a large skillet over medium-high heat, heat the olive oil until it shimmers.
2. Add the broccoli. Cook for about 6 minutes, stirring occasionally, until crisp-tender.
3. Stir in the soy sauce and sesame oil. Bring to a simmer. Reduce the heat to medium and cook for 3 minutes, stirring.
4. Toss with the sesame seeds before serving.

Nutrition Info:

- Calories:111; Total Fat: 10g; Saturated Fat: 1g; Carbohydrates: 5g; Fiber: 2g; Sodium: 466mg; Protein: 3g

Lemony Grilled Zucchini With Feta And Pine Nuts

Servings:4

Cooking Time: 8 Minutes

Ingredients:

- 3 ounces feta, crumbled
- 2 tablespoons chopped fresh mint leaves
- 2 tablespoons olive oil, divided
- 1 teaspoon fresh lemon juice
- 1 teaspoon lemon zest
- 2 scallions, green parts only, thinly sliced
- 2-3 zucchini (about 1½ pounds), halved lengthwise and cut into 3-inch pieces
- 1 teaspoon salt
- 2 tablespoons toasted pine nuts

Directions:

1. In a small bowl, stir together the feta, mint, 1 tablespoon of the oil, lemon juice, lemon zest, and scallions.
2. Brush the remaining tablespoon of oil onto the zucchini and sprinkle with the salt.

3. Heat a grill or grill pan to high heat. Cook the zucchini for 3 to 4 minutes per side, until grill marks appear and the zucchini is tender. Transfer the cooked zucchini to a serving platter, and spoon the topping over the top. Sprinkle the pine nuts over the top and serve immediately.

Nutrition Info:

- Calories: 176; Protein: 3g; Total Fat: 15g; Saturated Fat: 5g; Carbohydrates: 7g; Fiber: 2g; Sodium: 836mg;

Roasted Root Vegetable Salad

Servings:4
Cooking Time: 45 Minutes
Ingredients:

- 4 carrots, cut into ½-inch pieces
- 4 red potatoes, cut into ½-inch cubes
- 1 fennel bulb, cut into ½-inch pieces
- 2 tablespoons extra-virgin olive oil
- ¼ cup Lemon-Dill Vinaigrette

Directions:

1. Preheat the oven to 400°F.
2. Line two baking sheets with parchment paper.
3. In a large bowl, toss the carrots, potatoes, and fennel with the olive oil. Divide the vegetables between the two prepared sheets and spread in a single layer.
4. Roast for about 45 minutes, until the veggies are browned, stirring occasionally, rotating the pans and switching racks halfway through cooking. Cool slightly.
5. Drizzle the vinaigrette over the vegetables and toss to coat.

Nutrition Info:

- Calories:342; Total Fat: 15g; Saturated Fat: 3g; Carbohydrates: 49g; Fiber: 8g; Sodium: 85mg; Protein: 6g

Orange-maple Glazed Carrots

Servings:4
Cooking Time: 20 Minutes
Ingredients:

- 2 tablespoons pure maple syrup
- 1 tablespoon extra-virgin olive oil
- Juice of 1 orange
- Zest of 1 orange
- ½ teaspoon sea salt
- ¼ teaspoon freshly ground black pepper
- 2 cups baby carrots

Directions:

1. Preheat the oven to 400°F.
2. Line a baking sheet with parchment paper and set it aside.

3. In a medium bowl, whisk together the maple syrup, olive oil, orange juice, orange zest, salt, and pepper.
4. Add the carrots and toss to coat.
5. Spread the carrots in a single layer on the prepared sheet. Roast for 20 minutes, or until browned.

Nutrition Info:

- Calories:101; Total Fat: 4g; Saturated Fat: <1g; Carbohydrates: 17g; Fiber: 2g; Sodium: 298mg; Protein: 1g

Seared Green Beans With Sesame Oil

Servings:4
Cooking Time: 10 Minutes
Ingredients:

- 1½ pounds green beans, trimmed
- 2 tablespoons dark sesame oil
- Salt

Directions:

1. Bring a large saucepan of salted water to a boil over high heat. Add the green beans and cook just until tender but still bright green, for 2 to 3 minutes. Drain well.
2. Heat the oil in a large skillet over high heat. When the oil is very hot, add the green beans (you might have to cook the beans in batches to avoid crowding the pan), tossing occasionally, for 3 to 4 minutes, until the beans begin to blacken and blister in spots. Transfer to a serving platter and sprinkle with salt. Serve hot.

Nutrition Info:

- Calories: 113; Protein: 3g; Total Fat: 7g; Saturated Fat: 1g; Carbohydrates: 12g; Fiber: 6g; Sodium: 49mg;

Quick Creamy Coleslaw

Servings:4
Cooking Time: 0 Minutes
Ingredients:

- 1 head green cabbage, shredded, or 1 (8-ounce) package preshredded green cabbage
- 4 scallions, green parts only, chopped
- 2 carrots, grated
- ¼ cup Low-FODMAP Mayonnaise
- 1 tablespoon apple cider vinegar
- ¼ teaspoon ground mustard
- ½ teaspoon sea salt
- ¼ teaspoon freshly ground black pepper

Directions:

1. In a large bowl, combine the cabbage, scallions, and carrots.
2. In a small bowl, whisk together the mayonnaise, vinegar, mustard, salt, and pepper. Add the sauce to the coleslaw and toss to coat.

Nutrition Info:

- Calories:121; Total Fat: 5g; Saturated Fat: <1g; Carbohydrates: 18g; Fiber: 6g; Sodium: 394mg; Protein: 3g

Garden Medley

Servings:6
Cooking Time: 25 Minutes
Ingredients:
- ¾ cup water
- 4 carrots, cut into strips
- ¼ cup butter or margarine
- 1 yellow squash, cut lengthwise
- 3 tbsp green pepper, chopped
- 1 tbsp chopped basil
- Pinch of salt

Directions:
1. In a pot, bring the water to a boil and add the carrots. Cover the pot and let cook for 8-10 minutes.
2. Drain the water from the pot and add the butter to melt, stirring to keep the butter from burning. Add the pepper, basil, and salt to the pot and mix well.
3. Place the squash into the pot and cook covered for 8 minutes. The squash should be crispy but still tender.
4. Once the vegetables are tender, serve on a plate.

Nutrition Info:
- 149g Calories, 11g Total fat, 6g Saturated fat, 10.5g Carbohydrates, 2 g Fiber, 2g Protein, 12g Sodium.

Caprese Salad

Servings:4
Cooking Time: 0 Minutes
Ingredients:
- 2 cups torn romaine lettuce
- 20 cherry tomatoes, quartered
- ¼ cup loosely packed fresh basil leaves, chopped
- 4 ounces mozzarella cheese, chopped
- ¼ cup Italian Basil Vinaigrette

Directions:
1. In a large bowl, combine the lettuce, tomatoes, basil, and cheese.
2. Add the vinaigrette and toss to coat.

Nutrition Info:
- Calories:265; Total Fat: 14g; Saturated Fat: 5g; Carbohydrates: 26g; Fiber: 8g; Sodium: 202mg; Protein: 14g

Roast Vegetables

Servings:6
Cooking Time: 45 Minutes
Ingredients:
- Vegetables
- 1 ½ cups carrot

- 1 ½ cups parsnip
- 1 ½ cups pumpkin
- 2 red bell peppers
- 1 ¾ cup potatoes
- 1 ⅓ cup baby beetroot, drained
- Pinch of salt
- Pinch of pepper
- Glaze
- 4 tbsp olive oil
- 1 ½ tbsp ginger, crushed
- 1 tbsp maple syrup

Directions:
1. Preheat the oven to 375ºF and line a baking tray with parchment paper.
2. To prepare the vegetables, first, clean them and cut the carrots in half, if using large ones. Deseed the pepper and slice. Remove the skin of the pumpkin, parsnips, and potatoes before cutting into chunks. Cut the drained baby beetroots in half.
3. In the tray, place the vegetables in one layer and toss with a small amount of oil, salt, and pepper. Place in the oven.
4. The glaze is made by mixing the ingredients together in a bowl.
5. Baste the vegetables by coating them in a layer of glaze two to three times while cooking. Be sure to flip the vegetables halfway through the cooking process. Remove after 45 minutes, when they should be golden and crispy.

Nutrition Info:
- 316g Calories, 10.2g Total fat, 1.5g Saturated fat, 52.9g Carbohydrates, 10.3 g Fiber, 6.1g Protein, 15.8g Sodium.

Kale And Red Bell Pepper Salad

Servings:4
Cooking Time: 0 Minutes
Ingredients:
- 4 cups stemmed, chopped kale, or 1 (9-ounce) bag kale salad
- 1 red bell pepper, stemmed, seeded, and chopped
- ¼ cup pepitas (hulled pumpkin seeds)
- ¼ cup Balsamic Vinaigrette

Directions:
1. In a large bowl, combine the kale, bell pepper, and pepitas.
2. Add the vinaigrette and toss to coat.

Nutrition Info:
- Calories:149; Total Fat: 10g; Saturated Fat: 2g; Carbohydrates: 12g; Fiber: 2g; Sodium: 151mg; Protein: 4g

Pumpkin Cornbread

Servings:8
Cooking Time: 25 Minutes

Ingredients:

- 1 ¼ cups corn flour
- 1 cup gluten-free, all-purpose flour
- 2 tsp of baking powder
- ¾ tsp of baking soda
- 1 tbsp white sugar
- 1 tbsp brown sugar
- Pinch of salt
- 1 ½ tsp sage, dried
- ½ cup spring onions, green part only
- 1 cup cheese, cheddar or any other approved
- 1 cup pumpkin, puréed
- 1 cup lactose-free milk
- 2 tbsp olive oil

Directions:

1. Preheat the oven to 350°F.
2. Chop the spring onions finely and grate the cheese.
3. Mix the flour, baking powder, baking soda, sugar, salt, and sage together in a bowl.
4. Melt the butter and use it to grease an ovenproof skillet. Once greased, add the remainder of the butter in the bowl.
5. Mix all the ingredients together thoroughly, then scoop and spread the mixture into the skillet.
6. Bake for 30-35 minutes. When finished, the top should be golden. Insert a skewer into the middle of the pan, and if it comes out clean, the bread is fully cooked.

Nutrition Info:

- 230g Calories, 5.8g Total fat, 1.1g Saturated fat, 39.5g Carbohydrates, 2 g Fiber, 4.9g Protein, 9.8g Sodium.

Creamy Oven-baked Polenta With Corn And Parmesan Cheese

Servings:6
Cooking Time: 60 Minutes

Ingredients:

- Oil for preparing the baking dish
- 1 cup uncooked polenta
- 3½ cups water
- 1 cup fresh or frozen corn kernels
- 1 teaspoon salt
- ⅓ cup freshly grated Parmesan cheese
- 2 tablespoons butter

Directions:

1. Preheat the oven to 350°F.
2. Oil an 8-by-8-inch baking dish. In this dish, stir together the polenta, water, corn, and salt.
3. Bake, uncovered, in the preheated oven for 45 minutes. Stir in the cheese and butter, and bake for an additional 15 minutes. Serve hot.

Nutrition Info:

- Calories: 179; Protein: 6g; Total Fat: 6g; Saturated Fat: 4g; Carbohydrates: 26g; Fiber: 1g; Sodium: 508mg;

Chapter 8 Snacks & Desserts Recipes

Smoked Trout Brandade

Servings:6
Cooking Time: 35 Minutes
Ingredients:
- 1 pound russet potatoes, peeled and cut into chunks
- 8 ounces smoked trout, skin and bones removed, flaked into small pieces
- ¾ cup lactose-free milk
- 2 tablespoons lemon juice
- ¼ cup olive oil
- 2 tablespoons Garlic Oil (here)
- ½ teaspoon salt
- ½ teaspoon freshly ground black pepper
- 2 tablespoons freshly grated Parmesan cheese

Directions:
1. Bring a large saucepan of water to a boil over high heat. Add the potatoes and cook for 15 to 20 minutes, until they are tender. Drain potatoes and set aside.
2. Preheat the oven to 400°F.
3. In a large bowl, combine the trout and milk, and mash to a paste. Add the lemon juice and the cooked potatoes, and stir with a fork until well combined. Add the olive oil, Garlic Oil, salt, and pepper, and mix thoroughly. Taste and adjust the seasoning as needed.
4. Spoon the mixture into a shallow baking dish, top with the cheese, and bake in the preheated oven for about 15 minutes, until the cheese is melted and golden brown. Serve hot.

Nutrition Info:
- Calories: 239; Protein: 14g; Total Fat: 14g; Saturated Fat: 3g; Carbohydrates: 15g; Fiber: 2g; Sodium: 290mg;

Almond Cookies

Servings:x
Cooking Time:x
Ingredients:
- MAKES ABOUT 40
- ¾ cup (90 g) almond flour
- 1 tablespoon plus 1 teaspoon cornstarch
- ½ teaspoon gluten-free baking powder
- 1 large egg white
- ½ cup (110 g) superfine sugar
- 1 teaspoon finely grated lemon zest
- 3 drops almond extract
- 1 tablespoon (15 g) unsalted butter, melted

Directions:
1. Preheat the oven to 275°F (140°C). Line two baking sheets with parchment paper.
2. Combine the almond flour, cornstarch, and baking powder in a small bowl. Beat the egg white in a clean medium bowl with a handheld electric mixer until soft peaks form. Gradually beat in the sugar. Continue beating for 5 minutes more or until stiff peaks form. Add the almond flour mixture, lemon zest, almond extract, and melted butter and gently mix together with a large metal spoon.
3. Roll 2 teaspoons of the dough into a ball. Repeat with the remaining dough to make about 40 balls, placing them on the baking sheets and leaving a little room for spreading. Flatten slightly. Bake for 25 minutes, until they have started turning a light golden brown.
4. Cool on the sheets for 5 minutes, then transfer to a wire rack to cool completely.

Nutrition Info:
- 25 calories; 1 g protein; 1 g total fat; 0 g saturated fat; 3 g carbohydrates; 0 g fiber; 7 mg sodium

Amaretti

Servings:x
Cooking Time:x
Ingredients:
- MAKES 20–25
- 1 cup (120 g) almond flour (preferably finely ground)
- ¾ cup (120 g) confectioners' sugar
- 1 tablespoon plus 1 teaspoon cornstarch
- 2 large egg whites
- ⅓ cup (75 g) superfine sugar
- 1 teaspoon almond extract

Directions:
1. Preheat the oven to 325°F (170°C). Line two baking sheets with parchment paper.
2. Place the almond flour, confectioners' sugar, and cornstarch in a medium bowl and mix together well.
3. Beat the egg whites in a clean medium bowl with a handheld electric mixer until soft peaks form. Add the superfine sugar, 1 tablespoon at a time, and beat until shiny and stiff peaks form. Add the almond extract and beat to combine well. Gently fold in the almond flour mixture with a large metal spoon until just blended.
4. Place rounded teaspoons of the batter on the baking sheets, leaving room for spreading. Smooth the top of each cookie with the back of a metal spoon. Bake for 18 to 25

minutes, until lightly golden. Turn off the oven, leave the door ajar, and let the cookies cool and dry out in the oven.

Nutrition Info:

- 53 calories; 1 g protein; 2 g total fat; 0 g saturated fat; 8 g carbohydrates; 0 g fiber; 6 mg sodium

Dark Chocolate–macadamia Nut Brownies

Servings:18

Cooking Time:x

Ingredients:

- Nonstick cooking spray
- 10 tablespoons (1¼ sticks/150 g) unsalted butter, cut into cubes
- 10½ ounces (300 g) good-quality dark chocolate, broken into pieces
- 1¼ cups (275 g) packed light brown sugar
- ⅔ cup (85 g) superfine white rice flour
- ¼ cup (35 g) cornstarch
- 1 teaspoon xanthan gum or guar gum
- 3 large eggs
- 2 teaspoons vanilla extract
- ½ cup (95 g) dark chocolate chips
- ½ cup (125 ml) light cream
- ¾ cup (100 g) roughly chopped macadamia nuts (optional)

Directions:

1. Preheat the oven to 325°F (160°C). Grease an 11 x 7-inch (29 × 19 cm) baking pan with cooking spray and line with parchment paper.

2. Combine the butter and chocolate in a medium saucepan over low heat and stir until melted and smooth. Add the brown sugar and stir until dissolved. Transfer to a large bowl and let cool to room temperature.

3. Sift the rice flour, cornstarch, and xanthan gum three times into a separate bowl (or whisk in a bowl until well combined).

4. Stir the eggs into the chocolate mixture, one at a time. Add the sifted flour mixture, vanilla, chocolate chips, cream, and macadamia nuts (if using). Mix well, spoon into the baking pan, and smooth the surface.

5. Bake for 20 minutes, then cover with foil and bake for 20 to 25 minutes more, until just firm to the touch.

6. Remove from the oven and let cool in the pan to room temperature. Transfer to the refrigerator for 2 to 3 hours or overnight, until firm.

7. Turn out onto a cutting board, peel off the parchment paper, and cut into squares to serve.

Nutrition Info:

- 278 calories; 3 g protein; 18 g total fat; 9 g saturated fat; 31 g carbohydrates; 2 g fiber; 23 mg sodium

Banana Ice Cream

Servings:2

Cooking Time: 0 Minutes

Ingredients:

- 3 bananas, peeled and frozen
- 3 packets stevia
- ¼ teaspoon ground nutmeg

Directions:

1. In a blender or food processor, combine the bananas, stevia, and nutmeg.

2. Blend until smooth.

Nutrition Info:

- Calories:106; Total Fat: <1g; Saturated Fat: 0g; Carbohydrates: 27g; Fiber: 3g; Sodium: 1mg; Protein: 1g

Ginger Cookies

Servings:20

Cooking Time: 20 Minutes

Ingredients:

- ½ cup warm water
- 2 tbsp chia seeds
- ½ cup brown sugar
- 2 tbsp coconut oil
- 3 tbsp ginger, ground
- 1 tbsp cinnamon
- 1 cup buckwheat flour
- 1 cup brown rice flour
- Peanut butter or dark chocolate for filling

Directions:

1. Preheat the oven to 350°F and line a baking tray with parchment paper.

2. Put the chia seeds into warm water and let sit for 5 minutes.

3. In a bowl, mix the chia seeds and water, sugar, oil, ginger, and cinnamon.

4. Add the flour slowly then create balls with the dough, 1 tablespoon per ball to start with. You can add more dough to make larger cookies. Place them on the baking tray.

5. Make a hole in each ball of dough before baking for 20 minutes.

6. Add the filling while the cookies are still warm.

Nutrition Info:

- 85g Calories, 3g Total fat, 1.5g Saturated fat, 13g Carbohydrates, 1.8 g Fiber, 2g Protein, 1.8g Sodium.

Rich White Chocolate Cake

Servings:12
Cooking Time:x

Ingredients:

- Nonstick cooking spray
- 15 tablespoons (2 sticks minus 1 tablespoon/225 g) unsalted butter, cut into cubes
- 7 ounces (200 g) good-quality white chocolate, broken into pieces
- 2¼ cups (475 g) packed light brown sugar
- ¾ cup (65 g) soy flour
- ¾ cup (95 g) tapioca flour
- 1 cup (130 g) superfine white rice flour
- ½ cup (75 g) cornstarch
- 2 teaspoons xanthan gum or guar gum
- 1 teaspoon baking soda
- 1 teaspoon gluten-free baking powder
- 2 teaspoons vanilla extract
- 2 large eggs
- Confectioners' sugar, for dusting

Directions:

1. Preheat the oven to 300°F (150°C). Grease a 9-inch (23 cm) springform pan with cooking spray.
2. Combine the butter, white chocolate, brown sugar, and 1½ cups (375 ml) hot water in a medium heatproof bowl or the top part of a double boiler. Set over a saucepan of simmering water or the bottom part of the double boiler (make sure the bottom of the bowl does not touch the water) and stir until the chocolate and butter are melted and everything is well combined. Set aside to cool to room temperature.
3. Sift the soy flour, tapioca flour, rice flour, cornstarch, xanthan gum, baking soda, and baking powder three times into a medium bowl (or whisk in the bowl until well combined). Add the cooled white chocolate mixture, vanilla, and eggs and beat with a handheld electric mixer until smooth.
4. Pour the batter into the pan and bake for 45 minutes. Cover with foil and bake for 15 to 30 minutes more, until firm to the touch (a toothpick inserted into the center should come out clean).
5. Cool in the pan for 15 minutes, then remove the outer ring and turn out onto a wire rack to cool completely. Dust with confectioners' sugar before serving.

Nutrition Info:

- 496 calories; 7 g protein; 21 g total fat; 13 g saturated fat; 73 g carbohydrates; 1 g fiber; 196 mg sodium

Orange Biscuits

Servings:24
Cooking Time: 25 Minutes

Ingredients:

- Biscuits
- ½ tsp of baking soda
- Pinch of salt
- 2 cups flour, gluten-free or oat
- 1 tsp orange zest
- ½ cup butter
- ½ cup brown sugar
- ½ cup white sugar
- 1 egg, large
- 2 tbsp orange juice, fresh
- 1 tsp vanilla extract
- Glaze
- 1 cup powdered sugar
- 1 ½ tsp orange zest
- 1 ½ tbsp orange juice, fresh

Directions:

1. Preheat the oven to 350°F.
2. Use a grater to zest the orange. Do not grate the white layer.
3. Whisk the salt, baking soda, zest, and flour together in a large bowl.
4. In a different bowl, beat the butter and sugar together using an electric hand beater until the mixture is fluffy and not grainy. Add 2 tablespoons of orange juice, the egg, and the vanilla to the mixture.
5. Combine the dry and wet ingredients and mix until the dough is sticky. Form balls using about 2 tablespoons of dough. Place the balls on trays that are covered in parchment paper, then flatten the dough slightly before baking for 15-20 minutes. Rotate the trays halfway through. When the edges are golden brown, remove the trays and let them cool down on cooling racks.
6. For the icing, mix the powdered sugar, orange juice, and zest together. The icing should be sticky and not runny. Use a teaspoon to ice the biscuits once they are cool.

Nutrition Info:

- 154g Calories, 4.1g Total fat, 0.6g Saturated fat, 27.8g Carbohydrates, 1.7 g Fiber, 1.3g Protein, 14.6g Sodium.

Deviled Eggs

Servings:6
Cooking Time: 0 Minutes
Ingredients:

- 6 hardboiled eggs, peeled and halved lengthwise
- ½ cup Low-FODMAP Mayonnaise
- 2 tablespoons Dijon mustard
- 3 scallions, green parts only, minced
- ½ teaspoon sea salt
- ½ teaspoon ground paprika
- ⅛ teaspoon freshly ground black pepper

Directions:

1. Into a small bowl, scoop the egg yolks from the whites. Set the whites aside.
2. Add the mayonnaise, mustard, scallions, salt, paprika, and pepper to the yolks and mash them with a fork.
3. Spoon the mixture back into the egg whites.

Nutrition Info:

- Calories:240; Total Fat: 18g; Saturated Fat: 4g; Carbohydrates: 11g; Fiber: 1g; Sodium: 537mg; Protein: 10g

Herbed Polenta "fries"

Servings:16
Cooking Time: 40 Minutes
Ingredients:

- Olive oil for brushing
- 3¼ cups cold water
- 1 cup polenta
- 1 teaspoon chopped fresh sage
- 1 teaspoon chopped fresh rosemary
- ¾ teaspoon salt
- ½ cup grated Parmesan
- 2 tablespoons unsalted butter, cut into chunks

Directions:

1. Brush an 8-by-8-inch baking dish with olive oil.
2. In a medium saucepan set over medium heat, whisk together the water, polenta, sage, rosemary, and salt and bring to a boil. Reduce the heat to medium-low and cook, stirring continuously, until the mixture thickens, for 15 to 20 minutes. Add the cheese and butter, and stir to incorporate.
3. Spoon the polenta mixture into the prepared baking dish and spread it into a flat, even layer. Refrigerate, uncovered, for about 45 minutes, until set.
4. Preheat the broiler to high and line a large baking sheet with oiled aluminum foil.
5. Invert the pan of polenta to unmold it, then cut the polenta into sticks about 4 inches by 1 inch by 1 inch. Brush the sticks with oil and arrange them in a single layer on the prepared baking sheet. Broil for 15 to 20 minutes, until golden brown and crisp. Serve immediately.

6. Olives have a deep, rich umami flavor—especially helpful in seasoning when you can't use onions and garlic in your cooking.
7. This flavorful paste is fantastic spread on gluten-free crackers or cucumber rounds.
8. Dollop it in stew or soup to increase depth of flavor.
9. You won't taste any fishiness from the anchovies here, but feel free to omit them if you are vegetarian or they are simply not your cup of tea.
10. 1 cup pitted, cured black or green olives.
11. ¼ cup chopped flat-leaf parsley.
12. 1 tablespoon chopped fresh oregano.
13. 1 tablespoon capers, drained.
14. ½ teaspoon Dijon mustard.
15. 1 to 3 anchovy fillets (optional).
16. 1 tablespoon lemon juice.
17. 1½ teaspoons Garlic Oil (here).
18. 1½ teaspoons olive oil.
19. In a blender or food processor, combine all of the ingredients and pulse to a chunky paste.
20. You can also use a mortar and pestle to achieve the desired consistency.
21. Serve immediately or refrigerate for up to a week.

Nutrition Info:

- Calories: 314; Protein: 14g; Total Fat: 16g; Saturated Fat: 10g; Carbohydrates: 31g; Fiber: 1g; Sodium: 656mg;

Lemon Bar

Servings:16
Cooking Time: 50 Minutes
Ingredients:

- Crust
- 1 ½ cups gluten-free flour
- ½ cup white sugar
- ½ cup butter, unsalted
- 2 tbsp water
- Lemon
- 4 eggs, large
- ½ cup lemon juice
- 1 ½ cups sugar
- ¼ cup gluten-free flour
- Powdered sugar, to dust on top

Directions:

1. Preheat the oven to 350°F. Grease a square baking pan (9.5 inches by 9.5 inches) with butter and set aside.
2. Mix the flour and sugar together. Mix the butter into the flour until the mixture reaches a crumbly consistency. Add

the water and mix well. Press into the bottom of the pan and bake for 20-25 minutes.

3. In another bowl, whisk the eggs, lemon juice, sugar, and flour until smooth. Pour onto the baked crust.

4. Bake for another 25 minutes, remove from the oven, and allow to cool.

Nutrition Info:

- 212g Calories, 7.3g Total fat, 5.2g Saturated fat, 35.1g Carbohydrates, 1.4 g Fiber, 3.4g Protein, 25g Sodium.

Cinnamon-coconut Rice Pudding

Servings:4

Cooking Time: 40 Minutes

Ingredients:

- 1½ cups cold cooked rice
- 1 cup lactose-free milk
- 2½ cups coconut milk
- ⅓ cup sugar
- ¼ teaspoon salt
- ¾ teaspoon ground cinnamon
- ½ teaspoon vanilla extract

Directions:

1. In a medium saucepan, combine the rice, milk, coconut milk, sugar, and salt, and cook, uncovered, over medium heat, stirring frequently, for about 40 minutes, until the mixture thickens.

2. Remove from the heat, stir in the cinnamon and vanilla, and serve warm.

Nutrition Info:

- Calories: 261; Protein: 4g; Total Fat: 5g; Saturated Fat: 4g; Carbohydrates: 50g; Fiber: 1g; Sodium: 183mg;

Lemon Cheesecake

Servings:10

Cooking Time:x

Ingredients:

- 9 ounces (250 g) gluten-free vanilla cookies, crushed (about 2½ cups)
- 4 tablespoons (½ stick/60 g) unsalted butter, melted
- 1 heaping tablespoon unflavored gelatin powder
- One 8-ounce (225 g) package reduced-fat cream cheese, at room temperature
- ¾ cup (165 g) superfine sugar
- 2 tablespoons plus 2 teaspoons fresh lemon juice
- 1 to 2 heaping tablespoons grated lemon zest
- 1⅓ cups (300 ml) light whipping cream
- 1½ teaspoons unflavored gelatin powder
- 3 tablespoons (45 g) unsalted butter, cut into cubes, at room temperature

- ½ cup (110 g) superfine sugar
- 1 large egg yolk, lightly beaten
- 1 teaspoon grated lemon zest
- 2 tablespoons plus 2 teaspoons fresh lemon juice

Directions:

1. Mix together the crushed cookies and melted butter in a medium bowl. Press evenly into the bottom of an 8-inch (20 cm) springform pan. Refrigerate while you prepare the filling and topping.

2. To make the filling, add ½ cup (125 ml) cold water to a small heatproof bowl and whisk in the gelatin with a fork. Set aside for 5 minutes, or until the gelatin has begun to gel. Fill a larger bowl with boiling water, set the bowl containing the gelatin into it, and stir constantly until the gelatin has completely dissolved.

3. Combine the cream cheese, sugar, lemon juice, lemon zest, and dissolved gelatin in a food processor or blender and process for 1 to 2 minutes, until smooth.

4. Beat the cream in a medium bowl with a handheld electric mixer until thickened. Using a large metal spoon, fold the whipped cream into the cream cheese mixture. Pour the filling into the cookie crust. Cover and refrigerate for 3 hours, until set.

5. To make the topping, add ½ cup (125 ml) cold water to a small heatproof bowl and whisk in the gelatin with a fork. Set aside for 5 minutes, until the gelatin has begun to gel. Fill a larger bowl with boiling water, set the bowl containing the gelatin in it, and stir constantly until the gelatin has completely dissolved.

6. Combine the dissolved gelatin, butter, sugar, egg yolk, and lemon zest and juice in a small saucepan. Stir over low heat for about 15 minutes, until thick enough to coat the back of a spoon. Let cool to room temperature.

7. Pour the topping evenly over the filling, then return the cheesecake to the refrigerator for at least 3 hours, until set.

Nutrition Info:

- 380 calories; 7 g protein; 24 g total fat; 12 g saturated fat; 37 g carbohydrates; 1 g fiber; 160 mg sodium

Baked Veggie Chips

Servings:6

Cooking Time: 20 Minutes

Ingredients:

- 2 medium parsnips, peeled
- 2 medium zucchini
- 2 medium carrots, peeled
- Olive oil spray
- 1 teaspoon salt, plus more for garnish

Directions:

1. Using a handheld mandoline or a very sharp knife, slice the vegetables into very thin (1/16-inch) rounds.
2. Preheat the oven to 375°F.
3. Lightly oil 2 large baking sheets with olive oil spray.
4. Arrange the sliced vegetables on paper towels in a single layer, season with 1 teaspoon of salt, and let sit for 15 minutes. Dry the vegetables as thoroughly as possible with a paper towel.
5. Arrange the vegetable slices on the baking sheets in a single layer and coat with additional olive oil spray. Bake in the preheated oven for about 20 minutes.
6. Remove the chips from the oven, sprinkle them with additional salt, and let cool for 5 minutes. Serve immediately or cool to room temperature. The chips can then be stored in a sealed container on the countertop for up to 3 days.

Nutrition Info:
- Calories: 86; Protein: 2g; Total Fat: 1g; Saturated Fat: 0g; Carbohydrates: 20g; Fiber: 6g; Sodium: 417mg;

Crunchy Peanut Butter Cookies

Servings:18
Cooking Time: 10 Minutes

Ingredients:
- 1 cup all-natural peanut butter
- 1 cup sugar
- 1 teaspoon vanilla extract
- 1 egg, lightly beaten
- Pinch salt

Directions:
1. Preheat the oven to 350°F.
2. In a medium bowl, combine the peanut butter, sugar, vanilla, egg, and salt, and mix well. Drop the mixture by rounded spoonfuls onto an ungreased baking sheet, leaving about 1 inch of space between the cookies. Using the back of a fork, flatten the cookies, making a crosshatch pattern with the fork tines.
3. Bake in the preheated oven for about 10 minutes, until the edges of the cookies begin to turn golden brown. Transfer the cookies to a wire rack to cool. Serve at room temperature.

Nutrition Info:
- Calories: 135; Protein: 4g; Total Fat: 7g; Saturated Fat: 1g; Carbohydrates: 14g; Fiber: 1g; Sodium: 16mg;

Carrot Parsnip Chips

Servings:3
Cooking Time: 35 Minutes

Ingredients:
- 1 large parsnip, peeled and ends cut off
- 1 large carrot, peeled and ends cut off

- 2 tsp olive oil
- Pinch of salt
- 1 tsp thyme leaves

Directions:
1. Preheat the oven to 325°F.
2. Oil a baking tray lightly.
3. Peel the carrot and parsnip into long thin pieces and place onto the tray. Drizzle with oil and season.
4. Cook for 35 minutes, turning the vegetables 2 times during cooking.

Nutrition Info:
- 386g Calories, 10g Total fat, 1g Saturated fat, 73g Carbohydrates, 20 g Fiber, 6g Protein, 24g Sodium.

Summer Popsicle

Servings:4
Cooking Time: 2 Minutes

Ingredients:
- 4 carrots, large
- 3 oranges, large
- 1 lime, juiced
- 1 tsp orange zest
- 2 tbsp powdered sugar

Directions:
1. Grate the carrots.
2. In a clean cloth, wrap the carrots and squeeze the juice into a bowl.
3. Zest an orange. Juice the oranges and lime into the bowl of carrot juice and mix the zest in. Add the powdered sugar. If the mixture tastes too sour, add more powdered sugar, then pour into popsicle molds.
4. Place in the freezer overnight. If using wooden sticks, place them in after 2 hours in the freezer.

Nutrition Info:
- 156g Calories, 0.5g Total fat, 0.1g Saturated fat, 38.9g Carbohydrates, 9.7 g Fiber, 2.7g Protein, 19.2g Sodium.

Christmas Mince Pie

Servings:12
Cooking Time: 20 Minutes

Ingredients:
- Pastry
- 1 cup gluten-free flour
- ½ tsp guar gum
- 2 tbsp brown sugar
- ⅛ tsp cinnamon, ground
- ½ cup butter
- 1 tbsp lactose-free milk
- 1 egg, large

- Fruit mince
- ⅔ cup rhubarb, fresh
- ⅓ cup imperial mandarin
- 3 ½ tbsp cranberries, dried
- 2 ½ tsp ginger, crystallized
- 3 tbsp brown sugar
- ¼ cup water
- ½ tsp allspice
- ½ tsp cloves, ground
- ½ tsp cinnamon, ground
- ¼ tsp ginger, ground
- ½ cup pumpkin seeds, toasted and chopped
- Egg wash
- 1 egg
- 1 tbsp lactose-free milk

Directions:

1. Preheat the oven to 350°F. Grease a 12-hole shallow cupcake tin.

2. To make the pastry, sift the flour and guar gum into a large bowl, then stir the sugar and cinnamon in.

3. Chop the dairy into cubes and rub it into the flour until it looks like breadcrumbs.

4. In a bowl, heat the egg and mix it into the pastry with the milk. Bring the dough together and work it together until smooth. Pat the dough into a flat ball, wrap in plastic wrap, and chill in the fridge for 30 minutes.

5. For the fruit mince, start with the rhubarb by peeling and chopping it before roasting it in the preheated oven with a few tablespoons of water and brown sugar. After 10 minutes, the rhubarb should be soft.

6. Peel and chop the mandarin and crystallized ginger. Place a saucepan over medium heat. Add the fruit, water, and spices to the saucepan and bring it to a simmer. Once the rhubarb is cooked, add it to the saucepan and let it simmer for 10 minutes. Add more sugar and spices to taste, then mix in the pumpkin seeds.

7. Assemble the pie by first rolling the pastry out to ¼-inch thick and then cut the bases out to fit in the cupcake tin. Transfer the pastry to the tin and prick holes with a fork. Put 1 heaped spoon of fruit into each pie and top with strips of pastry.

8. Mix the egg and milk together, then brush that over the pastry and bake for 20 minutes.

Nutrition Info:

- 251g Calories, 11.1g Total fat, 1.8g Saturated fat, 33.9g Carbohydrates, 1.3 g Fiber, 4g Protein, 14.3g Sodium.

Chocolate-chia Pudding

Servings:6

Cooking Time: 5 Minutes

Ingredients:

- Chilling: Overnight
- 2 cups unsweetened almond milk
- ½ cup pure maple syrup
- 3 tablespoons unsweetened cocoa powder
- ½ teaspoon vanilla extract
- ½ cup chia seeds

Directions:

1. In a medium saucepan over medium heat, combine the almond milk, maple syrup, cocoa powder, and vanilla. Cook just until the cocoa powder dissolves, whisking constantly.

2. Remove the pan from heat and let cool slightly. Stir in the chia seeds.

3. Refrigerate overnight.

Nutrition Info:

- Calories:273; Total Fat: 20g; Saturated Fat: 17g; Carbohydrates: 24g; Fiber: 4g; Sodium: 15mg; Protein: 3g

Easy Trail Mix

Servings:4

Cooking Time: 0 Minutes

Ingredients:

- 1 cup dried bananas
- ½ cup raw unsalted almonds
- ¼ cup raw unsalted peanuts
- ¼ cup dried cranberries

Directions:

1. In a small bowl, mix all the ingredients.

2. Store in a resealable bag at room temperature for up to 1 month.

Nutrition Info:

- Calories:158; Total Fat: 11g; Saturated Fat: 1g; Carbohydrates: 13g; Fiber: 4g; Sodium: 2mg; Protein: 5g

Layered Tahitian Lime Cheesecake

Servings:10

Cooking Time:x

Ingredients:

- 9 ounces (250 g) gluten-free vanilla cookies, crushed (about 2½ cups)
- 4 tablespoons (½ stick/60 g) butter, melted
- 2 tablespoons unflavored gelatin powder
- Two 8-ounce (225 g) packages reduced-fat cream cheese, at room temperature
- One 14-ounce (396 g) can fat free sweetened condensed milk
- ⅓ cup (80 ml) coconut liqueur (see Notes)
- 3 tablespoons plus 1 teaspoon fresh lime juice

- Finely grated zest of 1 lime
- 1 to 2 drops green food coloring

Directions:

1. Mix together the crushed cookies and melted butter in a medium bowl. Press evenly into the bottom of a 9-inch (23 cm) springform pan. Place in the refrigerator while you prepare the topping.

2. Add ½ cup (125 ml) cold water to a small heatproof bowl and whisk in the gelatin with a fork. Set aside for 5 minutes, or until the gelatin has begun to gel. Fill a larger bowl with boiling water, set the bowl containing the gelatin in it, and stir constantly until the gelatin has completely dissolved.

3. Combine the dissolved gelatin, cream cheese, and condensed milk in a food processor or blender and process for 1 minute, or until smooth.

4. Pour half of the mixture into a clean bowl; there should be about 2 cups (500 ml). Add the coconut liqueur to the bowl and mix it in well. Pour over the cookie crust and freeze for 10 minutes.

5. Add the lime juice, lime zest, and food coloring to the remaining batter in the food processor and process for 30 seconds, or until well combined.

6. Remove the cheesecake from the freezer—it should be just set. Pour the lime mixture over the coconut layer, then refrigerate for 2 to 3 hours to set completely before serving.

Nutrition Info:

- 347 calories; 9 g protein; 16 g total fat; 8 g saturated fat; 39 g carbohydrates; 1 g fiber; 271 mg sodium

Raspberry–chia Seed Ice Pops

Servings:6
Cooking Time: None
Ingredients:

- 1½ cup raspberries (fresh or thawed frozen)
- 4 tablespoons sugar, divided
- ½ cup water
- 6 ice-pop molds and handles
- 1 (15-ounce) can light coconut milk
- 1½ tablespoons chia seeds

Directions:

1. In a blender, combine the raspberries, 2 tablespoons of the sugar, and water and blend until smooth.

2. Fill each ice-pop mold with about 1 inch of the raspberry mixture, and place in the freezer to harden (about 30 minutes). Place the remaining raspberry mixture in the refrigerator.

3. Whisk together the coconut milk, the remaining 2 tablespoons sugar, and the chia seeds in a small bowl.

4. Add the coconut milk mixture to the ice-pop molds, distributing evenly. Freeze for another 30 minutes.

5. Add the remaining raspberry mixture to the ice-pop molds, add the sticks or handles, and freeze for at least 4 hours, until completely frozen solid.

Nutrition Info:

- Calories: 115; Protein: 1g; Total Fat: 6g; Saturated Fat: 0g; Carbohydrates: 14g; Fiber: 3g; Sodium: 16mg;

Strawberry-rhubarb Crisp With Oat-pecan Topping

Servings:6
Cooking Time: 40 Minutes
Ingredients:

- FOR THE FILLING
- Butter or coconut oil for preparing the pan
- 2 cups sliced strawberries
- 1 cup finely chopped rhubarb
- ¼ cup sugar
- ⅛ teaspoon salt
- FOR THE TOPPING
- 1 cup gluten-free rolled oats
- ½ cup gluten-free oat flour
- ½ cup roughly chopped pecans
- ¼ cup packed light-brown sugar
- Pinch salt
- 4 tablespoons cold unsalted butter

Directions:

1. Preheat the oven to 350°F.

2. Grease a baking dish or 9-inch pie dish with butter or coconut oil.

3. In a medium bowl, combine the strawberries, rhubarb, sugar, and salt, and stir to mix. Transfer the mixture to the prepared baking dish.

4. To make the topping, combine the oats, oat flour, pecans, brown sugar, and salt in a medium bowl. Add the butter and mix with your hands until the butter is incorporated. Transfer the topping to the dish with the fruit, spreading it in an even layer over the top.

5. Bake in the preheated oven until the top is lightly browned and the filling is bubbly, for 35 to 40 minutes.

Nutrition Info:

- Calories: 277; Protein: 4g; Total Fat: 14g; Saturated Fat: 6g; Carbohydrates: 38g; Fiber: 4g; Sodium: 115mg;

Caramelized Upside-down Banana Cake

Servings:8
Cooking Time: 25 Minutes
Ingredients:
- Butter or coconut oil for preparing the pan
- 2 tablespoons unsalted butter
- 2 tablespoons brown sugar
- 2 bananas, 1 sliced and 1 mashed, divided
- 2 eggs, lightly beaten
- ⅓ cup maple syrup
- ¼ cup unsweetened coconut milk
- 1 teaspoon vanilla extract
- ½ teaspoon baking soda
- 1 teaspoon distilled vinegar
- ⅓ cup coconut flour

Directions:
1. Preheat the oven to 350°F.
2. Grease a 9-inch cake pan with butter or coconut oil. Put the butter in the cake pan and place the pan in the oven for a few minutes while it is preheating. Once the butter is melted, remove the pan from the oven and tilt it around so that the butter thoroughly coats the bottom of the pan. Sprinkle the brown sugar over the melted butter and arrange the banana slices in the pan on top of the butter and sugar.
3. In a large bowl, combine the eggs, maple syrup, coconut milk, vanilla, baking soda, vinegar, and mashed banana, and mix well. Add the coconut flour, and stir to mix and eliminate any clumps.
4. Pour the batter on top of the banana slices in the pan and spread into an even layer.
5. Bake in the preheated oven until the top of the cake is lightly browned and the cake is set in the center, for about 25 minutes. Remove from the oven and cool completely in the pan on a wire rack.
6. Slide a butter knife around the edge of the cake to loosen it from the pan, then invert the cake onto a serving platter. Serve at room temperature.

Nutrition Info:
- Calories: 173; Protein: 3g; Total Fat: 7g; Saturated Fat: 5g; Carbohydrates: 26g; Fiber: 3g; Sodium: 130mg;

Orange-scented Panna Cotta

Servings:4
Cooking Time:x
Ingredients:
- Nonstick cooking spray
- ORANGE TOPPING
- 2 tablespoons plus 2 teaspoons fresh orange juice, strained
- 2 tablespoons plus 2 teaspoons boiling water
- 2 tablespoons plus 2 teaspoons sugar
- 1½ teaspoons unflavored gelatin powder
- 1-⅔ cups (420 ml) light cream
- ½ cup (125 ml) milk, lactose-free milk, or suitable plant-based milk
- ½ cup (110 g) superfine sugar
- 3 to 4 heaping tablespoons finely grated orange zest
- 2 tablespoons plus 2 teaspoons fresh orange juice, strained
- 2¼ teaspoons unflavored gelatin powder
- Ice cubes
- Orange segments, for serving

Directions:
1. Grease four 4-ounce (125 ml) dariole molds, custard cups, or tall ramekins with cooking spray.
2. To make the topping, combine all the ingredients in a small heatproof bowl. Set the bowl over a larger bowl of boiling water and stir until the gelatin has completely dissolved.
3. Pour one quarter of the orange topping into each cup. Refrigerate for 1 to 2 hours, until set.
4. Combine the cream, milk, superfine sugar, orange zest, and orange juice in a medium saucepan over low heat. Cook, stirring regularly, taking care not to let it boil, for 20 minutes, or until it has thickened enough to coat the back of a spoon. Remove from the heat and pour into a medium heatproof bowl.
5. Pour 1 tablespoon cold water into a small heatproof bowl and whisk in the gelatin with a fork. Set it aside for 5 minutes, or until the gelatin has begun to gel. Fill a larger bowl with boiling water, set the bowl containing the gelatin in it, and stir constantly until the gelatin has completely dissolved. Whisk into the cream mixture.
6. Fill another large bowl with ice cubes. Place the bowl with the cream mixture on the ice and whisk every few minutes for about 10 minutes. The mixture will thicken as it cools. When it is thick enough to coat the back of a spoon, carefully pour it over the orange topping in the molds. Refrigerate, covered, for 2 to 3 hours, until set.
7. To serve, dip mold in hot water for a few seconds, then turn out onto plates. Serve garnished with fresh orange segments.

Nutrition Info:
- 359 calories; 6 g protein; 20 g total fat; 12 g saturated fat; 42 g carbohydrates; 1 g fiber; 62 mg sodium

Blueberry Muffins

Servings:24
Cooking Time: 30 Minutes
Ingredients:
- Topping
- ½ cup oats
- 2 tbsp pecans, chopped
- 2 tbsp flour (fodmap approved)
- 2 tbsp unsalted butter, melted
- 2 tbsp brown sugar
- Muffins
- 2 cups flour
- 1 cup oat flour
- 1 ½ cups brown sugar
- 1 ½ cups white sugar
- Pinch of salt
- 1 cup lactose-free milk
- ¼ cup maple syrup
- 4 cups unsalted butter, melted
- 2 cups blueberries, fresh

Directions:
1. Preheat the oven to 375ºF and line muffin tins with paper liners. Spray with non-stick spray.
2. In a blender, add the topping ingredients, pulse 5 times, and move to a bowl in the fridge.
3. Add the dry muffin ingredients (gluten-free flour, oat flour, sugars, salt) in a medium bowl and mix. Whisk the wet ingredients (milk, syrup, butter) together in a separate bowl. Slowly mix the dry ingredients into the wet ones. Fold the blueberries into the mixture.
4. In the muffin tins, scoop ¼ cup of batter, then crumble the topping over the mixture. Bake for 25-30 minutes. Cool for 10 minutes before removing from tin.

Nutrition Info:
- 533g Calories, 34g Total fat, 20g Saturated fat, 54.5g Carbohydrates, 3 g Fiber, 4g Protein, 27.6g Sodium.

Chocolate Tart

Servings:10
Cooking Time:x
Ingredients:
- Nonstick cooking spray
- 7 ounces (200 g) gluten-free chocolate cookies, crushed (about 2 cups)
- 5 tablespoons (75 g) unsalted butter, melted
- 8 ounces (225 g) good-quality dark chocolate, broken into pieces
- 10 tablespoons (1¼ sticks/150 g) unsalted butter, cut into cubes, at room temperature
- ¾ cup (165 g) superfine sugar
- 2 teaspoons vanilla extract
- ¼ cup (60 ml) coffee liqueur (optional)
- 5 large eggs, at room temperature
- Unsweetened cocoa powder, for dusting
- Gluten-free, lactose-free, ice cream, for serving

Directions:
1. Preheat the oven to 300°F (150°C). Grease a 9-inch (23 cm) fluted tart pan with cooking spray.
2. Mix together the crushed cookies and melted butter in a medium bowl. Press evenly into the bottom of the tart pan. Refrigerate while you prepare the filling.
3. To make the filling, place the chocolate in a small heatproof bowl or the top part of a double boiler. Set over a saucepan of simmering water or the bottom part of the double boiler (make sure the bottom of the bowl does not touch the water), stirring occasionally until melted. Set aside to cool slightly.
4. Combine the butter, sugar, vanilla, coffee liqueur (if using), and 1 egg in a medium bowl and beat with a handheld electric mixer until pale and creamy. Add the melted chocolate and beat until well combined. Set aside.
5. Clean the mixer beaters. Beat the remaining eggs in a large bowl for 3 to 5 minutes, until increased in volume by two or three times. Pour the chocolate mixture into the eggs and beat on low speed for 1 to 2 minutes, until combined.
6. Pour the filling evenly over the cookie crust and bake for 45 to 50 minutes, until set. Remove and let cool to room temperature, then refrigerate for 2 to 3 hours. Dust generously with cocoa and serve with ice cream.

Nutrition Info:
- 405 calories; 4 g protein; 26 g total fat; 15 g saturated fat; 36 g carbohydrates; 2 g fiber; 51 mg sodium

Coconut Rice Pudding

Servings:6
Cooking Time:x
Ingredients:
- ¾ cup (165 g) superfine sugar
- 3 cups (750 ml) milk, lactose-free milk, or suitable plant-based milk (more if needed)
- One 13.5-ounce (400 ml) can light coconut milk
- 2 teaspoons vanilla extract
- 1½ cups (300 g) Arborio rice
- Heaping ¼ cup (20 g) shredded sweetened or unsweetened coconut
- Maple syrup, for serving (optional)

Directions:

1. Combine the sugar, milk, coconut milk, and vanilla in a medium saucepan over medium-high heat and bring to a boil, stirring regularly. Add the rice. Reduce the heat and simmer, stirring regularly, for about 50 minutes, until the liquid has been absorbed and the rice is tender. Add extra milk if required.

2. Meanwhile, preheat the oven to 325°F (170°C) and line a baking sheet with foil. Sprinkle the coconut over the baking sheet and bake for 10 to 12 minutes, until it is just starting to turn golden brown.

3. Serve the rice pudding warm or at room temperature, topped with the toasted coconut and a drizzle of maple syrup, if desired.

Nutrition Info:

- 417 calories; 9 g protein; 7 g total fat; 5 g saturated fat; 78 g carbohydrates; 1 g fiber; 85 mg sodium

Irish Cream Delights

Servings:6
Cooking Time:x

Ingredients:

- ½ cup (125 ml) light cream
- ½ cup (110 g) packed light brown sugar
- 2 cups (500 ml) milk, lactose-free milk, or suitable plant-based milk
- ½ cup (125 ml) Irish cream liqueur, such as Baileys
- ¼ cup (35 g) cornstarch
- Shaved chocolate, for serving

Directions:

1. Combine the cream, brown sugar, and 1¾ cup (435 ml) of the milk in a medium saucepan and cook over medium heat until almost boiling. Stir in the liqueur.

2. Blend the cornstarch with the remaining ¼ cup (60 ml) of milk to form a smooth paste. Gradually add to the warm cream mixture, stirring constantly to ensure there are no lumps, then cook, stirring, over medium heat for about 5 minutes, until thickened. (Don't let it boil.)

3. Pour the pudding into six 4-ounce (125 ml) ramekins. Allow to cool, then cover with plastic wrap and refrigerate for 3 to 4 hours, until set.

4. Decorate with the shaved chocolate just before serving.

Nutrition Info:

- 230 calories; 4 g protein; 8 g total fat; 5 g saturated fat; 32 g carbohydrates; 0 g fiber; 76 mg sodium

Carrot Cake With Cream Cheese Frosting

Servings:10
Cooking Time:x
Ingredients:

- Nonstick cooking spray
- ⅓ cup (45 g) superfine white rice flour
- ⅓ cup (50 g) cornstarch
- 2 teaspoons gluten-free baking powder
- 1 teaspoon baking soda
- 1 teaspoon xanthan gum or guar gum
- 1 heaping tablespoon ground cinnamon
- 1 heaping tablespoon pumpkin pie spice
- 2 cups (240 g) almond flour
- 1 cup (220 g) packed light brown sugar
- 2 medium carrots, grated
- ⅓ cup (35 g) walnuts, chopped
- 4 large eggs, separated
- One 8-ounce (225 g) package reduced-fat cream cheese
- 1 tablespoon plus 1 teaspoon fresh lemon juice
- ½ cup (80 g) confectioners' sugar

Directions:

1. Preheat the oven to 325°F (160°C). Grease an 8½ x 4½-inch (22 x 15 cm) loaf pan with cooking spray and line with parchment paper, leaving an overhang on the two long sides to help lift out the cake later.

2. Sift the rice flour, cornstarch, baking powder, baking soda, xanthan gum, cinnamon, and pumpkin pie spice three times into a large bowl (or whisk in the bowl until well combined). Stir in the almond flour, brown sugar, grated carrots, walnuts, and egg yolks.

3. Beat the egg whites in a medium bowl with a handheld electric mixer until stiff peaks form. Gently fold the egg whites into the carrot batter with a large metal spoon.

4. Pour the batter into the pan and bake for 45 to 50 minutes, until firm to the touch (a toothpick inserted into the center should come out clean). Cool in the pan for 10 minutes, then turn out onto a wire rack to cool completely.

5. To make the cream cheese frosting, combine the cream cheese, lemon juice, and confectioners' sugar in a bowl and mix until smooth. Spread the frosting over the cooled cake and serve.

Nutrition Info:

- 384 calories; 11 g protein; 18 g total fat; 5 g saturated fat; 47 g carbohydrates; 4 g fiber; 348 mg sodium

Salted Caramel Pumpkin Seeds

Servings:16
Cooking Time: 25 Minutes
Ingredients:

- Roasted seeds
- 2 cups pumpkin seeds
- 2 ½ tbsp sugar
- ¼ tsp cinnamon, ground

- ½ tsp ginger, ground
- Pinch of nutmeg
- 2 tsp water
- Salted caramel sauce
- 1 ½ tbsp butter
- 1 tbsp white sugar
- 1 ½ tbsp brown sugar
- ½ tsp rock salt

Directions:

1. Preheat the oven to 300ºF.
2. Mix the pumpkin seeds, spices, and sugar with water. The seeds should be damp to allow the spices and sugar to stick.
3. Line a tray with parchment paper and grease it. Spread the seeds evenly over the tray, then bake in the oven for 25 minutes. The seeds should be golden and crunchy. Remember to mix the seeds up halfway through cooking.
4. When the seeds finish baking, place a saucepan over medium heat and melt the butter. Mix the sugar and salt into the butter, then cook for 2 minutes until the mixture is a deep golden color. Lower the heat. Mix the seeds into the caramel, transfer back to the tray, and let cool.

Nutrition Info:

- 124g Calories, 9.8g Total fat, 1.7g Saturated fat, 5.7g Carbohydrates, 1.1 g Fiber, 5.4g Protein, 4g Sodium.

Pineapple Salsa

Servings:2
Cooking Time: None
Ingredients:

- 2 cups chopped pineapple
- 2 jalapeño chiles, seeded and finely chopped
- ¼ cup finely chopped cilantro
- ½ teaspoon salt
- Juice of 1 lime
- 1 tablespoon olive oil

Directions:

1. In a medium bowl, stir all of the ingredients together until well combined.
2. Let sit at room temperature for 15 to 20 minutes before serving to allow the flavors to blend.

Nutrition Info:

- Calories: 73; Protein: 1g; Total Fat: 4g; Saturated Fat: 1g; Carbohydrates: 11g; Fiber: 1g; Sodium: 292mg;

Amaretti Tiramisu

Servings:6
Cooking Time:x
Ingredients:

- 4 large eggs, separated
- ½ cup (110 g) superfine sugar, plus more for the coffee (optional)
- 12 ounces (340 g) reduced-fat cream cheese, at room temperature
- 1 cup (250 ml) strong brewed coffee
- ¼ cup (60 ml) Marsala or amaretto (optional)
- About 30 Amaretti
- ½ teaspoon instant coffee
- ⅔ cup (110 g) confectioners' sugar
- 2 heaping tablespoons unsweetened cocoa powder, plus more for dusting

Directions:

1. Combine the egg yolks and superfine sugar in a large bowl and beat with a handheld electric mixer until thick, pale and creamy. Beat in the cream cheese for 3 to 4 minutes, until the mixture is smooth and well combined.
2. Clean the mixer beaters. Place the egg whites in a large clean bowl and beat until stiff peaks form. Using a large metal spoon, gently fold the egg whites into the cream cheese mixture.
3. Combine the coffee, sugar to taste, and the liqueur (if using) in a small bowl. Dip each Amaretti cookie into the coffee. Place 1 cookie in each of six glass dessert dishes and top with a few tablespoons of the cream cheese filling. Repeat with the remaining cookies and filling, finishing with a cream cheese layer.
4. To make the chocolate sauce, dissolve the instant coffee in 2 to 3 tablespoons hot water. Sift the confectioners' sugar and cocoa into a small bowl, add the coffee mixture, and stir until smooth.
5. Drizzle the chocolate sauce over the tiramisu and dust with additional cocoa. Cover and refrigerate for at least 2 hours, preferably overnight, before serving.

Nutrition Info:

- 415 calories; 13 g protein; 20 g total fat; 8 g saturated fat; 45 g carbohydrates; 2 g fiber; 236 mg sodium

Low-fodmap Hummus

Servings:4
Cooking Time: 0 Minutes
Ingredients:

- 1 zucchini
- 2 tablespoons tahini
- 2 tablespoons Garlic Oil
- Juice of 1 lemon
- ½ teaspoon sea salt
- Assorted low-FODMAP veggies, for dipping

Directions:

1. In a blender, combine the zucchini, tahini, garlic oil, lemon juice, and salt. Process until smooth.

2. Serve with the veggies for dipping.

Nutrition Info:

- Calories:116; Total Fat: 11g; Saturated Fat: 2g; Carbohydrates: 4g; Fiber: 1g; Sodium: 251mg; Protein: 2g

Peanut Butter Cookies

Servings:24

Cooking Time: 10 Minutes

Ingredients:

- 1 cup sugar-free natural peanut butter
- ½ cup packed brown sugar
- 1 egg, beaten
- 1 teaspoon baking soda
- ½ teaspoon vanilla extract
- Pinch sea salt

Directions:

1. Preheat the oven to 350°F.

2. Line a baking sheet with parchment paper and set it aside.

3. In a medium bowl, mix the peanut butter and brown sugar.

4. Stir in the egg, baking soda, vanilla, and salt until well combined. Roll the dough into 24 teaspoon-size balls and place them on the prepared sheet. Flatten slightly with a fork in a crosshatch pattern.

5. Bake for about 10 minutes, or until the cookies puff and turn golden brown.

Nutrition Info:

- Calories:78; Total Fat: 6g; Saturated Fat: 1g; Carbohydrates: 5g; Fiber: <1g; Sodium: 113mg; Protein: 3g

Warm Lemon Tapioca Pudding

Servings:6

Cooking Time:x

Ingredients:

- 4 lemons
- 4 cups (1 liter) low-fat milk, lactose-free milk, or suitable plant-based milk
- ½ cup (100 g) pearl tapioca or sago
- ⅓ cup (75 g) superfine sugar

Directions:

1. Using a vegetable peeler, slice the zest of all 4 lemons into ¾-inch (2 cm) strips. Juice the lemons until you have ½ cup juice.

2. Combine the milk and lemon zest in a medium saucepan and bring to a simmer over high heat. Reduce the heat to low and simmer for 2 minutes. Remove and discard the lemon zest.

3. Add the tapioca to the milk, stirring well to combine. Simmer over low heat, stirring regularly, for 20 to 25 minutes, until the tapioca resembles translucent jellylike balls.

4. Remove from the heat. Stir in the sugar and lemon juice and pour into six glass dessert dishes. Serve immediately.

Nutrition Info:

- 161 calories; 5 g protein; 2 g total fat; 1 g saturated fat; 32 g carbohydrates; 0 g fiber; 83 mg sodium

Banana Fritters With Fresh Pineapple

Servings:4

Cooking Time:x

Ingredients:

- 1 cup (120 g) dried gluten-free, soy-free bread crumbs*
- ⅓ cup (75 g) packed light brown sugar
- 1 tablespoon ground cinnamon
- 2 large eggs
- ½ teaspoon confectioners' sugar
- 4 small bananas, peeled and halved lengthwise
- 2 tablespoons (30 g) unsalted butter
- Gluten-free, lactose-free vanilla ice cream, for serving
- ½ small pineapple, peeled, cored, and finely chopped
- Pulp of 2 passion fruits (optional)

Directions:

1. Preheat the oven to 300°F (150°C).

2. Combine the bread crumbs, brown sugar, and cinnamon on a large plate. Lightly beat the eggs with the confectioners' sugar in a shallow bowl.

3. Dip the banana halves into the egg mixture, then toss in the bread crumbs until well coated.

4. Melt 1 tablespoon of the butter in a large nonstick frying pan over medium-low heat. Add half of the banana pieces and cook for 3 to 4 minutes on each side, until golden brown. Transfer to a baking sheet and keep warm in the oven. Melt the remaining 1 tablespoon butter and cook the remaining banana halves the same way.

5. Place two banana halves each on four plates. Top with ice cream, pineapple, and passion fruit pulp (if desired). Serve immediately.

Nutrition Info:

- 357 calories; 6 g protein; 9 g total fat; 5 g saturated fat; 66 g carbohydrates; 6 g fiber; 74 mg sodium

Rice Pudding

Servings:4
Cooking Time: 17 Minutes

Ingredients:

- 2 cups unsweetened almond milk, divided
- 1½ cups cooked white rice
- ⅓ cup sugar
- Pinch sea salt
- 1 egg, beaten
- ½ teaspoon vanilla extract
- Freshly grated nutmeg, for garnishing (optional)

Directions:

1. In a medium saucepan over medium heat, stir together 1½ cups almond milk, the rice, sugar, and salt. Cover and cook for about 15 minutes, or until thick.
2. Add the remaining ½ cup almond milk and the egg. Cook for 2 minutes, stirring constantly.
3. Remove the pan from the heat and stir in the vanilla.
4. Serve warm garnished with freshly grated nutmeg (if using).

Nutrition Info:

- Calories:49; Total Fat: 2g; Saturated Fat: 0g; Carbohydrates: 7g; Fiber: <1g; Sodium: 91mg; Protein: <1g

Coconut Bites

Servings:14
Cooking Time: 2 Minutes

Ingredients:

- 2 cups cornflakes, gluten-free
- ½ cup brown sugar
- ¼ cup oats
- 6 tbsp dried coconut, shredded
- 4 tbsp pumpkin seeds
- 6 tbsp butter

Directions:

1. Crush the cornflakes and soften the butter. Place all the ingredients, except the coconut, into a food processor and pulse until large crumbs form.
2. Press and roll the mixture into balls, approximately 1 tbsp per ball (add more if there is leftover dough), then roll in the coconut.
3. Store in the fridge.

Nutrition Info:

- 139g Calories, 8,2g Total fat, 2.5g Saturated fat, 14.9g Carbohydrates, 0.8 g Fiber, 1.8g Protein, 8g Sodium.

Chocolate–peanut Butter Balls

Servings:16
Cooking Time: 5 Minutes

Ingredients:

- ½ cup sugar-free natural peanut butter
- ¼ cup unsalted butter, at room temperature
- 1 cup confectioners' sugar
- 1 cup semi-sweet chocolate chips
- 2 tablespoons coconut oil

Directions:

1. Line a baking sheet with parchment paper and set it aside.
2. In a large bowl, stir together the peanut butter, butter, and confectioners' sugar until well mixed. Form the mixture into about 16 tablespoon-size balls.
3. In a medium saucepan over low heat, melt the chocolate chips and coconut oil for about 5 minutes, stirring constantly until melted and smooth.
4. Dip the balls in the chocolate mixture and place on the prepared sheet. Freeze for 10 minutes to set the chocolate coating.

Nutrition Info:

- Calories:165; Total Fat: 11g; Saturated Fat: 5g; Carbohydrates: 15g; Fiber: <1g; Sodium: 92mg; Protein: 2g

Parmesan Potato Wedges

Servings:4
Cooking Time: 25 Minutes

Ingredients:

- 4 red potatoes, cut into wedges
- 2 tablespoons Garlic Oil
- ¼ cup grated Parmesan cheese
- ½ teaspoon sea salt
- ¼ teaspoon freshly ground black pepper

Directions:

1. Preheat the oven to 425°F.
2. In a small bowl, combine the potatoes, garlic oil, Parmesan cheese, salt, and pepper and toss to coat the potatoes with the cheese and oil. Spread the potatoes in a single layer on a rimmed baking sheet.
3. Bake for about 25 minutes, or until the potatoes are tender.

Nutrition Info:

- Calories:232; Total Fat: 9g; Saturated Fat: 2g; Carbohydrates: 34g; Fiber: 4g; Sodium: 313mg; Protein: 6g

Herbed Veggie-and-tofu Skewers

Servings:10
Cooking Time: 10 Minutes
Ingredients:

- 28 ounces extra-firm tofu, drained, frozen, and thawed
- ¼ cup balsamic vinegar
- 1 tablespoon Dijon mustard
- 1½ teaspoons chopped fresh thyme
- 3 tablespoons olive oil, plus more for oiling
- 1 teaspoon Garlic Oil (here)
- 1 tablespoon lemon juice
- 1 teaspoon coarse salt
- Pinch cayenne pepper
- 1 globe eggplant (about 1 pound), cut into ½-inch chunks
- 1 green bell pepper, cut into 1-inch squares
- 1 red bell pepper, cut into 1-inch squares

Directions:

1. Cut the block of tofu into 4 or 5 slabs, and place them on a towel-lined baking sheet. Place another towel and then another baking sheet on top, and weight it with several cans of tomatoes or other heavy items. Let sit for 15 to 20 minutes to drain excess water.
2. Cut the drained tofu into 1-inch cubes.
3. In a large bowl, combine the vinegar, mustard, and thyme, and stir to mix well. Add the cubed tofu and toss gently to coat well. Cover and refrigerate overnight.
4. Heat a grill or grill pan to medium-high heat.
5. In a large bowl, stir together the olive oil, Garlic Oil, lemon juice, salt, and cayenne. Add the eggplant and bell peppers, and toss to coat.
6. Thread the tofu cubes and vegetable chunks onto skewers, alternating and distributing the ingredients evenly.
7. Grill the skewers, turning every few minutes, until the tofu is browned and the veggies are tender, for 8 to 10 minutes total. Serve immediately.

Nutrition Info:

- Calories: 274; Protein: 18g; Total Fat: 18g; Saturated Fat: 2g; Carbohydrates: 14g; Fiber: 6g; Sodium: 474mg;

Chocolate Lava Cakes

Servings:4
Cooking Time: 15 Minutes
Ingredients:

- 4 tablespoons unsalted butter, plus more for preparing the ramekins
- 5 ounces dark chocolate, chopped
- 2 eggs
- 2 egg yolks
- ¼ cup granulated sugar
- ½ teaspoon vanilla extract
- 3 tablespoons gluten-free all-purpose flour
- ⅛ teaspoon xanthan gum
- 1 tablespoon unsweetened cocoa powder
- ⅛ teaspoon salt
- Powdered sugar, whipped cream, or Whipped Coconut Cream (here) for serving (optional)

Directions:

1. Preheat the oven to 425°F.
2. Butter the insides of 4 (4-ounce) oven-safe ramekins and place the ramekins in a baking dish.
3. In the top of a double boiler set over simmering water, combine the chocolate and 4 tablespoons butter, stirring frequently, until melted.
4. In a large bowl, whisk together the eggs, egg yolks, sugar, and vanilla until the mixture becomes thick and very pale yellow. While whisking, slowly add the melted chocolate-butter mixture to the egg mixture until well combined.
5. Stir in the flour, xanthan gum, cocoa powder, and salt. Transfer the mixture to the prepared ramekins in the baking dish, dividing equally.
6. Place the baking dish in the preheated oven and add water to the baking dish so that it comes halfway up the sides of the ramekins. Bake for about 15 minutes, until the centers of the cakes are just barely set.
7. Carefully remove the ramekins from the baking dish and transfer them to a wire rack. Cool for about 10 minutes. Before serving, run a butter knife around the edge of each cake to loosen it from the ramekin and then invert it onto a serving plate. Serve immediately, with a dusting of powdered sugar or a dollop of whipped cream or Whipped Coconut Cream.

Nutrition Info:

- Calories: 415; Protein: 7g; Total Fat: 27g; Saturated Fat: 16g; Carbohydrates: 38g; Fiber: 2g; Sodium: 146mg;

Lemon Tartlets

Servings:x
Cooking Time:x
Ingredients:

- MAKES 12
- Nonstick cooking spray
- ½ cup (75 g) cornstarch
- 1¼ cups (300 ml) water
- Grated zest of 2 lemons
- ¾ cup (180 ml) fresh lemon juice

- 4 tablespoons (½ stick/60 g) unsalted butter, cut into cubes, at room temperature
- ⅔ cup (150 g) sugar
- 2 large egg yolks
- 1 batch Tart Crust dough, chilled
- Gluten-free, lactose-free ice cream, for serving

Directions:

1. Preheat the oven to 325°F (170°C). Grease twelve tartlet pans or a 12-cup muffin pan with cooking spray.

2. To make the filling, blend the cornstarch with 1 tablespoon of the water in a small saucepan to form a smooth paste. Add the remaining water, stirring to ensure there are no lumps, then add the lemon zest, lemon juice, butter, and sugar and stir over medium-low heat until thickened, 3 to 5 minutes. Remove from the heat and let cool for 10 minutes. Stir in the egg yolks. Pour into a bowl, cover, and refrigerate until cold.

3. Meanwhile, place the chilled dough between two sheets of parchment paper and roll out to a thickness of about ⅛ inch (2 to 3 mm). Cut out 12 rounds with a pastry cutter to fit the pan or cups. Place in the pan or cups and trim the edges to neaten. Bake for 12 to 15 minutes, until golden. Let cool on a wire rack.

4. Spoon the chilled lemon filling into the tartlet crusts and serve with ice cream.

Nutrition Info:
- 297 calories; 4 g protein; 15 g total fat; 9 g saturated fat; 39 g carbohydrates; 1 g fiber; 12 mg sodium

Caramel Nut Bars

Servings:18
Cooking Time:x

Ingredients:
- Nonstick cooking spray
- ½ cup (65 g) superfine white rice flour
- ¼ cup (45 g) potato flour
- ⅓ cup (50 g) cornstarch
- ¼ cup (55 g) superfine sugar
- ¼ teaspoon baking soda
- ¼ teaspoon gluten-free baking powder
- 1 teaspoon xanthan gum or guar gum
- 4 tablespoons (½ stick/60 g) unsalted butter, cut into cubes, at room temperature
- 1 large egg, beaten
- 1 teaspoon vanilla extract
- 1 cup (220 g) packed light brown sugar
- 10 tablespoons (1 stick plus 2 tablespoons/150 g) unsalted butter, cut into cubes, at room temperature
- ⅓ cup (80 ml) light cream
- 3 tablespoons plus 1 teaspoon cornstarch
- ½ cup (65 g) roasted unsalted pecans, roughly chopped
- ⅔ cup (110 g) roasted unsalted Brazil nuts (skin on), roughly chopped
- ½ cup (70 g) roasted unsalted macadamia nuts, halved

Directions:

1. Preheat the oven to 350°F (180°C). Grease an 11 x 7-inch (28 x 18 cm) baking pan with cooking spray and line with parchment paper, leaving an overhang on the two long sides to help lift out the bars later.

2. Sift the rice flour, potato flour, cornstarch, superfine sugar, baking soda, baking powder, and xanthan gum together three times into a bowl (or whisk in the bowl until well combined). Rub in the butter with your fingertips. Add the egg and vanilla and mix with a large metal spoon until well combined. As the mixture becomes more solid, use your hands to bring it together to form a ball.

3. Roll out the dough between two sheets of parchment paper to a thickness of ¼ inch (5 mm). Gently fit into the bottom of the pan and prick all over with a fork. Refrigerate for 10 minutes.

4. Bake for 10 to 12 minutes, until the crust is firm and lightly golden. Set aside to cool, but leave the oven on.

5. To make the topping, combine the brown sugar and butter in a large saucepan over medium heat and stir until the butter has melted and the mixture comes to a boil. Remove from the heat and stir in the cream and cornstarch, mixing until smooth. Add the pecans, Brazil nuts, and macadamia nuts. Return the pan to medium heat and stir until the mixture comes to a boil. Reduce the heat to low and cook gently for 2 to 3 minutes more, until the mixture is thick and sticky.

6. Spread the nut topping evenly over the crust and bake for 15 minutes, or until the topping is bubbling. Let cool completely in the pan, then transfer to a board, remove the parchment paper, and cut into small (or large!) pieces to serve.

Nutrition Info:
- 278 calories; 3 g protein; 20 g total fat; 8 g saturated fat; 25 g carbohydrates; 1 g fiber; 39 mg sodium

Baked Blueberry Cheesecakes

Servings:9

Cooking Time:x

Ingredients:

- 7 ounces (250 g) gluten-free vanilla cookies, crushed (about 2 cups)
- 4 tablespoons (½ stick/60 g) unsalted butter, melted
- 2 cups (300 g) fresh or frozen blueberries
- Two 8-ounce (225 g) packages reduced-fat cream cheese, at room temperature
- One 14-ounce (396 g) can fat-free sweetened condensed milk
- 2 teaspoons vanilla extract
- ½ cup (125 ml) light whipping cream
- 2 large eggs
- ¼ cup (35 g) cornstarch

Directions:

1. Preheat the oven to 325°F (160°C).
2. Mix together the crushed cookies and melted butter, then press into the bottom of nine 4-inch (10 cm) springform pans. Divide the blueberries evenly over the cookie crusts.
3. Combine the cream cheese, condensed milk, vanilla, cream, eggs, and cornstarch in a food processor or blender and process until smooth. Pour the batter over the crusts. Bake for 15 to 20 minutes, until lightly golden and firm to the touch.
4. Allow to cool completely in the pans, then cover and refrigerate for 3 hours before serving.

Nutrition Info:

- 512 calories; 9 g protein; 18 g total fat; 9 g saturated fat; 37 g carbohydrates; 1 g fiber; 252 mg sodium

Cream Puffs With Chocolate Sauce

Servings:6

Cooking Time:x

Ingredients:

- 5 tablespoons (75 g) unsalted butter
- 1 cup (130 g) superfine white rice flour
- 1 teaspoon xanthan gum or guar gum
- 1 heaping tablespoon sugar
- 3 large eggs
- 2 cups (500 ml) low-fat milk, lactose-free milk, or suitable plant-based milk
- 6 large egg yolks
- ½ cup (110 g) superfine sugar
- ⅓ cup (50 g) cornstarch
- 2 teaspoons vanilla extract
- ⅓ cup (50 g) cornstarch

- 2½ cups (625 ml) low-fat milk, lactose-free milk, or suitable plant-based milk
- 3½ teaspoons sugar
- 4 ounces (115 g) good-quality dark chocolate, broken into small pieces
- 2 tablespoons plus 2 teaspoons coffee liqueur or brewed strong espresso mixed with a bit of unsweetened cocoa powder
- ½ teaspoon vanilla extract
- 4 ounces (115 g) good-quality dark chocolate, broken into pieces
- ⅓ cup (80 ml) light cream

Directions:

1. Preheat the oven to 400°F (200°C). Line two baking sheets with parchment paper.
2. Combine the butter and ¾ cup (185 ml) water in a medium saucepan and bring to a boil. Mix the rice flour and xanthan gum in a bowl until well combined, then add to the pan and beat quickly with a wooden spoon. The mixture will come away from the side of the pan and form a smooth ball.
3. Transfer the dough to a medium bowl. With a handheld electric mixer, beat in the sugar. Beat in the eggs one at a time.
4. Place rounded teaspoons of the dough on the sheets, about 1½ inches (4 cm) apart. Bake for 7 minutes, or until the pastries puff up. Reduce the temperature to 350°F (180°C) and bake for 10 minutes more or until crisp and lightly browned.
5. Reduce the temperature to 275°F (140°C) and remove one sheet from the oven. Quickly and carefully cut a small opening in the side of each pastry. Return the sheet to the oven and repeat with the second sheet. Bake for 5 minutes, or until the pastries have dried out.
6. Remove from the oven and let cool to room temperature. Carefully cut the pastries open. Remove and discard the soft centers without crushing the pastry cases.
7. While the pastries are cooling, to make the crème custard, pour the milk into a small heavy-bottomed saucepan over medium heat and bring to just below a boil. Beat the egg yolks and superfine sugar in a large bowl with a handheld electric mixer until thick and creamy. Beat in the cornstarch. Pour in the hot milk and cream and whisk until smooth. Return the mixture to the pan and whisk gently over medium-low heat until the custard has thickened. Remove from the heat and beat in the vanilla. Pour into a bowl, cover, and refrigerate for 1 to 2 hours, until cold.
8. To make the chocolate custard, blend the cornstarch with ½ cup (125 ml) of the milk to form a smooth paste. Combine the sugar and the remaining 2 cups (500 ml) of milk in a small saucepan and bring to just below a boil.

Gradually add the cornstarch mixture, stirring constantly until the custard has thickened. When very thick, remove from the heat and stir in the chocolate, coffee liqueur, and vanilla until the mixture is smooth and the chocolate has melted. Pour into a bowl, cover, and refrigerate for 1 to 2 hours, until cold.

9. To make the chocolate sauce, combine the chocolate and cream in a heatproof bowl or the top part of a double boiler. Set over a saucepan of simmering water or the bottom part of the double boiler (make sure the bottom of the bowl does not touch the water), and stir until the chocolate is melted and well combined with the cream.

10. Gently open each pastry and spoon in the fillings, using the crème custard in half of them and the chocolate custard in the other half. Serve topped with the warm chocolate sauce.

Nutrition Info:

- 536 calories; 11 g protein; 28 g total fat; 16 g saturated fat; 63 g carbohydrates; 4 g fiber; 120 mg sodium

Cinnamon Panna Cotta With Pureed Banana

Servings:4
Cooking Time:x
Ingredients:

- Nonstick cooking spray
- 1⅔ cups (420 ml) light cream
- ½ cup (125 ml) milk, lactose-free milk, or suitable plant-based milk
- ½ cup (110 g) superfine sugar
- 1 teaspoon ground cinnamon
- 1 teaspoon vanilla extract
- 2¼ teaspoons unflavored gelatin powder
- Ice cubes
- 2 ripe bananas, peeled
- 2 teaspoons light brown sugar

Directions:

1. Grease four 4-ounce (125 ml) dariole molds, custard cups, or tall ramekins with cooking spray.

2. Combine the cream, milk, superfine sugar, cinnamon, and vanilla in a medium saucepan over low heat. Cook, stirring regularly, taking care not to let it boil, for 20 minutes, or until the mixture is thick enough to coat the back of a spoon. Remove from the heat and pour into a medium heatproof bowl.

3. Add 1 tablespoon of cold water to a small heatproof bowl and whisk in the gelatin with a fork. Set it aside for 5 minutes, or until the gelatin has begun to gel. Fill a larger bowl with boiling water, set the bowl containing the gelatin

in it, and stir constantly until the gelatin has completely dissolved. Whisk into the cream mixture.

4. Fill a large bowl with ice cubes. Place the bowl with the cream mixture on the ice and whisk every few minutes for about 10 minutes. The mixture will thicken as it cools. When it is thick enough to coat the back of a spoon, carefully pour it into the molds. Refrigerate, covered, for 2 to 3 hours, until set.

5. Combine the bananas and brown sugar in a bowl and mash with a fork until smooth and well combined.

6. To serve, dip each mold in hot water for a few seconds, then turn out onto plates. Spoon the pureed banana into a piping bag and use to decorate the plates (or dollop directly onto the panna cotta, if preferred).

Nutrition Info:

- 370 calories; 5 g protein; 20 g total fat; 12 g saturated fat; 46 g carbohydrates; 2 g fiber; 60 mg sodium

Rhubarb Custard Cup

Servings:4
Cooking Time: 20 Minutes
Ingredients:

- Rhubarb
- 1 ¼ cups rhubarb, fresh
- 2 ½ tbsp raspberries, fresh or frozen
- Custard
- 4 tbsp custard powder, without milk or whey powder
- 4 cups lactose-free milk
- 1 ½ tbsp white sugar
- 1 tsp vanilla extract
- Layer
- Low-FODMAP muesli or crumble

Directions:

1. Weigh and chop the rhubarb. Place the rhubarb and raspberries into a saucepan, cover with warm water, and place over medium heat and bring to a simmer. Allow to simmer for 10 minutes, then drain the liquid using a sieve. Mash the fruit in the saucepan.

2. In a microwave bowl, mix together the custard powder, milk, and white sugar. Cook on high for 2 minutes and stir, repeating until thick. Add vanilla extract if the flavor is not sweet enough.

3. Layer the rhubarb, custard, and muesli/crumble into cups.

Nutrition Info:

- 431g Calories, 13.8g Total fat, 3.4g Saturated fat, 70.7g Carbohydrates, 5 g Fiber, 4.9g Protein, 26.1g Sodium.

Pb&j Mug Cake

Servings:2

Cooking Time: 2 Minutes

Ingredients:

- 1 egg large
- 3 tbsp almond milk
- 3 tbsp peanut butter
- 5 tbsp gluten-free flour
- 2 tbsp sugar
- 1 tbsp jam/jelly, preferred flavor

Directions:

1. In a large mug, mix the ingredients, except the jam/jelly.
2. Swirl the jam in the mug before cooking.
3. Microwave on high until the center is just cooked.

Nutrition Info:

- 396g Calories, 15.5g Total fat, 3.5g Saturated fat, 54.5g Carbohydrates, 4 g Fiber, 11.5g Protein, 21g Sodium.

Cappuccino And Vanilla Bean Mousse Duo

Servings:6

Cooking Time:x

Ingredients:

- Nonstick cooking spray
- 8 ounces (225 g) good-quality white chocolate, broken into pieces
- ⅔ cup (150 ml) light cream
- 1 heaping tablespoon unflavored gelatin powder
- 4 large eggs, separated, at room temperature
- 1 cup (250 ml) light whipping cream
- ¼ cup (55 g) superfine sugar
- 1 teaspoon vanilla bean paste or 1 to 2 teaspoons vanilla extract
- 2 teaspoons instant coffee
- Edible organic flowers (optional)

Directions:

1. Grease six 5-ounce (150 ml) glasses or ramekins with nonstick cooking spray.
2. Combine the chocolate and light cream in a heatproof bowl or the top part of a double boiler. Set over a saucepan of simmering water or the bottom part of the double boiler (make sure the bottom of the bowl does not touch the water) and stir until melted and well combined. Set aside to cool for 15 to 20 minutes.
3. Pour ½ cup (125 ml) cold water into a small heatproof bowl and whisk in the gelatin with a fork. Set aside for 5 minutes, or until the gelatin has softened. Fill a larger bowl with boiling water, set the bowl containing the gelatin in it, and stir constantly until the gelatin has completely dissolved.
4. Stir the gelatin into the cooled chocolate mixture, then stir in the egg yolks, one at a time. Pour half of the chocolate mixture into another bowl.
5. Combine the whipping cream and sugar in a clean bowl and beat with a handheld electric mixer until the mixture is thick and the sugar has dissolved. Spoon half of the whipped cream into a smaller bowl.
6. Clean the mixer beaters. Beat the egg whites in a large clean bowl until stiff peaks form.
7. Add the vanilla to one of the bowls of chocolate mixture. With a large metal spoon, fold this into one of the bowls of whipped cream until well combined. Finally, gently fold in half of the beaten egg whites. Pour into the glasses. Cover and refrigerate for 1 hour, or until set. Let the other bowls sit at room temperature.
8. After an hour, dissolve the coffee in 2 tablespoons hot water and stir it into the remaining chocolate mixture. Fold this into the remaining whipped cream, then gently fold in the remaining egg whites. Pour into the glasses over the vanilla layer. Cover and refrigerate for 2 hours more or until set.
9. Just before serving, garnish with flowers, if desired.

Nutrition Info:

- 470 calories; 9 g protein; 33 g total fat; 20 g saturated fat; 33 g carbohydrates; 0 g fiber; 108 mg sodium

Brownie Cupcakes With Vanilla Icing

Servings:12

Cooking Time: 20 Minutes

Ingredients:

- Cupcakes
- ½ cup butter
- 9 tbsp dark chocolate
- 2 eggs, large
- ¼ cup lactose-free milk
- 1 tsp vanilla extract
- 1 cup gluten-free flour
- 3 tbsp cocoa powder
- ¾ cup brown sugar
- ¼ tsp of baking powder
- ¾ tsp of baking soda
- Pinch of salt
- Icing
- ½ cup butter
- 1 ½ cups powdered sugar
- ½ tsp vanilla extract
- 2 drops food coloring of choice

- Edible cake decorating pearls, optional

Directions:

1. Preheat the oven to 350°F. Line a muffin tray with cupcake liners.

2. Chop the chocolate roughly and melt it in the microwave with the butter for 15 seconds at a time, stirring in between.

3. Whisk the eggs, milk, and vanilla extract together until smooth, then add in the melted butter and chocolate.

4. In a separate bowl, mix the dry ingredients together then add in the wet mixture. Mix until the batter is smooth. Spoon an even amount of mixture into each cupcake liner.

5. Bake for 15 minutes, then check with a skewer. The top of the cupcakes should look slightly cracked and the skewer should come out clean. Remove the cupcakes from the oven and let the tin cool for 5 minutes before placing the cupcakes onto a cooling rack.

6. To make the icing, soften the butter, but don't melt it. Mix the butter, powdered sugar, vanilla extract, and 2 drops of food coloring in a bowl until it is smooth and creamy. If it is too dry, add a small amount of water. Ice the cupcakes once they are cool and decorate.

Nutrition Info:

- 365g Calories, 19,9g Total fat, 4.7g Saturated fat, 43.9g Carbohydrates, 1.7 g Fiber, 3.2g Protein, 30.8g Sodium.

Strawberry Ice Cream

Servings:4
Cooking Time: -

Ingredients:

- 2 small bananas, firm and frozen
- 7 oz strawberries, frozen
- 5 tbsp coconut yogurt
- 2 tbsp maple syrup
- 1 tsp vanilla extract

Directions:

1. Chop the frozen fruit into small pieces, then place the ingredients into a food processor. Blend until smooth, making sure to scrape down the sides.

2. Taste the mixture and add maple syrup or vanilla extract as desired. Serve soft or freeze for a few hours before serving. Serve with chocolate fudge sauce.

Nutrition Info:

- 177g Calories, 4g Total fat, 3.5g Saturated fat, 37g Carbohydrates, 2.7 g Fiber, 1.2g Protein, 28.4g Sodium.

Triple-berry Shortcakes

Servings:6
Cooking Time: 15 Minutes
Ingredients:

- ¼ cup butter
- ½ cup plus 2 tablespoons powdered sugar, divided
- 2 eggs
- ½ teaspoon vanilla extract
- ½ cup cornstarch
- ¾ teaspoon baking powder
- 1 cup sliced strawberries
- 1 cup blueberries
- 1 cup raspberries
- 1 cup heavy cream
- ¼ cup maple syrup

Directions:

1. Preheat the oven to 375°F and spray 6 muffin cups with cooking spray.

2. In a large bowl cream butter and ½ cup sugar together using an electric mixer set on medium speed. Add the eggs and vanilla and beat until the mixture is pale yellow and fluffy.

3. In a small bowl, combine the cornstarch and baking powder, and add it a little at a time to the butter mixture. Beat until well combined.

4. Scoop the mixture into the prepared muffin cups, filing each about halfway.

5. Bake in the preheated oven for about 15 minutes, or until a toothpick inserted into the center comes out clean.

6. Remove from the pan from the oven and transfer the cakes to a rack to cool.

7. In a medium bowl, combine the berries and toss together gently.

8. In another medium bowl, whip the cream with an electric mixer until fluffy and soft peaks form. Add the remaining 2 tablespoons of sugar and beat until incorporated.

9. Split the cakes and place them in wide shallow bowls. Top with the berries and whipped cream to serve.

Nutrition Info:

- Calories: 318; Protein: 3g; Total Fat: 17g; Saturated Fat: 10g; Carbohydrates: 41g; Fiber: 3g; Sodium: 86mg;

Pecan And Maple Tarts

Servings:x
Cooking Time:x
Ingredients:

- MAKES 24
- Nonstick cooking spray
- 2 batches Tart Crust dough, chilled
- 1 tablespoon (15 g) unsalted butter, at room temperature
- ¼ cup (55 g) packed light brown sugar
- ½ teaspoon vanilla extract
- 1 large egg

- ¼ cup (60 ml) maple syrup
- ½ cup (60 g) pecans, roughly chopped
- Confectioners' sugar, for dusting (optional)

Directions:

1. Preheat the oven to 325°F (170°C). Grease two 12-cup mini tartlet or mini muffin pans with cooking spray. Line a baking sheet with parchment paper.

2. Place the chilled pastry dough between two sheets of parchment paper and roll out to a thickness of about ⅛ inch (2 to 3 mm). Cut out 24 round crusts with a scalloped 1- to 1½-inch (3 to 4 cm) pastry cutter to fit the mini tartlet pans. Place in the cups and trim the edges to neaten. Using a star-shaped cookie cutter (or other desired shape), cut out 24 small stars. Place the stars on the baking sheet. Bake the crusts and stars until golden (the crusts will take about 10 minutes, but the stars will only need 7 to 8 minutes). Remove from the oven and cool on a wire rack.

3. Increase the oven temperature to 350°F (180°C).

4. To make the filling, combine the butter, brown sugar, and vanilla in a small bowl and beat with a handheld electric mixer until creamy. Beat in the egg and maple syrup, then stir in the chopped pecans.

5. Pour the filling evenly into the crusts and bake for 5 to 10 minutes, until the filling is set (it should remain firm when given a gentle shake). Place a star on each tart while still warm.

6. Cool in the pans for 10 minutes before removing and cooling completely on a wire rack. Dust with confectioners' sugar, if desired.

Nutrition Info:

- 218 calories; 4 g protein; 12 g total fat; 7 g saturated fat; 24 g carbohydrates; 1 g fiber; 114 mg sodium

Chinese Chicken In Lettuce Cups

Servings:4

Cooking Time: 5 Minutes

Ingredients:

- 2 tablespoons gluten-free soy sauce
- 2 tablespoons rice vinegar
- ½ teaspoon salt
- ½ teaspoon sugar
- 2 tablespoons vegetable oil
- 2 teaspoons Garlic Oil (here)
- 2 teaspoons minced fresh ginger
- 1 pound boneless, skinless chicken breasts, minced
- ½ cup water chestnuts, minced
- 8 to 10 inner leaves iceberg lettuce, edges trimmed and chilled
- Handful of fresh cilantro leaves, coarsely chopped

- ¼ cup unsalted roasted peanuts, coarsely chopped (optional)

Directions:

1. In a small bowl, stir together the soy sauce, rice vinegar, salt, and sugar.

2. Heat the vegetable oil and Garlic Oil in a skillet or wok set over high heat. Add the ginger and cook, stirring, for 10 seconds. Add the chicken and cook, stirring, for about 1 minute, until the chicken is opaque all over. Add the water chestnuts and reduce to medium-low. Stir in the soy sauce mixture and cook for about 2 minutes more, until the chicken is cooked through.

3. Arrange the lettuce cups on a platter or serving plates and spoon some of the chicken mixture into each, dividing equally. Garnish each serving with cilantro and peanuts, if using, and serve immediately.

Nutrition Info:

- Calories: 378; Protein: 36g; Total Fat: 19g; Saturated Fat: 4g; Carbohydrates: 14g; Fiber: 1g; Sodium: 778mg;

Energy Bars

Servings:14

Cooking Time: -

Ingredients:

- ⅓ cup sunflower seed butter or peanut butter
- 6 tbsp maple syrup
- 1 ½ cups puffed rice
- ½ cup pumpkin seeds, roughly chopped
- 4 tbsp dried cranberries, chopped roughly
- ½ tsp ginger, ground
- ½ tsp cinnamon, ground
- 1 tbsp dark chocolate, chopped roughly

Directions:

1. Line a square baking pan with parchment paper.

2. Melt the butter and the syrup over medium heat. Once melted, remove from the heat and stir in the pumpkin seeds, puffed rice, dried cranberries, ginger, and cinnamon. Coat the ingredients evenly.

3. Spread the mixture across the pan evenly, then place another piece of parchment paper over the mixture and apply pressure evenly to compress.

4. Melt the dark chocolate, then drizzle over the mixture. Refrigerate for 2 hours before cutting.

Nutrition Info:

- 121g Calories, 6.4g Total fat, 1g Saturated fat, 14.4g Carbohydrates, 1.2 g Fiber, 3g Protein, 8.8g Sodium.

Cinnamon And Chestnut Flan

Servings:10
Cooking Time:x
Ingredients:
- Nonstick cooking spray
- 1 batch Tart Crust dough, chilled
- ¾ cup (165 g) superfine sugar
- 2 tablespoons ground cinnamon
- One 14-ounce (396 g) can fat-free sweetened condensed milk
- One 8-ounce (225 g) package mascarpone or reduced-fat cream cheese, at room temperature
- 1½ cups (225 g) chestnut meal
- 4 large eggs
- Confectioners' sugar, for dusting
- Gluten-free, lactose-free ice cream, for serving

Directions:
1. Preheat the oven to 350°F (170°C). Grease a 9-inch (23 cm) fluted quiche pan with cooking spray.
2. Place the chilled dough between two sheets of parchment paper and roll out to a thickness of about ⅛ inch (2 to 3 mm). Ease the crust into the flan dish and trim the edges to neaten.
3. Line the crust with parchment paper, fill with pie weights or rice, and bake for 10 minutes, or until lightly golden. Remove from the oven and reduce the oven temperature to 325°F (160°C). Remove the weights and parchment.
4. Meanwhile, to make the filling, combine the superfine sugar, cinnamon, condensed milk, mascarpone, chestnut meal, and eggs in a food processor or blender and blend until smooth and well combined. Pour the filling into the warm crust.
5. Bake for 50 to 60 minutes, until set. Remove and let cool completely in the pan before serving.
6. Dust with confectioners' sugar and serve with ice cream.

Nutrition Info:
- 506 calories; 8 g protein; 21 g total fat; 7 g saturated fat; 71 g carbohydrates; 3 g fiber; 188 mg sodium

Maple Syrup Bavarian Cream With Quick Pecan Brittle

Servings:6
Cooking Time:x
Ingredients:
- Nonstick cooking spray
- 3 large egg yolks, at room temperature
- ½ cup (110 g) superfine sugar
- ½ cup (125 ml) maple syrup
- ½ cup (125 ml) low-fat milk, lactose-free milk, or suitable plant-based milk
- 1 heaping tablespoon unflavored gelatin powder
- Ice cubes
- 1 cup (250 ml) light whipping cream
- 1¾ ounces (50 g) gluten-free butterscotch candies
- ½ cup (60 g) pecans, coarsely crushed

Directions:
1. Grease six 4-ounce (125 ml) dariole molds, custard cups, or tall ramekins with cooking spray.
2. Place the egg yolks and sugar in a medium bowl and beat with a handheld electric mixer for 2 to 3 minutes, until thick and pale.
3. Combine the maple syrup and milk in a medium saucepan over low heat. Whisk in the egg mixture and stir with a wooden spoon over very low heat for 5 minutes, or until thick enough to coat the back of the spoon. Don't let it boil. Remove from the heat and pour into a medium heatproof bowl.
4. Add 3 tablespoons of cold water to a small heatproof bowl and whisk in the gelatin with a fork. Set it aside for 5 minutes, or until the gelatin has begun to gel. Fill a larger bowl with boiling water, set the bowl containing the gelatin in it, and stir constantly until the gelatin has completely dissolved. Whisk the gelatin into the maple mixture until smooth.
5. Fill a large bowl with ice cubes. Place the bowl with the maple mixture on the ice and whisk every few minutes for about 10 minutes. The mixture will thicken as it cools.
6. Beat the cream in a medium bowl with a handheld electric mixer until thick. Fold into the cooled maple mixture with a large metal spoon until well combined. Pour evenly into the molds, then place the molds on a baking sheet, cover with plastic wrap, and refrigerate for 4 to 5 hours.
7. To make the pecan brittle, combine the butterscotch and pecans in a small food processor or blender and process until coarsely crushed (don't overdo it or you will be left with crumbs).
8. To serve, dip each mold into hot water for a few seconds, then turn out onto plates. Sprinkle generously with the pecan brittle.

Nutrition Info:
- 391 calories; 5 g protein; 23 g total fat; 9 g saturated fat; 45 g carbohydrates; 1 g fiber; 62 mg sodium

Berry Crumble

Servings:3
Cooking Time: 20 Minutes
Ingredients:
- Filling
- 1 cup blueberries, fresh or frozen
- 2 tbsp water
- 1 cup strawberries, fresh or frozen
- 1 ½ tsp white sugar
- 1 tbsp cornstarch, corn-based
- Crumble
- 1 cup gluten-free cornflakes
- ¼ cup packed brown sugar
- ¼ cup gluten-free flour
- 3 tbsp dried coconut, shredded
- 2 tbsp pumpkin seeds
- 4 tbsp butter, softened

Directions:
1. Preheat the oven to 350°F.
2. In a bowl, crush the cornflakes into small bits and mix them with the brown sugar, flour, coconut, and pumpkin seeds. Use the softened butter to work the dry mix into small crumbs, making sure there are no large lumps.
3. In an ovenproof dish, place the strawberries and blueberries, cutting the strawberries into smaller pieces if necessary. Over the berries, sprinkle the white sugar and cornstarch. Spread the crumble over the top evenly. Place the dish on a flat baking tray and cook in the oven for 20 minutes. The topping should be golden brown.
4. It is best served hot.

Nutrition Info:
- 425g Calories, 22.2g Total fat, 5.7g Saturated fat, 52.2g Carbohydrates, 3.6 g Fiber, 5.7g Protein, 22.6g Sodium.

Spiced Tortilla Chips

Servings:4
Cooking Time: 15 Minutes
Ingredients:
- 12 (6-inch) corn tortillas
- 1 tablespoon vegetable oil
- 1 teaspoon ground cumin
- 1 teaspoon gluten-free, onion- and garlic-free chili powder
- 1 teaspoon salt

Directions:
1. Preheat the oven to 350°F.
2. Cut each tortilla into 8 wedges. Brush the wedges on both sides with the oil and arrange them in a single layer on a large baking sheet.

3. In a small dish, combine the cumin, chili powder, and salt. Sprinkle the spice mixture onto the chips, distributing evenly.
4. Bake the chips for about 7 minutes. Turn the pan around and bake for an additional 7 to 8 minutes, until the chips are golden brown and crisp. Serve immediately or cool to room temperature. Cooled chips may be stored in a sealed container on the countertop for up to 3 days.

Nutrition Info:
- Calories: 189; Protein: 4g; Total Fat: 6g; Saturated Fat: 1g; Carbohydrates: 32g; Fiber: 5g; Sodium: 615mg;

Banana Friands (mini Almond Cakes)

Servings:x
Cooking Time:x
Ingredients:
- MAKES 12
- Nonstick cooking spray
- 9 tablespoons (1 stick plus 1 tablespoon/135 g) unsalted butter, cut into cubes
- 1¼ cups (200 g) confectioners' sugar, plus more for dusting
- ¼ cup (35 g) cornstarch
- ¼ cup (35 g) superfine white rice flour
- 1¼ cups (150 g) almond flour
- 5 large egg whites, lightly beaten
- 1 tablespoon plus 1 teaspoon fresh lemon juice
- 1 teaspoon vanilla extract
- 1 small ripe banana, peeled and roughly chopped

Directions:
1. Preheat the oven to 350°F (180°C). Lightly grease a 12-cup muffin pan, friand pan, or petite loaf pan with cooking spray.
2. Melt the butter in a small saucepan over low heat, then cook for 3 to 4 minutes more, until flecks of brown appear. Set aside.
3. Sift the confectioners' sugar, cornstarch, and rice flour three times into a large bowl (or whisk in the bowl until well combined). Stir in the almond flour, then add the egg whites, lemon juice, vanilla, and melted butter and mix with a large metal spoon until combined. Stir in the chopped banana.
4. Spoon the batter into the pan until each cup is two-thirds full. Bake for 12 to 15 minutes, until lightly golden and firm to the touch (a toothpick inserted into the center should come out clean).
5. Cool in the pan for 5 minutes, then turn out onto a wire rack to cool completely. Dust with confectioners' sugar before serving.

Nutrition Info:

- 229 calories; 4 g protein; 15 g total fat; 6 g saturated fat; 22 g carbohydrates; 2 g fiber; 29 mg sodium

Orange And Poppy Seed Cake

Servings:10
Cooking Time:x
Ingredients:
- Nonstick cooking spray
- 2 oranges
- 1¼ cups (150 g) almond flour
- 1 teaspoon gluten-free baking powder
- ½ cup (65 g) superfine white rice flour
- 2 tablespoons poppy seeds
- 5 large eggs
- 1¼ cups (275 g) sugar

Directions:
1. Preheat the oven to 325°F (170°C). Grease a 9-inch (23 cm) springform pan with cooking spray and line with a parchment paper circle.
2. Place the oranges in a medium saucepan of boiling water and boil, covered, for 20 minutes. Drain. Place the softened oranges in a food processor or blender and process (seeds, pith, and all!) for 3 to 4 minutes to form a smooth paste. Set aside to cool.
3. Sift the almond flour, baking powder, and rice flour three times into a bowl (or whisk in the bowl until well combined). Stir in the poppy seeds.
4. Beat the eggs in a medium bowl with a handheld electric mixer for 5 minutes, or until thick and creamy. Add the sugar and beat until well combined.
5. Stir the orange paste into the dry ingredients, then fold into the egg mixture with a large metal spoon. Pour the batter into the pan and bake for 50 to 60 minutes, until golden brown and firm to the touch (a toothpick inserted into the center should come out clean).
6. Cool in the pan for 15 minutes, then remove the outer ring and turn out onto a wire rack to cool completely.

Nutrition Info:
- 355 calories; 11 g protein; 19 g total fat; 2 g saturated fat; 43 g carbohydrates; 5 g fiber; 80 mg sodium

Chia Pudding

Servings:3
Cooking Time: -
Ingredients:
- ¼ cup chia seeds
- 1 tbsp cocoa powder
- 1 tbsp peanut butter
- 1 tbsp maple syrup
- 1 can coconut milk

Directions:
1. Fill an airtight jar with all the ingredients.
2. Close the jar and shake, then remove the top and stir the ingredients. Ensure that the bottom of the jar is clear. Shake again and place in the fridge for a minimum of 4 hours.

Nutrition Info:
- 386g Calories, 10g Total fat, 1g Saturated fat, 73g Carbohydrates, 20 g Fiber, 6g Protein, 24g Sodium.

Sweet And Savory Popcorn

Servings:7
Cooking Time: 5 Minutes
Ingredients:
- ½ cup vegetable oil
- 1 cup popcorn kernels
- ⅓ cup brown sugar
- ⅓ cup white sugar
- 2 tsp salt, or to taste

Directions:
1. Blend together cranberries, butter, Greek yogurt, milk, banana, and chia seeds.
2. Add ice until the desired consistency is achieved.

Nutrition Info:
- 258g Calories, 16g Total fat, 2.2g Saturated fat, 24.8g Carbohydrates, 6.2 g Fiber, 3.7g Protein, 23.2g Sodium.

Maple-spiced Walnuts

Servings:2
Cooking Time: 8 Minutes
Ingredients:
- 2 tablespoons maple syrup
- 2 teaspoons olive oil
- 1 tablespoon water
- 2 cups walnut halves
- 1 tablespoon sugar
- 1 teaspoon coarse salt
- 1 teaspoon ground cumin
- ½ teaspoon ground coriander
- ⅛ teaspoon cayenne pepper

Directions:
1. Combine the maple syrup, oil, and water in a large skillet. Heat, stirring, over medium heat for about 5 minutes. Stir in the walnuts.
2. Add the sugar, salt, cumin, coriander, and cayenne pepper. Cook, tossing to coat the nuts well, for about 3 minutes more, until the nuts are lightly browned.

3. Transfer to a sheet of parchment paper, spread the nuts out into a single layer, separate them, and cool completely. Serve at room temperature.

Nutrition Info:

- Calories: 223; Protein: 8g; Total Fat: 20g; Saturated Fat: 1g; Carbohydrates: 8g; Fiber: 2g; Sodium: 242mg;

Lemon Coconut Cupcakes

Servings:12
Cooking Time: 25 Minutes
Ingredients:

- Cupcakes
- 1 ½ cups gluten-free, all-purpose flour
- ½ tsp xanthan gum
- 2 tsp of baking powder
- Pinch of salt
- 1 tbsp lemon zest
- ½ cup butter, room temperature
- ½ cup white sugar
- ½ cup brown sugar
- 2 eggs
- 1 tsp vanilla extract
- 2 ½ tbsp lemon juice
- ½ cup coconut yogurt
- Lemon butter icing
- ¾ cup butter
- 1 ½ cups powdered sugar
- 1 ½ tbsp lemon juice

Directions:

1. Preheat the oven to 350°F and grease a 12-muffin tin.
2. For the cupcakes, mix together the dry ingredients and put to the side.
3. In a large bowl, mix the butter and sugar until combined, then whisk together the eggs and vanilla until smooth before adding the lemon juice and blending. Add the dry ingredients and yogurt, alternating between them, beginning and ending with the dry ingredients. Mix well.
4. Spoon into muffin cups, filling ⅔ of the way. Place into the center of the oven and bake for 25 minutes. The tops should be golden. When a skewer or toothpick is inserted into them, it should come out clean. Leave to cool.
5. The icing is optional. To make the icing, mix room temperature butter and powdered sugar together with lemon juice until smooth. Then, use a knife to cover the top of the cupcakes after they have cooled.

Nutrition Info:

- 366g Calories, 17.5g Total fat, 4.4g Saturated fat, 49.4g Carbohydrates, 0.4 g Fiber, 2.7g Protein, 34.3g Sodium.

Gingerbread Men

Servings:20
Cooking Time:x
Ingredients:

- 1 large egg
- ⅓ cup (75 g) superfine sugar
- ½ cup (175 g) brown rice syrup
- 5 tablespoons (75 g) unsalted butter, melted
- 1 cup (130 g) superfine white rice flour
- ½ cup (90 g) potato flour
- 1 cup (90 g) soy flour
- 1 teaspoon xanthan gum or guar gum
- 1 teaspoon gluten-free baking powder
- 1 to 1½ heaping tablespoons ground ginger
- Cornstarch, for rolling out dough
- Gluten-free icing (optional)

Directions:

1. Preheat the oven to 300°F (150°C). Line three baking sheets with parchment paper (or work in batches).
2. Beat the egg and sugar together in a large bowl with a wooden spoon. Stir in the brown rice syrup and melted butter.
3. Sift the rice flour, potato flour, soy flour, xanthan gum, baking powder, and ginger together three times into a separate bowl (or whisk in a bowl until well combined). Add to the syrup mixture and mix well to combine. Refrigerate for 15 minutes to firm up slightly.
4. Lightly sprinkle your work surface with cornstarch. Roll out the dough on the floured surface to a thickness of ¾ to 1 inch (2 to 3 mm). Use a cookie cutter to cut out shapes (it doesn't have to be people, of course—you could do stars, pine trees, or any shape you like). Place on the baking sheets, allowing room for spreading.
5. Bake for 8 to 10 minutes. Cool on the sheets for 10 to 15 minutes, then transfer to a wire rack to cool completely. When cool, decorate with gluten-free icing, if desired.

Nutrition Info:

- 92 calories; 3 g protein; 3 g total fat; 2 g saturated fat; 15 g carbohydrates; 0 g fiber; 34 mg sodium

Quinoa Muffins

Servings:24
Cooking Time: 20 Minutes
Ingredients:

- 1 ½ cups quinoa flour
- 1 cup quinoa flakes
- ⅓ cup walnuts, chopped
- 1 tbsp cinnamon
- 4 tsp baking powder

- 2 tsp baking soda
- Pinch of salt
- 4 eggs
- 4 bananas, mashed
- ½ cup almond milk
- ¼ cup maple syrup

Directions:

1. Preheat the oven to 375°F.
2. Mix the dry ingredients in one bowl. In a separate bowl, combine the wet ingredients. Combine the ingredients until mixed fully.
3. Spoon into greased muffin pans and bake for 20 minutes. Check if the center is dry by poking the center of a muffin with a skewer. If it comes out clean, they are ready.

Nutrition Info:

- 175g Calories, 10.5g Total fat, 4g Saturated fat, 6g Carbohydrates, 1.5 g Fiber, 14g Protein, 4g Sodium.

Banana Birthday Cake With Lemon Icing

Servings:16
Cooking Time: 55 Minutes

Ingredients:

- Cake
- ½ cup white sugar
- ½ cup brown sugar
- 1 cup butter, softened
- 3 eggs, large
- 2 tsp vanilla extract
- 4 bananas, firm, mashed
- 1 tsp chia seeds, can be substituted with 1 ½ tsp guar gum
- 1 tbsp boiling water
- 2 tsp of baking soda
- ½ cup lactose-free milk
- 3 cups gluten-free flour
- 2 tsp of baking powder
- Icing
- 1 ½ tbsp lemon juice
- 5 tbsp butter
- 1 ½ cups powdered sugar
- 1 tbsp lemon zest

Directions:

1. Preheat the oven to 350°F. Grease a 10-inch round tin and line it with parchment paper.
2. In a bowl, mix the softened butter and sugar with a hand mixer until smooth and fluffy.
3. Add the vanilla and the eggs, one at a time.

4. Mash the bananas until there are 2 cups worth. Zest and juice the lemon and place the zest to the side. Add the banana and juice to the wet mix.
5. Dissolve the chia seeds in 1 tbsp of boiling water. Stir until the consistency is thick and then add to the wet mixture.
6. Heat the milk in the microwave for 30 seconds, then mix the baking soda into it. Fold into the wet mixture.
7. Sift together the flour and baking powder. Mix the dry ingredients into the wet mixture and stir until fully mixed. Pour into the cake tin and bake in the center of the oven for 45-60 minutes. When the cake turns golden, check the middle of the cake with a skewer to see if it is cooked. Remove it from the oven and allow to cool.
8. For the icing, pour the powdered sugar into a bowl. Soften the butter, but do not melt it. Add the dairy into the bowl. Begin mixing and add the lemon juice. Mix until smooth.
9. Ice the cake once it is cool and top with the lemon zest.

Nutrition Info:

- 405g Calories, 18g Total fat, 2.8g Saturated fat, 56.8g Carbohydrates, 1.1 g Fiber, 3.7g Protein, 31g Sodium.

Lamb Meatballs

Servings:4
Cooking Time: 20 Minutes

Ingredients:

- Oil for preparing the pan
- 1 pound ground lamb
- ½ cup cooked rice
- ⅓ cup crumbled feta cheese
- Zest of 1 lemon
- 3 tablespoons minced parsley
- 1 teaspoon salt
- 1 teaspoon ground cumin
- 1 teaspoon ground allspice
- ½ teaspoon ground cinnamon
- 1 egg, lightly beaten
- 1 tablespoon Garlic Oil (here)

Directions:

1. Preheat the oven to 400°F.
2. Line a large, rimmed baking sheet with lightly oiled parchment paper.
3. In a mixing bowl, combine the lamb, rice, cheese, lemon zest, parsley, salt, cumin, allspice, cinnamon, and egg, and mix well.
4. Form the lamb mixture into 1½-inch balls and arrange them on the prepared baking sheet.
5. Bake the meatballs in the preheated oven until they are browned and cooked through, for about 20 minutes.

6. Drizzle the Garlic Oil over the meatballs just before serving and serve hot.

Nutrition Info:

- Calories: 361; Protein: 37g; Total Fat: 13g; Saturated Fat: 6g; Carbohydrates: 21g; Fiber: 1g; Sodium: 844mg;

No-bake Chocolate Cookies

Servings:15

Cooking Time: 5 Minutes

Ingredients:

- Cooling: 10 to 20 minutes
- 1 cup sugar
- ½ cup unsweetened almond milk
- 2 tablespoons unsweetened cocoa powder
- 1½ cups quick-cooking oatmeal
- ¾ cup almond butter
- 1 teaspoon vanilla extract
- Pinch sea salt

Directions:

1. Line a baking sheet with parchment paper and set it aside.

2. In a large saucepan over high heat, stir together the sugar, almond milk, and cocoa powder. Bring the mixture to a boil and boil for 1 minute, stirring constantly.

3. Remove the pan from the heat and immediately stir in the oatmeal, almond butter, vanilla, and salt. Spoon 1-tablespoon portions onto the prepared sheet.

4. Refrigerate for 20 minutes or freeze for 10 minutes to cool.

Nutrition Info:

- Calories:107; Total Fat: 3g; Saturated Fat: 2g; Carbohydrates: 20g; Fiber: 1g; Sodium: 14mg; Protein: 2g

21 DAY MEAL PLAN

Day 1

Breakfast: Hawaiian Toasted Sandwich 19

Lunch: Snapper With Tropical Salsa 51

Dinner: Curried Potato And Parsnip Soup 65

Day 2

Breakfast: Pesto Noodles 20

Lunch: Chicken Tenders 36

Dinner: Smoked Gouda And Tomato Sandwich 66

Day 3

Breakfast: Cranberry Almond Bowl 21

Lunch: Spicy Pulled Pork 37

Dinner: Potato Leek Soup 66

Day 4

Breakfast: Feta, Chicken, And Pepper Sandwich 22

Lunch: Easy Shepherd's Pie 37

Dinner: Potato And Corn Chowder 66

Day 5

Breakfast: Spicy Scrambled Chickpeas 23

Lunch: Sesame-crusted Cod 37

Dinner: Creamy Seafood Soup 67

Day 6

Breakfast: Chicken Wrap 24

Lunch: Crunchy Homemade Fish Sticks 38

Dinner: Vegetable Soup 67

Day 7

Breakfast: Sweet Green Smoothie 25

Lunch: Tuna And Pineapple Burgers 37

Dinner: Pesto Ham Sandwich 68

Day 8

Breakfast: Pesto Toasted Sandwich 26

Lunch: Turkey And Sweet Potato Chili 39

Dinner:

Day 9

Breakfast: Ginger-berry Rice Milk Smoothie 27

Lunch: Chile Chicken Stir-fry 39

Dinner: Philly Steak Sandwich

Day 10

Breakfast: Pumpkin Pie Pancakes 28

Lunch: Ginger-sesame Grilled Flank Steak 40

Dinner: Vietnamese Beef Noodle Salad 68

Day 11

Breakfast: Melon And Berry Compote 29

Lunch: Chili-lime Shrimp And Bell Peppers 40

Dinner: Roasted Squash And Chestnut Soup 69

Day 12

Breakfast: Sausage And Egg Omelet 30

Lunch: Lemon-dill Cod On A Bed Of Spinach 41

Dinner: Spicy Clear Soup 69

Day 13

Breakfast: Carrot Cake Porridge 31

Lunch:20-minute Pulled Pork 42

Dinner: Chicken Noodle Soup 70

Day 14

Breakfast: Rhubarb Ginger Granola Bowl 33

Lunch: Spaghetti And Meat Sauce 42

Dinner: Turkey-ginger Soup 70

Day 15

Breakfast: Summer Berry Smoothie 32

Lunch: Fish With Thai Red Curry Sauce 42

Dinner: Greens And Lemon Soup 70

Day 16

Breakfast: Smoothie Bowl 32

Lunch: Turkey And Red Pepper Burgers 43

Dinner: Peppered Beef And Citrus Salad 71

Day 17

Breakfast: Melon And Yogurt Parfait 34

Lunch: Asian-style Pork Meatballs 44

Dinner: Shrimp Chowder 71

Day 18

Breakfast: Banana Toast 35

Lunch: Soy-infused Roast Chicken 44

Dinner: Egg Salad Sandwich 72

Day 19

Breakfast: Maple–brown Sugar Oatmeal 36

Lunch: Lamb And Vegetable Pilaf 45

Dinner: Carrot And Ginger Soup 72

Day 20

Breakfast: Protein Smoothie 19

Lunch: Teriyaki Salmon 53

Dinner: Smoked Chicken And Walnut Salad 73

Day 21

Breakfast: Pineapple-coconut Smoothie 19

Lunch: Quick Shepherd's Pie 46

Dinner: Vegetable Beef Soup 73

RECIPES INDEX

Mussels In Chili, Bacon, And Tomato Broth 66

N

No-bake Chocolate Cookies 130

O

Olive Tapenade 88

Open-faced Bacon, Tomato, And Cheese Sandwich 65

Orange And Poppy Seed Cake 127

Orange Biscuits 106

Orange-ginger Salmon 47

Orange-maple Glazed Carrots 101

Orange-scented Overnight Oatmeal 19

Orange-scented Panna Cotta 112

Oven-baked Zucchini And Carrot Fritters With Ginger-lime Sauce 33

P

Pan-seared Scallops With Sautéed Kale 57

Parmesan Baked Zucchini 97

Parmesan Mayo Corn On The Cob 94

Parmesan Potato Wedges 117

Pasta With Pesto Sauce 84

Pasta With Tomato And Lentil Sauce 84

Pb&j Mug Cake 122

Pb&j Smoothie 24

Peanut Butter Bowl 25

Peanut Butter Cookies 116

Peanut Butter Granola 31

Peanut Butter Pancakes 29

Peanut Butter Soba Noodles 79

Pecan And Maple Tarts 123

Pecan-crusted Maple-mustard Salmon 62

Peppered Beef And Citrus Salad 71

Pesto Ham Sandwich 68

Pesto Noodles 15

Pesto Toasted Sandwich 16

Philly Steak Sandwich 68

Pico De Gallo Salsa 90

Pineapple Fried Rice 76

Pineapple Salsa 115

Pineapple, Strawberry, Raspberry Smoothie 32

Pineapple-coconut Smoothie 19

Polenta With Roasted Vegetables And Spicy Tomato Sauce 80

Pork Sausages With Cheesy Potato Rösti 49

Pork Tenderloin Chops With Potatoes And Pan Sauce 35

Pork Tenderloin On Creamy Garlic Polenta With Cranberry Sauce 57

Potato And Corn Chowder 66

Potato Frittata 79

Potato Leek Soup 66

Potato Pancakes 28

Protein Smoothie 19

Pumpkin Cornbread 103

Pumpkin Pie Pancakes 17

Q

Quiche In Ham Cups 22

Quick Creamy Coleslaw 101

Quick Shepherd's Pie 46

Quick Steak Tacos 50

Quinoa Breakfast Bowl With Basil "hollandaise" Sauce 27

Quinoa Muffins 128

Quinoa Porridge 20

Quinoa With Cherry Tomatoes, Olives, And Radishes 94

Quinoa With Swiss Chard 99

Quinoa-stuffed Eggplant Roulades With Feta And Mint 80

R

Raspberry Sauce 87

Raspberry Smoothie 29

Raspberry–chia Seed Ice Pops 111

Red Snapper With Creole Sauce 48

Red Snapper With Sweet Potato Crust And Cilantro-lime Sauce 41

Rhubarb Custard Cup 121

Rhubarb Ginger Granola Bowl 18

Rib-eye Steak With Creamy Shrimp Sauce 63

Rice & Zucchini Slice 25

Rice Paper "spring Rolls" With Satay Sauce 98

Rice Pilaf With Vegetables 100

Rice Pudding 117

Rich White Chocolate Cake 106

Risotto With Smoked Salmon And Dill 46

Roast Vegetables 102

Roasted Chicken, Potatoes, And Kale 52

Roasted Garlic Shrimp And Red Peppers 61

Roasted Lamb Racks On Buttered Mashed Rutabaga 53

Roasted Lemon-parmesan Broccoli 96

Roasted Potato Wedges 99

Roasted Root Vegetable Salad 101

Roasted Squash And Chestnut Soup 69

Roasted Sweet Potato Salad With Spiced Lamb And Spinach 68

Roasted-veggie Gyros With Tzatziki Sauce 75

Rosemary-lemon Chicken Thighs 59

S

Salsa Verde 91

Salted Caramel Pumpkin Seeds 114

Sausage And Egg Omelet 17

Sausage-stuffed Kabocha Squash 20

Sautéed Shrimp With Cilantro-lime Rice 61

Savory Muffins 33

Scrambled Tofu 30

Seared Green Beans With Sesame Oil 101

Sesame Rice Noodles 96

Sesame-broccoli Stir-fry 100

Sesame-crusted Cod 37

Shrimp Chowder 71

Sirloin Chimichurri 56

Smoked Chicken And Walnut Salad 73

Smoked Gouda And Tomato Sandwich 66

Smoked Trout Brandade 104

Smoky Corn Chowder With Red Peppers 74

Smoothie Bowl 32

Snapper With Tropical Salsa 35

Soy-infused Roast Chicken 44

Spaghetti And Meat Sauce 42

Spanish Chicken With Creamy Herbed Rice 59

Spanish Meatloaf With Garlic Mashed Potatoes 47

Spanish Rice 81

Spiced Tortilla Chips 126

Spicy Clear Soup 69

Spicy Pulled Pork 37

Spicy Salmon Burgers With Cilantro-lime Mayo 55

Spicy Scrambled Chickpeas 16

Spinach And Bell Pepper Salad With Fried Tofu Puffs 69

Steamed Mussels With Saffron-infused Cream 52

Stir-fry Sauce 87

Strawberry Ice Cream 123

Strawberry Smoothie 20

Strawberry-kiwi Smoothie With Chia Seeds 31

Strawberry-rhubarb Crisp With Oat-pecan Topping 111

Stuffed Rolled Roast Beef With Popovers And Gravy 54

Stuffed Zucchini Boats 79

Summer Berry Smoothie 32

Summer Popsicle 109

Sun-dried Tomato Spread 90

Sweet And Savory Popcorn 127

Sweet Green Smoothie 16

Sweet-and-sour Sauce 86

Sweet-and-sour Turkey Meatballs 50

Swiss Chicken With Mustard Sauce 44

Printed in Great Britain
by Amazon

17999156R00079